A Catholic Guide TO THE BIBLE

REVISED AND EXPANDED

Other Books by Oscar Lukefahr, C.M.

"We Believe..."
A Survey of the Catholic Faith

We Worship
A Guide to the Catholic Mass

We Pray
Living in God's Presence

We Live
To Know, Love, and Serve God

The Search for Happiness
Four Levels of Emotional and Spiritual Growth

Christ's Mother and Ours
A Catholic Guide to Mary, Revised and Updated

The Privilege of Being Catholic

The Catechism Handbook

A Catholic Guide to the Bible (Revised)
is also available in Spanish:
Guía Católica para la Biblia

A Catholic Guide

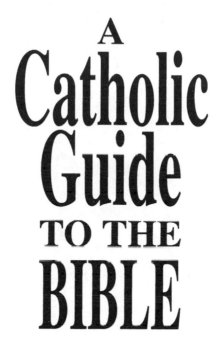

TO THE

BIBLE

REVISED AND EXPANDED

FATHER OSCAR LUKEFAHR, C.M.

Liguori
ONE LIGUORI DRIVE
LIGUORI MO 63057-9999

Dedication

To Mary, Joann, Joe and Barb
Our names are in the book together
To Hank and Jeanne
"Our feet are standing within your gates, O Jerusalem!"
(Psalm 122:2)

Imprimi Potest:
Richard Thibodeau, CSsR
Provincial, Denver Province
The Redemptorists

Imprimatur:
Most Reverend Michael J. Sheridan
Auxiliary Bishop, Archdiocese of St. Louis

ISBN 978-0-7648-0201-0
Library of Congress Catalog Card Number: 97-75918

Copyright © 1992, revised and expanded 1998, Liguori Publications
Printed in United States of America
14 13 / 16 15 14

Liguori Publications, a nonprofit corporation, is an apostolate of the Redemptorists. To learn more about the Redemptorists, visit Redemptorists.com.

To order, call 800-325-9521
www.liguori.org

Table of Contents

Introduction

O ne of the questions God will ask us at the Judgment will be, "How did you like my book?" God's book is the Bible, a work we should read and enjoy

But as anyone who's opened the Bible knows, it is also a book that can be hard to understand. Many have attempted to read the Bible from start to finish, only to be discouraged by difficult passages, pages of names and numbers, unfamiliar styles of writing, and the sheer size of the Bible.

It is the purpose of this book to help readers overcome such obstacles by explaining where the Bible came from and what it is about and to help people *read* the Bible by offering them a guided tour with background information and selected passages for every book in the Bible.

Readers will be investigating such topics as languages of the Bible, literary forms, history, and theology. This will require time and effort. As students of the piano must first learn to read notes in order to play beautiful music, so students of the Bible must learn the basics of biblical scholarship in order to read the Bible with ease and understanding.

Students of the piano are usually advised to practice daily. Students of the Bible who use this *Guide* are advised to set aside some time each day to read a few pages, to look up pertinent Bible references, and to answer questions from the workbook which accompanies this book (also available from Liguori Publications). You will probably gain more from short daily study times than from an occasional cram session.

In writing A *Catholic Guide to the Bible*, I have made every effort to be faithful to the teachings of the Catholic Church. In the many areas where the Church has not issued an official statement regarding matters of interpretation, I have done my best to state opinions within the boundaries of reason and fidelity to Church dogma. References to the *Catechism of the Catholic Church* are given as follows: the citation (C 1-10) directs the reader to sections one through ten in the *Catechism*.

This *Guide* is an invitation to study the Bible. It is also an invitation to embark on an adventure: to hear the word of God, to read the very words Jesus once read, to open the very pages the saints have touched! It is also an invitation to discover that the Bible can be a treasured companion on our journey through life, for once we understand the basics of biblical scholarship and become familiar with the Bible, God speaks to us through its pages.

And we'll have the right answer to that question on Judgment Day: "Your book, Lord? I loved it. It's guided me to your presence!"

FATHER OSCAR LUKEFAHR, C.M.

P.S. A note of thanks to all who have guided me in the writing of this book. Thanks... To Father David Polek, C.SS.R., who first suggested the project. To Cecelia Portlock, whose expertise and advice have been invaluable. To all who have read the entire manuscript and workbook, especially to Frank and Gail Jones, Delores Lindhurst, and Kathy and Dennis Vollink. To all who helped with various stages of the project: Carol Meyer, Kasey Nugent, Henry and Jeanne Moreno, Father John Tackaberry, C.M., Mary Ann Toczylowski, Brock and Kathy Whittenberger, and Dr. Michael Wulfers. To the Bible Study Class at St. Vincent de Paul Parish in Perryville, Missouri, whose encouragement and advice were essential. To my sister, Joann Lukefahr, D.C., who made arrangements for the class. To my seminary Scripture professors, Father James Fischer, C.M. and Father Gilmore Guyot, C.M. To Penny Elder, Cheryl Callier, and Sherrie Hotop, who helped with the second edition of the book and workbook, and to Kass Dotterweich for editing this edition. May God bless you all!

PART I

ENTERING
THE BIBLE

CHAPTER ONE

Bibles, Beliefs, and Beginnings

O ne Saturday morning I answered the rectory doorbell to find two well-dressed young men standing on my front porch. Both carried Bibles and briefcases. Both seemed surprised to be face to face with a Catholic priest (the rectory carried no sign to indicate that it was any different from the other homes in our little town), but they asked if they might come in.

I invited them into the living room and introduced myself as the pastor of the local Catholic Church. They gave their names and related that they were volunteers for their church, going door to door, explaining their beliefs and passing out tracts. The younger of the two apologized saying that he was fairly new to such evangelization, but that it was his turn to speak. He proceeded to give a verse-by-verse interpretation of the Our Father, growing more and more nervous as he became aware of the incongruity of explaining the Lord's Prayer to a minister more than twice his age. Finally, flustered to the point of forgetting what followed "Give us this day our daily bread," he stopped and asked if we could just talk.

He then inquired how he should address me. "Any way you like," I replied, "but most people call me 'Father.'" He wondered why, for hadn't Jesus stated that we should call no one on earth our father? I explained that, according to our Catholic interpretation of Matthew 23:9, Jesus was speaking against false attitudes of pride and superiority, not forbidding the use of words like *father* or *teacher;* otherwise, these words could not be used in reference to parents or instructors! I explained also that we were following the practice of Saint Paul, who wrote to those he served: "Indeed, in Christ Jesus I became your father through the gospel" (1 Cor 4:15).

We then went on to discuss methods of interpreting the Bible. They stated their belief that the Bible gives a timetable for the future, including the date for the end of the world. I explained how the Catholic Church teaches that the time is known only to God (Mk 13:32), and that we should always be ready to meet Christ.

Soon it was time for them to move on. Their visit had been a friendly one, marked by politeness and mutual respect. But I haven't circled a date on my calendar for the end of the world, and I doubt that those young men call their minister "Father"!

What Does the Bible Mean?

That Saturday morning visit illustrates the fact that those who call themselves Christians may read the Bible, but may not understand it in the same way. This is due partly to the complexities of language. We've all had the experience of saying something in an effort to express a particular idea, only to have our hearers misunderstand us. The complexities are multiplied when people attempt to communicate across barriers of time, culture, or language.

We speak English. Shakespeare spoke English. But we struggle at times to grasp his meaning, for many words no longer convey the same ideas they did in his time. He spoke of *fardels* borne; we'd more likely use the word *burdens*. A phrase that is a compliment in one culture can be an insult in another. An appropriate word in one language might be a poor choice in another. Some years ago, for example, the Chevrolet Motor Company had a model called the "Nova." The car was exported to Mexico, where its name caused a good deal of confusion. In Spanish, *No va* means "It doesn't go."

The Bible was written long ago over a span of a thousand years by people who belonged to a culture far different from ours and who spoke languages we do not understand. The Bible uses literary forms (types of literature) that vary greatly from ours. Many of the most important words of the Bible (those of Jesus) were spoken in one language (Aramaic), written down in another (Greek), and translated into a third (English). Small wonder then that we have problems discerning the meaning of the Bible.

It is the belief of the Catholic Church and many other Christian churches that the Bible also has God as its author. This means that we can expect a degree of reliability available nowhere else. But it adds further complications. How can God and human beings be authors of the same writings? How should such writings be interpreted?

The official position of the Catholic Church is that God inspired the human authors of the Bible to write using their own talents, abilities, and styles. God did not just dictate messages to them or use them as a ventriloquist uses a dummy. Therefore, we can best understand any part of the Bible by going back to the time and place of its human author and discovering what that author intended to express.

The interpretation of the Bible will be studied in detail later. But by now it should be obvious that the Bible *must* be interpreted. There are those who say that we can discern the meaning of the Bible from the words alone. But the passage of thousands of years and the fact that the Bible was written in other languages for people of different cultures mean that study and interpretation are necessary if we want to gain a proper understanding of the Bible.

To further demonstrate this point, we need only look at a few quotations from the Bible. Psalm 144:1 says of God: "Blessed be the LORD, my rock." Does this mean that God is solid mineral matter or does it mean that God is an all-powerful creator on whom we can depend? Interpretation is necessary. Another example may be found in Luke 14:26, where Jesus says, "Whoever comes to me and does not hate father and mother, wife and children, brothers and sisters, yes, and even life itself, cannot be my disciple." Does Jesus mean that we must literally *detest* our own relatives? Or did the Aramaic language spoken by Jesus mean something else? Again, interpretation is absolutely necessary!

Scholarly Research and the Bible

The idea of interpreting the Bible makes some Catholics feel uneasy. They may hear that some biblical passages once assumed to be historical are now being interpreted in another way. Does this mean that the whole Bible is just a fairy tale?

Certainly not. There *have* been changes in our understanding of parts of the Bible in recent years. These changes are due to discoveries by scholars in the fields of language, archaeology, and history.

Language: The nineteenth and twentieth centuries brought to light thousands of documents unknown since biblical times. Records in Egyptian, Assyrian, Babylonian, Persian, Aramaic, and many other languages have enabled scholars to decipher ancient ways of writing and thinking. Discoveries like those of the Dead Sea Scrolls (ancient copies of Bible books and other literature found in desert caves southeast of Jerusalem) in 1947 have helped researchers make spectacular progress in their understanding of both the Old and New Testaments.

Archaeology: In the last two centuries, archaeologists have shed new light on the Bible. Ancient monuments and entire cities have been unearthed and studied in Egypt, Palestine, and other areas important to the Bible. Almost every aspect of life mentioned in the Bible has been clarified in one way or another.

History: Aided by archaeological finds, historians have obtained a more accurate picture of ancient times. They have been able to document real historical truth in the Bible and to differentiate the nonhistorical parts of the Bible from the historical.

As a result, we are perhaps in a better position to understand the original meaning of the biblical authors than anyone since the time of Jesus. We may have to revise our ways of looking at some parts of the Bible, but this does not imply that the whole Bible is a fairy tale. There is history in the Bible. But there are also parables, poetry, short stories, songs, drama, fables, and other kinds of writing.

All of this might seem overwhelming. It is true that the kind of research requiring knowledge of ancient languages, cultures, and history may be beyond the reach of most people. But biblical scholars have done much of the groundwork for us. With their help, we can learn to recognize and understand the literary forms of the Bible just as we recognize and understand the literary forms commonly used today.

We benefit from the research of scholars each time we open good modern translations of the Bible. Such translations are closer to the original manuscripts (handwritten documents) than were the old Catholic *Douay* and the Protestant *King James* versions. They may provide introductions to the books of the Bible as well as notes that give historical background and explain difficult passages.

A note of clarification: This book mentions Scripture scholars often and refers to their works. Every effort has been made here to follow scholarship faithful to the teachings of the Catholic Church and to express views that are in keeping with directions set by the Church. But the opinions of scholars can change as new evidence is discovered by archaeologists, linguists, and historians. This should not alarm us. Our faith rests not on the latest speculations of scholars, but on God's wisdom and authority. While scholarly theories and opinions change, the basic doctrines upon which the Catholic Church is founded are certain and everlasting because they come from Jesus Christ, our Lord and God, who "is the same yesterday and today and forever" (Heb 13:8).

Modern Translations of the Bible

No manuscripts in the handwriting of the original authors survive today. The oldest manuscripts available are copies and translations, some of them two thousand years old, a few even older. In centuries past, there were many disagreements about what the original books actually said. But progress in archaeology, linguistics, and history has helped scholars reach agreement about the substance of the original texts.

As a result, many of the drastic differences formerly found in Protestant and Catholic translations of the Bible have been eliminated. For example, the non-biblical addition to the Lord's Prayer, "For thine is the kingdom, the power, and the glory" has been removed from modern Protestant editions. Nevertheless, there are many modern English translations, Protestant and Catholic. People often ask, "Why so many?" and "Which one should I use?"

There are many translations simply because words have so many meanings and are subject to different interpretations. One translator might want to use the word *help,* while another might prefer *assist.* To one linguist *love* might seem preferable in a certain instance to *charity,* while to another *charity* might seem the better choice.

Some translations follow the original language closely, while freer translations, or paraphrases (such as *The Living Bible*), reword and restate ideas. The first approach can provide a version that faithfully presents the thought of the original author, but the language may be stilted. The second approach might have the advantage of producing a more readable text, but it can also impose a translator's biases on the content.

There are many English versions approved for Catholics in the United States today. Among them are the *Jerusalem Bible*, the *New American Bible*, and the *New Revised Standard Version of the Bible.* They are good translations, reliable without being stilted on the one hand or mere paraphrases on the other. The *New Revised Standard Ver-*

sion of the Bible (the translation chosen for the *Catechism of the Catholic Church*) will be used throughout this book.

Beginning to Read the Bible

The Bible is actually a collection of many books. (The word *bible* comes from the Greek *biblia,* meaning "books." The Bible is also referred to as the sacred Scriptures, the sacred writings, or as Scripture.) There are two major divisions of the Bible: the Old Testament, written before the time of Jesus Christ, and the New Testament, written during the one hundred years after Christ's death and Resurrection. Most Bibles have a table of contents enumerating the various books in the Old and New Testaments as well as a list of abbreviations commonly used for the books.

Each of the books is divided into chapters and verses. The system in use today was not a part of the original Bible, and breaks for chapters and verses are frequently not synchronized with the meaning of the text. But it does provide a universally accepted method for finding citations from the Bible.

The usual way of giving a citation from the Bible is first to name the book (often abbreviated): Mt refers to the Gospel of Matthew, 1 Pet to the First Letter of Peter. Next comes a number, indicating the chapter. Mt 2 would mean the Gospel of Matthew, Chapter 2. The chapter number is followed by a punctuation mark of some kind (usually a colon, but sometimes a comma or a period), after which come more numbers signifying the verses. Thus, Mt 2:19-23 means the Gospel of Matthew, Chapter 2, Verses 19 to 23.

If the citation refers to more than one chapter, it is printed Mt 2:19– 3:6, meaning the Gospel of Matthew, Chapter 2, Verse 19 through Chapter 3, Verse 6.

Sometimes specific verses within the same chapter are referred to, while others are skipped. A comma is used to indicate verses that are skipped. For example, 1 Kings 2:1-4,10-11 refers to the First Book of Kings, Chapter 2, Verses 1 to 4 and 10 to 11. (Verses 5 to 9 are omitted.)

This system may seem confusing at first, but it becomes easier as the reader becomes familiar with the Bible and with the process of looking up passages. From this point on, all biblical citations will be given using abbreviations as found in the *New Revised Standard Version of the Bible.* Other Bibles may use slightly different abbreviations, and some versions of the Bible may occasionally vary the numbering of selected verses and chapters. The reader can usually find these chapters and verses by looking in the general area of the passage that has been cited.

Helps for Reading the Bible

This book will guide its readers through the Bible. Further assistance may be found in many available Bible study aids. A Bible *commentary* offers verse-by-verse explanations of Bible passages. A Bible *atlas* gives maps showing the world as it was during the various stages of Old and New Testament history. Atlases may also offer details about daily life in ancient times. A *concordance* lists each occurrence of every word in the Bible and gives the chapter and verse where the word may be found. A Bible *dictionary* offers explanations for important words, names, and places in the Bible. *Audiotapes* of the Bible make the sacred Scriptures available to listeners at times when reading is not possible or convenient. They are especially valuable to the blind and visually handicapped. *Computer programs* available for many versions of the Bible allow the user to access any word or verse and permit comparisons of versions in parallel columns on the computer screen.

There are literally thousands of books offering information about the Bible. Some of them are very helpful and in conformity with Catholic teaching. Other materials, even some that claim to be nondenominational, contradict Catholic doctrine and attack the Catholic faith. Students of the Bible may judge the value of materials by looking through them at a library or by browsing through the Bible section in a Catholic bookstore.

Faith and the Bible

The Bible has been a bestseller for two thousand years. It addresses every human situation, reflects every emotion, and paints vivid pictures of all kinds of people—good and bad. It is great literature: lively history, spirited poetry, unforgettable stories. Passages like "The Lord is my shepherd" (Psalm 23) and Jesus' parable of the Prodigal Son (Luke 15:11-32) are known and loved by hundreds of millions throughout the world.

But the main reason why the Bible is a bestseller is that it is inspired by God. This means that God influenced the human authors of the Bible to teach the truths needed for our salvation. God, then, gave us the Bible to answer the great questions in life. "Why are we here?" "What is the source of created things?" "Is there a God, and, if so, what is God like?" "How ought we to live?" "What will happen to us when we die?"

It is possible, but incorrect, to see the Bible only as great literature to be investigated in the same way other great books are studied. We may know its content and talk in scholarly fashion about its themes, but we are failing to address the most important issue unless we ask ourselves: *Is the Bible inspired by God? Does God really speak to us through the pages of the Bible? Does the Bible show us how to live? Do we trust in the Bible's message of salvation and eternal life through Jesus Christ?*

The Bible calls for a response. We may read and enjoy a fine novel without having to make any changes in our lifestyle. But when we read the Bible, we are challenged to believe and hope, to love and give, to sacrifice and share, to forgive and be forgiven, to grow and trust. We may appreciate the Bible as great literature, but we fully comprehend the Bible only when we see it as a means for dialogue with the living God.

Some years ago I met an elderly woman who had been diagnosed as having terminal cancer. After we discussed her illness, I asked her if she feared death. "Oh, no," she replied. "Jesus will take me by the hand and lead me to heaven. I want to be with my husband, with my parents. I know that God will take care of me."

She *knew* her Bible! She may not have been able to quote chapter and verse, but she knew what Jesus had promised, and she believed! On the other hand, it is possible for a scholar to know all that Jesus says about eternal life without believing a word of it. Our goal in studying the Bible should be to learn what God says in the Bible *and* to believe it *and* to act upon it.

At times we may turn to the Bible with study of its contents uppermost in our minds. At times we may open the Bible primarily as a starting point for prayer. At times we may look into the Bible for guidance. But in every case, we should preface our use of the Bible with humble prayer to God: "O Lord, help me to understand your word. Enable me to believe in your word. Strengthen me to act upon your word. Amen."

Questions for Discussion and Reflection

What is your favorite Bible passage? Why? What part of the Bible is most puzzling to you? Why?

When you pick up the Bible, or when the Bible is read at a worship service, do you consciously try to think that God is speaking to you through these words? What are some ways you can be reminded of this reality? (An example: Some people picture Christ standing at the pulpit on Sunday mornings, reading the Bible to them.)

Activities

Reflect for a few minutes on the most important questions in your life. Then write out your own prayer, asking God to help you find answers to these questions in the Bible. Keep this prayer in your Bible, and use it each time you study or read the Bible.

CHAPTER TWO
Authors of the Bible: God and People

Whirling all around us are sights and sounds, symphonies and Shakespeare's plays, newscasts and baseball games, popular music and talk shows. Transmitted from television stations, these sights and sounds become visible and audible to us the moment we turn on a TV set.

Whirling all around us are other sights and sounds, messages of love and truth, images of grandeur and beauty. Flowing forever from the Creator of the universe, these sights and sounds become visible and audible when we turn our hearts and minds to God.

Most of us are aware of how events are captured by a television camera, broadcast from a station, and received into our homes. We may not understand so clearly how God sends messages to us or how we receive them. But through our Jewish-Christian tradition, we learn that God communicates with us through the beauty of nature, through events in our lives, through other people, and through the experience of prayer. We learn also that we listen to God by tuning our senses and our intellect, our memory and our will, our imagination and our emotions, to the reality of God's presence, action, and communication.

The quality of the pictures and sounds we pick up on a TV depends on many factors. Sunspots or an electrical appliance can cause static. A defective antenna or a faulty tuning dial can cloud the picture and distort the sound. Similarly, the quality of the images and messages we receive from God can be clouded by many factors. Our minds can be blinded by sin. Conflicting messages that deny the existence of God can confuse our hearts. Our senses and intellect, memory and will, imagination and emotions, may be so burdened down with earthly pursuits that we find it almost impossible to direct our attention toward heaven.

Biblical Inspiration

In recent years technology has made it possible for us to overcome many of the obstacles to good television reception. Signals are bounced off satellites. Cable TV gives a direct line to a transmission source. Movies recorded on videotape or DVD can be played back with great clarity.

Technology cannot eliminate the obstacles hindering communication between God and us, but God's inspiration can. In Jewish-Christian history, there have been people who searched for God with such intensity that they "saw God's face" and "heard God's voice." They were *inspired* by God.

Their experience of God in nature, people, events, and prayer may have been similar to the ways in which we encounter God. In some cases, they may have been inspired in scholarly research without realizing that God was working through them (2 Macc 2:19-32 and Lk 1:1-4). In other instances, they may have received God's inspiration in dramatic revelations, as Isaiah did through visions (Isa 6).

But whether they were inspired through natural processes or miraculous occurrences, they reported their experiences to others. Eventually, the Jewish or Christian community to which they belonged recognized their perceptions of God to be authentic, recorded those perceptions, and treasured them as sacred. In time, under God's guidance, the community collected such sacred writings into a book which expressed its beliefs and helped shape the beliefs of generations to come.

Because the Bible came from inspired authors through a community, the perceptions of God preserved in the Bible differ from non-biblical perceptions. Those in the Bible have special standing because they are recognized by the community, the Church, as inspired by God.

The Bible Today

Because God inspired the authors of the Bible in such a way that the inspiration was recognized by the Church, the Bible speaks to us today.

We can, and should, communicate with God in personal prayer. But we struggle. Like a television set depending on a faulty antenna located far from the station, we often receive an image clouded by the interference of conflicting voices and a message garbled by the static of sin. The Bible is like a videotape or DVD we can insert into our awareness and receive a vision and message that are unmistakably from God.

In the Bible are visions of God handed on to us by Abraham, by Moses, by the Jewish community. In the Bible are visions of God given to us by Luke, by Paul, by the Christian community. Through the books of the Bible, our ideas of God are clarified and our ability to speak with God is improved. The Bible puts us in touch with God in a unique and powerful way!

The History Behind the Bible—"B.C."

The development of the Bible occurred in human history. Anyone wanting to become familiar with the Bible should be acquainted with the history of the Jewish and Christian communities that gave birth to the Bible. We will examine this history in later chapters. Here we briefly survey the main events to provide a framework for further study.

The survey begins with Abram, a native of Ur, an ancient city north of the Persian Gulf. In about 1900 B.C. Abram's family migrated to Haran, a city near the present-day Turkish-Syrian border. (Many dates related to Old Testament history are approximate.) In Haran, Abram received a call from God to move to Canaan (the territory known at various times as the Promised Land, Israel, Judah, Judea, Palestine, and the Holy Land). God made a covenant (a ceremonial agreement) with Abram, changing his name to Abraham and promising that he and his wife, Sarah (changed from Sarai), would have a son, the first in a long line of descendants. That son, Isaac, became the father of Jacob, who had twelve sons. In about 1720 B.C. Jacob and his family migrated to Egypt, where their descendants, the Hebrews, eventually became slaves.

About 1250 B.C. a Hebrew named Moses heard God telling him to guide his people to freedom in the land of Canaan, the Promised Land. Moses led the Hebrews (also known as Israelites and later as Jews) in a daring escape. At Mount Sinai he received a new sign of God's covenant in the Ten Commandments, then shepherded the Israelites as they wandered in the desert for forty years. Moses died before entering the

Promised Land, and his lieutenant, Joshua, led the people into Canaan. A period of conquest followed, with the twelve tribes (divisions of the Hebrew people named after the sons of Jacob) settling in various parts of Canaan. They fought with the land's inhabitants (Philistines and others) through a long frontier period called the time of the Judges.

About 1020 B.C. Saul, a charismatic leader, began to bring the tribes together and was named king. He eventually went insane and was killed in battle. He was replaced by a young soldier named David. Beginning about 1000 B.C., David united the tribes, set up Jerusalem as the center of his government, and made Israel a force to be reckoned with in the Middle East. In 961 B.C. his son, Solomon, succeeded him as king and built a magnificent Temple in Jerusalem. But in his later years, Solomon fell into the worship of false gods and alienated his people with heavy taxes and forced labor. His son, Rehoboam, continued these policies, and in 922 B.C. a civil war split the people into two kingdoms—Israel in the north with its capital in Samaria and Judah in the south with its capital in Jerusalem (some scholars give the date as 927 B.C. or 931 B.C.).

Both kingdoms were plagued by poor leadership and by the people's infidelity toward God. In 721 B.C. Israel was attacked by Assyria (part of modern Iraq); its leading citizens were slaughtered or dragged into exile. Other captives from foreign lands were brought into Israel by the Assyrians; they intermarried with Israelites who had been left behind, forming the people known as the Samaritans. In 587 B.C. Judah was conquered by Babylon (also part of modern Iraq). Jerusalem was sacked, its walls destroyed, and its Temple demolished. The survivors were taken into exile in Babylon.

A few decades later, Cyrus, king of Persia, defeated Babylon. He allowed the Israelites to return home in 539 B.C. Those who went back found Jerusalem a heap of ruins. Harassed on every side by enemies, they finished building a new Temple about 515 B.C. and rebuilding the city walls in 445 B.C. But their hopes of regaining the glory of King David's time were doomed to disappointment.

Alexander the Great took command of their government in 332 B.C. After his death, Egypt and Syria vied for control of the Jewish nation, and in 167 B.C. the Syrians launched a terrible persecution of the Jews. They were resisted by a family of warriors, the Maccabees, who succeeded in gaining independence in 142 B.C. This lasted until 63 B.C. when the Romans conquered Jerusalem and made Palestine (Idumea,

Judea, Samaria, and Galilee) a vassal state. In 37 B.C. Herod the Great was set up by the Romans as king; both a despot and a tireless builder, he ruled until 4 B.C. About two years before the end of his reign, Jesus Christ was born. (Those who originally tried to calculate the date of Christ's birth missed by six or seven years.)

The History Behind the Bible—"A.D."

Jesus was raised in the town of Nazareth, about sixty miles north of Jerusalem. He learned the trade of his foster father, Joseph, a carpenter. At about the age of thirty, Jesus began to preach a message that stirred the hearts of many Israelites: The kingdom of God was being established on earth and the hopes of believers would be fulfilled through Jesus. He demonstrated remarkable powers by working miracles of healing. He gathered a band of twelve apostles as special assistants. Many who heard his teaching and saw his miracles hoped that Jesus would be the new King David, a messiah (savior) who would overthrow the Romans and make their country a world power once again. Jesus refused to endorse such hopes, for his kingdom was not of this world.

Nevertheless, Jesus' popularity caused alarm among the Sadducees and Herodians, the ruling classes among the Jewish people. Collaborators with the Romans, they were afraid that the large crowds surrounding Jesus might be incited to revolt. Another important class in Palestine, the Pharisees, were infuriated when Jesus criticized their insistence that people could be saved only by observing the thousands of detailed rules they handed down. Eventually, the Sadducees, Herodians, and Pharisees plotted against Jesus. With the cooperation of Judas Iscariot, one of the twelve apostles, Jesus was arrested, subjected to an unfair trial before the Jewish high court, the Sanhedrin, and was sentenced to death. Because the Jewish leaders did not want to be blamed for Jesus' death, and because they wanted him to undergo the humiliation of a Roman crucifixion, they had him condemned to death by the Roman governor, Pontius Pilate. He was crucified on a Friday afternoon between two criminals at a place called Golgotha, outside the walls of Jerusalem. He died after hours of agony, and a Roman soldier thrust a spear into his side to guarantee the fact of his death. Jesus was buried and his tomb sealed by a huge stone. Soldiers were posted to guard the spot, and his enemies felt that they were rid of him forever.

But on the following Sunday morning, the tomb was found open and empty. No one knew what to make of it until Jesus appeared to his followers risen and glorious, no longer limited by time or space. For a period of forty days, Jesus appeared often to his apostles and to others. He reminded them of how he had foretold his death and Resurrection as God's way of overcoming death and of bringing eternal life to all. He told his followers to preach the Good News of this salvation to the world, taught them that they were to be the sign of his continuing presence on earth, and then ascended into heaven. Ten days later the followers of Jesus were touched by the power of God's Spirit. Led by Peter, first among the apostles, they began to preach to huge crowds that the risen Jesus was the Messiah hoped for by the Jewish people. They invited their hearers to put their faith in Christ and to be joined to Christ by Baptism.

The number of believers grew into the thousands, but opposition from Jewish leaders grew also. In A.D. 36, six years after Christ's Resurrection, a persecution broke out, led by a Pharisee named Saul. He oversaw the execution of a Church leader, Stephen, and threw many believers into prison.

Then came a dramatic and unexpected development. Saul had a vision of the risen Christ and began to proclaim Jesus as the Messiah. Other believers, forced out of Jerusalem by persecution, began to preach the Good News of Jesus to Jews and Gentiles (non-Jews). In spite of further persecutions, Christians continued to preach, grow in number, and care for one another. Gradually, they moved away from their Jewish ties because of the persecutions and because so many Jews refused to accept Jesus as the Messiah.

Christianity soon spread throughout the civilized world. Saul, now known as Paul, and other missionaries preached Christ in Asia Minor, Europe, Africa, and Asia, their task made easier by Roman roads and Roman peace. But then Rome became a foe. The Emperor Nero started a persecution against Christians in the mid-sixties and, according to tradition, martyred both Peter and Paul in Rome. By every logic, the mighty Roman Empire should have crushed Christianity, but persecutions only spurred further growth.

Rome played a major part in another important development. After the death of Herod Agrippa in A.D. 44, rebels in Judea known as Zealots pressed for a holy war against the Romans. In A.D. 66 the unrest exploded into a full-blown revolt. In A.D. 70 the Romans besieged

Jerusalem, slaughtered its inhabitants, and reduced the city to ruins. The Temple was no more, and Christianity was separated even further from its Jewish roots.

Christians soon developed a sense of their own identity as a Church. Patterns of Church structure were established. Local churches were led by bishops and assisted by priests and deacons. Those who succeeded Peter as Bishop of Rome were seen to possess the same authority Peter had received from Jesus; they were first among bishops as Peter had been first among the apostles.

Periodic persecutions by Roman authorities continued, but the Church flourished. By the year A.D. 100 there were 300,000 to 500,000 believers. In A.D. 313, when Christians numbered several million, the Roman Emperor Constantine issued the decree of Milan, granting religious tolerance to the Church. Christianity had become a *catholic* (universal) Church as Christ had intended.

The Formation of the Old Testament

The Jewish people see Abraham as their father in faith and Moses as the leader who brought them from slavery into freedom. We might assume, given the importance of Abraham and Moses, that the sacred books of the Jewish people (the Old Testament) would date back to these great leaders. The descendants of Abraham and Moses certainly passed down stories about these heroes as well as their teachings from generation to generation. They also related traditions about their background and religious beliefs in song and saga, poetry and parable, legend and law.

But these stories, traditions, and beliefs did not reach their present form until later. There are many theories about how this happened. One theory (modified and refined over the years) holds that the Old Testament developed from different sources. A first set of traditions was recorded during the reigns of David and Solomon. These traditions, including some of the best known and most loved stories of the Bible, used "Yahweh" as the name for God, and so are called Yahwist. After the civil war of 922 B.C., another set of traditions, which used "Elohim" as the name for God and is called Elohist, was put into writing in the northern kingdom. When the northern kingdom was destroyed by the Assyrians in 721 B.C., the Elohist documents were taken south where they were merged with the Yahwist tradition. About this time, laws of north and south were codified in a document now known as the Deuter-onomist ("second law") tradition. After the southern kingdom fell to the Babylonians, leaders of the Israelites began to focus more closely on the spiritual meaning of their identity as God's people. They put into writing a fourth set of documents known as the Priestly tradition. Finally, an editor or group of editors blended together the four traditions to form the first five books of the Bible, known as the Pentateuch (Genesis, Exodus, Leviticus, Numbers, and Deuteronomy)—dearly loved by Jews as their Torah or Law.

During the long period of the formulation of the Pentateuch, other books of the Bible were being written. The Deuteronomist tradition produced Joshua, Judges, 1 and 2 Samuel, and 1 and 2 Kings, which put a theological interpretation on the events of Israelite history from the Exodus through the fall of Jerusalem. Great preachers and spiritual leaders, known as the prophets, urged the people of Israel and Judah to be faithful to God's covenant. Their sermons and many of the details of their lives were recorded in the prophetic books of the Old Testament.

With the building of the Temple came temple worship. For centuries, songs used in this worship were collected with other religious and instructional poetry, then arranged several centuries before Christ into the Book of Psalms (Psalter). From the tenth through the fifth centuries before Christ, other kinds of writing evolved: collections of wise sayings like Proverbs, stories like Ruth designed to teach religious lessons, and reflections on the problems of life like Job.

In the fourth century before Christ, efforts to see God's providence in the events of history found expression in the writings of the Chronicler (1 and 2 Chronicles, Ezra, and Nehemiah). As Israel found itself under attack by Greece, Egypt, and Syria, great writers composed stories like Tobit, Judith, and Esther, teaching the virtues of fidelity, devotion, courage, and trust in God. The trials endured by the Israelites during such hard times caused wise teachers to examine the meaning of life in books like Ecclesiastes and Sirach. The Syrian persecution and Maccabean revolt became the focus of 1 and 2 Maccabees, written about 100 B.C.

A special kind of literature called apocalypse developed during the Syrian persecution. Using visions, numerical codes, and symbols, the authors of such literature, represented by the Book of Daniel (Chapters 7–12), tried to encourage the oppressed to persevere. Finally, about the middle of the first century before Christ, a Jew who was familiar with

Greek thinking and Hebrew traditions wrote the Wisdom of Solomon to proclaim God's presence in the world, the immortality of the human soul, and God's Final Judgment rewarding the just and punishing the wicked.

When were these books formed into the collection we know as the Old Testament? By the time of the return from exile, there were compilations of sacred writings that were proclaimed to the people on special occasions. For example, the Book of Nehemiah describes how Ezra, the priest-scribe, read to the people of Jerusalem the book of the law of Moses, most likely a portion of the Pentateuch (Neh 8). Mention is made, one hundred years or so before Christ, of the "sacred books" (1 Macc 12:9) and the "law and the prophets" (2 Macc 15:9).

By this time there were apparently two collections of sacred books in common use. One, in Hebrew, came to be known as the Palestinian. The other, in Greek, was called the Septuagint (from the Greek word for seventy, following a tradition that it came from seventy translators) or Alexandrian (from the city in Egypt where it originated). This version included some books written in Greek and Aramaic (spoken language of the Jews before and during the time of Christ) as well as those translated from Hebrew, and so was larger than the Palestinian collection. The Palestinian and Alexandrian collections were honored by different Jewish communities, but since Greek was then the common language of the Mediterranean world, the Alexandrian collection became more widespread. Neither of these collections reached its definitive form until after the time of Christ. The Alexandrian collection was accepted by Christians as their Old Testament. The Palestinian collection was set by a group of Jewish scholars about A.D. 100, partially in reaction to the Christian use of the Alexandrian collection.

The Formation of the New Testament and the Christian Bible

After Christ's Resurrection, missionaries spread the Good News of Jesus by preaching. Eventually, Christians felt a need to preserve their heritage in writing. Collections of the sayings of Jesus, liturgical prayers, and professions of faith began to appear. In A.D. 51 or 52 Paul started to write letters to the cities he had evangelized. These letters were preserved and shared. Soon they were recognized as having a special authority. By A.D. 65 or 70 the Gospel of Mark was written. Other gospels and writings followed. Some were accepted by the Church as inspired by God, while others were rejected. By A.D. 125 (at the latest) all twenty-seven books of our New Testament were written. By A.D. 250 or so they were compiled into a list (canon) and were generally recognized as inspired.

During these years, the sacred books of the Jewish people were evaluated by Christians. Since the entire New Testament was written in Greek for Greek-speaking Christians of Jewish and gentile origin, New Testament writers used the Alexandrian (Septuagint) version of the Old Testament. They usually quoted the Old Testament from the Alexandrian version and frequently referred to the books found only in this version. Church councils (gatherings of Church leaders) at Rome in A.D. 382, Hippo in 393, and Carthage in 397 gave lists of the books of the Christian Bible based on the Alexandrian version. The early Church accepted the Bible as Catholics accept it today (twenty-seven New Testament books and forty-six Old Testament books; C 120).

There was little dissent until the sixteenth century, when Martin Luther and other Protestants rejected the Alexandrian (Christian) list in favor of the Palestinian (Jewish) list. Luther also questioned the inspiration of four New Testament books: Hebrews, James, Jude, and Revelation; however, his followers maintained the traditional list, and it soon prevailed. In 1546 the Council of Trent defined the Alexandrian as the official list of Old Testament books for Catholics and reaffirmed the traditional list of New Testament books. As a result, while Catholics and Protestants today share the same New Testament of twenty-seven books, the Catholic Old Testament contains seven more books than the Protestant: Tobit, Judith, First and Second Maccabees, Wisdom, Sirach (sometimes called Ecclesiasticus), and Baruch (plus additions to Esther and Daniel). These are placed in some Protestant Bibles as the Apocrypha (hidden books).

The Languages of the Bible

The Old Testament was largely written in Hebrew. The Book of Tobit and parts of Daniel, Ezra, and Esther were written in Aramaic. The Wisdom of Solomon and the Second Book of Maccabees were written in Greek, as was the entire New Testament. Thanks to cooperation among Scripture scholars of all faiths, modern English translations are in substantial agreement with one another and accurately relay the ideas and feelings conveyed in the original languages. To the extent that they do, God, the divine Author of the Bible, speaks to us through the human authors of the Bible.

Questions for Discussion and Reflection

Can you think of a situation in the Bible where someone encountered God in nature? in people? in events? in prayer? Be as specific as you can in recalling the circumstances of God's self-revelation in each of these cases. (Some examples: 1 Kings 19:9-13 [nature]; Acts 9:1-9 [people]; Ps 78 [events]; Ex 33:7-11 [prayer].) Can you recall incidents in your own life when you experienced God in nature, people, events, prayer?

Activities

Try to memorize or at least become familiar with these important dates:

B.C. 1900—Abraham; 1720—Joseph and brothers in Egypt; 1250—Moses and the Exodus; 1000—David; 922—divided kingdoms; 721—fall of northern kingdom to Assyria; 587—fall of southern kingdom to Babylon; 539—exiles return; 515—Temple rebuilt; 445—Jerusalem's walls rebuilt; 332—Alexander the Great conquers Palestine; 167—Syrian persecution and Maccabee revolt; 142—independence for Judea; 63—Romans conquer Jerusalem; 37—Herod the Great; 6—birth of Jesus Christ.

A.D. 26—Christ begins his preaching; 30—Christ's crucifixion and Resurrection; 36—persecution of Christians under Saul; 51—first book of New Testament; 70—destruction of Jerusalem; 125—New Testament books completed; 313—Edict of Milan; 382—Council of Rome lists seventy-three books of Bible; 1546—Council of Trent defines books of Bible.

Most Bibles have maps of lands inhabited by the Jewish people. Try to become familiar with these lands. Note that at different times the Jewish homeland was known as the Promised Land, Canaan, Israel, Judah, Judea, Palestine, and the Holy Land.

Quietly reflect for a few minutes on the sights and sounds whirling all around you. Then turn on a radio, and tune in several different programs. The sounds were there all the time, but a radio was necessary to capture them. Turn off the radio, and sit quietly once again. Reflect on the sights and sounds that are messages from God to you. Notice something beautiful in nature. Think of a person you love. Consider an event that brought you joy or sorrow. Then open your heart to God, and pray for the grace to see what God wants you to see, to hear what God wants you to hear.

CHAPTER THREE
Reading and Interpreting the Bible

E very morning thousands of Americans sit down to a cup of coffee and the morning paper. Typical readers might look through the front-page news, check out the sports headlines, browse through a number of advertisements, read an editorial or two, scan some popular columns, and enjoy the comics.

Without realizing it, they are engaging in a sophisticated form of literary analysis. As they page through the various sections of the paper, they instinctively categorize many different forms of writing and interpret them accordingly. They look for one thing on the front page, another in the editorials. They draw one kind of information from their favorite columnist, another from the advertisements. They eagerly read about "Giants" and "Angels" on the sports page and laugh at the antics of talking dogs and feisty cats in the comics.

Analyzing Literary Forms Across Cultures

We might wonder what is so sophisticated about reading the morning paper. But imagine the following scenario. In the year 2025 the earth is struck by an immense meteor. Most people are killed by the impact and by the geological disturbances that follow. The few who survive are reduced to living in caves. They begin the difficult process of rebuilding civilization. By the year 5000 they have reached the point of doing scholarly research about ancient cultures, including the United States of America in the early twenty-first century. Under the rubble of three thousand years, they discover old documents and analyze them until they can begin to translate English into their own language.

One day archaeologists discover pieces of a newspaper. They laboriously decipher a front-page story about a robbery. "Guard guns down bandit trying to steal company payroll," they read, helped in their analysis by a picture of the bandit lying in a pool of blood. Next they discover part of a sports section that says: "Crowd cheers as New York catcher guns down St. Louis runner trying to steal second base." The archaeologists are shocked. They come to the conclusion that Americans enjoyed sporting events where contestants fought to the death.

They are further confused by these Americans when they find a portion of the comics. They wonder: "Did dogs talk in the old days and did cats actually push their owners around?"

The archaeologists remain baffled until other finds of newspapers and literature give them an improved knowledge of English and of American culture. They discover that "gunning down a runner" on the sports page means something quite different from "gunning down a bandit" on the front page. They study books about cartoons and soon are chuckling over the funnies, wondering how they could have misunderstood them so completely.

The task of these fiftieth century archaeologists would be to enter into the minds of twenty-first century Americans, to learn the culture, to understand the language, to find out what each writer had intended. Much study and research would be required before they could interpret our writings. What we Americans do easily and without thinking might be a very demanding chore after the passage of three thousand years!

Analyzing Literary Forms of the Bible

This imaginary scenario can help us realize some of the difficulties involved in understanding the Bible. About three thousand years have passed since the first parts of the Bible were written. As was pointed out in Chapter One, archaeologists have only recently uncovered many elements necessary for a proper understanding of the Bible. So it is not surprising that a reevaluation of biblical books has taken place. While this might be disturbing to some people, it has in fact greatly enhanced our ability to grasp the real meaning of the Bible. It is true that some books formerly thought to be historical are now classified in other categories. But it is also true that the essential historical foundation of our Christian faith is now more demonstrable than ever. For example, no serious historian would question the reality of Christ's life. The more we study the Bible, the more assurance we have that our faith is solidly built on rock.

The method of interpreting the Bible, which attempts to go back to the original intent of its authors by analyzing their times, culture, language, and other circumstances, is called the *contextual* approach. This is the approach recommended by Pope Pius XII in his 1943 encyclical letter, *Divino Afflante Spiritu,* by the Second Vatican Council, and by the *Catechism of the Catholic Church* (C 109-110).

Another approach to the Bible is the *fundamentalist interpretation*, which usually holds that the words of the Bible must be taken at face value. There are many different kinds of fundamentalism, and all of them involve *interpreting* the Bible in one way or another.

Some fundamentalists say the story of creation in the first chapter of Genesis must be taken exactly as it is: God created the world in six 24-hour days, then rested on the seventh. Other fundamentalists teach that the days stand for longer periods of time. Fundamentalists actually interpret every passage of the Bible; they explain how the Bible should be understood.

This only shows that the Bible *must* be interpreted. We've seen that passages calling God a "Rock" and those demanding that we "hate" members of our family require interpretation. So does nearly every passage of the Bible. The real issue is: What principles will we use to interpret the Bible?

Catholic Principles for Interpreting the Bible

Fundamentalists tend to interpret the Bible according to the subjective principles of an individual preacher or according to their own personal interpretation. Catholics are encouraged to interpret the Bible according to objective principles endorsed by the Church. Catholics are guided to a proper interpretation of the Bible in essential matters of Faith because the Church clearly defines such doctrines as the Resurrection of Christ and his Real Presence in the Eucharist. The *Catechism of the Catholic Church* teaches that we must read the Scriptures within the living Tradition of the Church. God entrusted the Bible to the Church and sent the Holy Spirit to guide the Church to all truth, and we can understand the Bible only with the Church's guidance (C 113).

The first principle of interpretation is that given by Pope Pius XII, the Second Vatican Council, and the *Catechism of the Catholic Church* (C 109-110). We should use the contextual approach to discover the literal meaning of any passage, the meaning intended by the authors. To find it, we study the time, place, way of life, mode of thinking, purpose in writing, and manners of expression of those authors.

Another important principle expressed in the *Catechism of the Catholic Church* (C 112) is that we must be attentive to the content and unity of the whole Bible. We should interpret a given passage in light of the other passages that relate to it. A classic example of this is Matthew 26:26-28, where Jesus said over the bread and wine: "Take, eat; this is my body....Drink from it, all of you; for this is my blood." Curiously enough, this is one passage which fundamentalists refuse to take literally. But Catholics interpret it in the light of John 6, where Jesus proclaims himself to be the bread of life. When Jesus said that we must eat his flesh and drink his blood, many of his hearers abandoned him. Jesus did not call them back and tell them, "You misunderstood. I only meant that in a symbolic way." What he was asking them to believe was hard to accept, and when they refused, Jesus sadly let them go. Other passages, such as 1 Corinthians 11:27, also point to the Real Presence of Jesus under the appearances of the bread and wine. Catholics look at the content of the whole Bible, and believe that Jesus is truly present in the Eucharist.

A third principle for interpreting the Bible is that there is a unity and consistency to the truths God has revealed for our salvation. The *Catechism of the Catholic Church* calls this the analogy of faith (C 114). Some interpreters mistakenly pit faith and works against each other, arguing that we are saved by faith alone. But faith and works cannot be separated. In Galatians 3:1-9, Paul emphasizes that justification comes through faith in Christ rather than through observance of the Jewish law. By saying this, Paul is not denying the importance of good works, for in Galatians 5–6 he emphasizes them as "the fruit of the Spirit" (5:22). Passages that affirm the importance of faith are consistent with those that speak of the need for works. "The only thing that counts is faith working through love" (5:6). When this principle of unity and consistency is ignored, confusion results. It is possible, for example, to argue almost any position by quoting certain parts of the Bible to the exclusion of others. Catholics are urged to recognize the harmony in God's plan. (At times Catholics are attacked for their beliefs by someone citing some passages while ignoring others. Our response should be to explain our position if the other person is open-minded. If not, then we should state that we respect the beliefs of others and we expect them to respect ours.)

A fourth principle is that the languages of the Bible use colorful expressions not meant to be taken at face value. Some samples: "If you had faith the size of a mustard seed, you would say to this mulberry tree, 'Be uprooted and planted in the sea,' and it would obey you" (Lk 17:6). "If your right eye causes you to sin, tear it out and throw it away" (Mt 5:29). And the previously mentioned "Whoever comes to me and does not hate father and mother, wife and children, brothers and sisters, yes, and even life itself, cannot be my disciple" (Lk 14:26). This kind of language is not easily translated into English, but we ought to remember that we have untranslatable expressions in English too. As the mother said to her daughter, "I've told you a million times not to exaggerate!"

A fifth principle is that Old Testament passages should be interpreted in light of Jesus Christ and of the New Testament (C 129). Some excerpts from the Old Testament make us wonder: "Can this really be part of the spiritual message God sends to guide us?" The Psalmist's cry for revenge, "O daughter Babylon, you devastator, / happy shall they be who pay you back… / who take your little ones / and dash them against the rock!" (Ps 137:8-9), is such a passage. It is certainly not a part of the message of Jesus! We can presume, therefore, that it is a reflection of the imperfect theology of the Old Testament, not an indication of God's will for us.

As a general rule, it is safe to say that if an Old Testament passage attributes something to God which we cannot attribute to Jesus Christ, then that passage should be interpreted in light of Christ's life and teaching. For example, it is not likely that God actually commanded Old Testament military leaders to slaughter every man, woman, and innocent child in the cities they overran. It is far more likely that these leaders mistakenly believed God to be behind their directives and that their erroneous attitudes are reported as they perceived them. (This matter will be addressed in more detail in chapter 5.)

Inspiration and Truth in the Bible

The contextual approach to the Bible does not deny the truth of the Bible. The Catholic Church teaches that God is the author of the Bible. This is what is meant by biblical inspiration. "All scripture is inspired by God and is useful for teaching, for reproof, for correction, and for training in righteousness" (2 Tim 3:16; see also 2 Pet 1:20-21).

Since God is the author of the Bible, the books of Scripture teach without error the truths that God intends to reveal for the sake of our salvation (C 107). But truth is expressed in different ways in various literary forms, such as history, prophecy, poetry, law, proverbs (wise sayings), myths (stories or descriptions of actual events that explain ultimate reality), legends (popular unverifiable stories handed down from the past, often conveying a moral), fables (fictitious stories, often with animal characters, that teach a lesson), and parables (simple stories that illustrate a moral or a religious lesson).

All these literary forms are capable of communicating truth in dramatic fashion. Poetry, for example, expresses truth in ways a dictionary cannot. These opening lines from Percy Bysshe Shelley's "To a Skylark"...

Hail to thee, blithe spirit!
Bird thou never wert....

seem to say the skylark was never a bird. The dictionary affirms that the skylark is a bird. Yet both Shelley and the dictionary tell the truth. Shelley expresses in poetic fashion the beauty and grace of the skylark. The dictionary gives us a technical definition. If we know how to read poetry, we will see the truth of Shelley's lines and understand that they convey realities the dictionary cannot.

It is interesting to note that the more important any subject matter is to us, the more we tend to use poetry and other nonscientific literary forms. Scientific, factual language may be adequate for the laboratory, but when we are dealing with the deepest things in life, we find such speech lacking. We turn instead to poetry, images, symbols, and song. The Bible deals with life and death, love and hate, good and evil, God and nothingness. Mere laboratory language cannot do justice to such issues!

Worth noting, too, is the distinction between truth and historical actuality. A story which is not historical can convey truth, as the parables of Jesus show. The "prodigal son" may not have been a real person, but the point of the parable is true: God loves us more than we can imagine and is always ready to forgive us.

At times historical persons become the focal point for stories that are not historical but teach lessons that are true. For example, George Washington existed in history. But one story often told about George Washington—that as a child he chopped down his father's cherry tree, then admitted his guilt ("I cannot tell a lie")—is probably not historical. Yet the story teaches a moral that is true: Honesty is the best policy. So in the Bible, historical persons like Abraham became heroes of stories which, while not historical, teach religious lessons. For example, the story about God asking Abraham to sacrifice his son Isaac goes beyond history because it describes interaction between God and a human being (Gen 22:1-19). What actually occurred in this event seems impossible to express in mere historical terms. In the Bible, parables, poetry, myths, fables, and other literary forms become vehicles for the expression of important religious truths, many of which transcend history.

Inspiration and Human Limitations

In the Catholic understanding of inspiration, God did not merely dictate words, but influenced the authors to use their own talents and abilities. As a result, the Bible is both the Word of God and the work of human beings. The Church teaches that those truths which God inspired for our salvation are without error (C 107), but there are many elements in the Bible (such as contemporary notions of science and history) which are not directly related to our salvation. So the Bible can have limitations which come from its human origins. In particular, the Old Testament contains matters that are imperfect and provisional (C 122).

The human authors of the Bible were people of their own times in terms of their scientific knowledge. They took for granted that the earth rested on pillars, for example, and apparently had no idea that it is a globe spinning through space. God inspired those very people, with their limited knowledge of science and their mistaken notions about the created universe, to teach basic truths that still apply today. God used their inaccurate ideas to get across a true message: God created all that exists.

The human authors of the Bible were people of their own times in their inability to grasp the fullness of God's revelation. God guided them to the extent that they could accept divine inspiration. Those who lived five hundred years before Christ did not comprehend the difference between causing and allowing. They thought that God caused everything, including evil. (See Ex 11:10.) In this they were mistaken, and God did not inspire their limitations (which are entirely human). But God could inspire these limited human authors to convey truths about other important matters. As the centuries passed, and as people grew in spiritual maturity, they could grasp more and more of God's truth. In later books of the Old Testament and in the New Testament, we find a clearer understanding of God's causality.

A young man once remarked to me, "I don't understand how Catholics can believe that Mary prays for us when the Bible says that the dead don't know anything. As far as I am concerned, Ecclesiastes 9:5 settles the issue." This statement is a classic example of how to *mis*use the Bible. Ecclesiastes 9:5 declares: "The living know that they will die, but the dead know nothing." The young man took this passage as the last word in the Bible on life after death. But it is far from the last word. We human beings learn things step by step. From ignorance we move gradually to knowledge. The Holy Spirit progressively guides us to a fuller understanding of the truth (Jn 16:13). The author of Ecclesiastes, who wrote three hundred years before Christ, was mistaken about eternal life. But the inspired message of Ecclesiastes is not the last word on eternal life. Rather, it is the fact that we need a Savior. Later Old Testament books, such as 1 and 2 Maccabees and Wisdom, taught the existence of life after death. Jesus made the reality of eternal life absolutely clear, and his teaching is proclaimed throughout the New Testament.

God did not change, but people did in terms of their ability to hear what God was saying to them. There is a development of doctrine in the biblical books, and the more we know of the history and formation of the Bible, the better we will understand it. Many older passages from the Bible are dated; they are valuable because they show how humanity has evolved in its understanding of God's message, but they should no longer guide our actions. They must be interpreted and understood in the light of the whole Bible, especially the teaching of Jesus.

Inspiration and Uncertainty

Biblical authors sometimes put different versions of an event in the same book, possibly because they were not sure which version was correct or because they came from separate traditions that the authors wanted to preserve. Thus, we read in Acts 9:7 that when Jesus appeared to Paul, those who accompanied Paul "heard the voice but saw no one." In Acts 22:9 they "saw the light but did not hear the voice." Perhaps Luke learned two versions of what had happened years before, could not decide which was the more accurate, and so included both. Obviously, Luke was not trying to prove the truth of one or the other. What he wanted to convey, and what God said through him without error, was that Jesus had appeared to Paul and changed his entire life. If such uncertainties or conflicting accounts did not bother the authors of the Bible, then clearly they should not trouble us. They are peripheral to the central purpose of the Bible, the expression of spiritual realities.

The Bible and Tradition: Revelation

All that has been said about the Bible being handed on through the Catholic Church and about the Church's role in interpreting the Bible can help us understand that the Bible came from the Church, not the Church from the Bible.

By proclaiming that the seventy-three books of the Bible were inspired by God and by rejecting other books as not inspired, the early Church was saying: "*This* is what we believe about God, about Jesus Christ, about life and death, about who we are as a Church. *That* is what we reject." The books of the Bible, in turn, helped shape the beliefs of each new generation of Christians.

This was a dynamic process involving conflict. In the first four centuries after Christ, there were some people who wanted to put limits on the saving action of Jesus by claiming that all Christians should follow the law of Moses. Some heretics said that Jesus was God, but not human. Others asserted that Jesus was human, but not God. Still others denied that Jesus revealed God as Father, Son, and Holy Spirit.

The Church refuted such errors and expressed God's revealed truth about important doctrines in the books of the Bible it accepted as inspired. It repudiated false teachings by rejecting books such as the Gnostic gospels and other works sometimes called the "hidden books" of the Bible. The Church expressed its beliefs also in the way it interpreted the Bible, in the decisions of councils, in formulas of faith called creeds, and in its worship. In this way, Christ guided the Church we recognize as "Catholic," and inspired the Bible as a "Catholic" book.

In this process the Church did not create its own set of beliefs. Rather, the Church could teach only the truths God has made known to humanity. God has revealed some truths in natural ways. The universe, for example, shows us something of God's greatness. But God has also spoken to us in miraculous ways, teaching us supernatural truths we could not have arrived at on our own. In Old Testament times God revealed truths to inspired writers. Then, in the fullness of time, God sent Jesus Christ as the perfect Word of Revelation (Jn 1). What Jesus taught the apostles was handed on by them orally through preaching and in writing. God's supernatural Revelation, then, is transmitted in two ways: through sacred Tradition and through Scripture.

The content of sacred Tradition and Scripture is called the Deposit of Faith. Jesus revealed all the truths necessary for our salvation, and in this sense the Deposit of Faith is complete. The Church adds nothing to this Deposit, but under the guidance of the Holy Spirit it does grow in its understanding of what Christ has revealed. As the Church hands on the Deposit of Faith from generation to generation, it develops a keener awareness of the beauty of God's Revelation (C 74-100).

Tradition means "handing on," and sacred Tradition includes the way the Church has handed on and interpreted the Bible, as well as conciliar decisions, creeds, worship, and the consistent teaching of the Church. These may not contradict the Bible but are closely related to the Bible, are based on the Bible, and expand upon the Bible.

Some churches contend that all doctrine must be found explicitly in the Bible. Catholics do not think that our beliefs can be limited to what the Bible says, because early in the life of the Church there was no New Testament. The first Christians believed in sacred Tradition before a complete Bible existed.

The Catholic Church teaches that every doctrine must be in harmony with the Bible, but need not be explicitly declared in the Bible. An example is the doctrine of the Trinity. The Bible mentions Father, Son, and Holy Spirit, but never uses the word Trinity. What is implicitly contained in the Bible is made explicit in the sacred Tradition of the Church.

Sacred Tradition is necessary also if the Church is to apply the teaching of the Bible to changing circumstances. The Church does this under the guidance of the Holy Spirit, for Jesus said to the apostles: "I still have many things to say to you, but you cannot bear them now. But when the Spirit of truth comes, he will guide you into all the truth" (Jn 16:12-13). (See Chapter 12 for a more detailed explanation of the relationship between Scripture and sacred Tradition.)

The Bible: A Catholic Book

We have spoken of the Bible as a "Catholic" book. This is not to deny it to anyone else. But the original Christian Bible was formed in communities of believers presided over by Catholic bishops and finalized into a collection through the decisions of councils of Catholic bishops.

The Bible was preserved and handed down through the centuries by the Catholic Church. Before the invention of the printing press, Catholic monks and nuns copied each letter of every word of the Bible by hand. Many of these handwritten manuscripts survive today, testimonials to the love and artistic skill of those who created them.

For two thousand years the Bible has been read daily at Catholic celebrations of the Eucharist. In catacombs, in private homes, and in great cathedrals, God's word has been proclaimed to Catholics, a continuing witness to the Church's reverence for the Bible. The Catholic *Lectionary,* a book of Scripture readings following a three-year cycle for Sundays, was the model for the *Common Lectionary* used in many Protestant churches.

The Catholic Church encourages its members to read the Bible. The Second Vatican Council in its *Dogmatic Constitution on Divine Revelation*:

> ...forcefully and specifically exhorts all the Christian faithful...to learn "the surpassing knowledge of Jesus Christ" (Phil 3:8) by frequent reading of the divine Scriptures. "Ignorance of the Scriptures is ignorance of Christ." Therefore, let them go gladly to the sacred text itself, whether in the sacred liturgy, which is full of the divine words, or in devout reading....Let them remember, however, that prayer should accompany the reading of sacred Scripture, so that a dialogue takes place between God and man. For, "we speak to him when we pray; we listen to him when we read the divine oracles" (#25; see also C 131-133).

The Senses of Scripture

The *Catechism of the Catholic Church* notes that in addition to the literal sense intended by the authors of the Bible, there can also be a spiritual sense (C 115-119). Because of the unity of God's plan for our salvation, God could intend connections of which the human authors

34

were unaware. Scripture passages can therefore convey relationships through symbolism and analogy, and many biblical events can be signs that call our attention to deeper realities. God knows and intends these relationships, and the Church seeks them out through prayer and reflection. The *Catechism* subdivides the spiritual sense into three types.

The first is the *allegorical* sense. This means that a biblical event can carry a symbolism that transcends the literal meaning of the text. For example, the crossing of the Red Sea is an allegory, a sign, which prefigures and suggests Christian baptism.

The second is the *moral* sense, meaning that events in Scripture should guide us to act justly. The Book of Ruth, for instance, not only tells the story of a woman who was committed to God and to her family but also invites us to imitate Ruth's commitment.

The third sense is the *anagogical*. This word comes from a Greek verb meaning to lead, and it indicates that events in the Bible have an eternal significance. By anagogy the city Jerusalem on earth is a sign of the heavenly Jerusalem, and the Church on earth is a sign of our eternal home in heaven.

The Bible: God Speaks to Us

In chapter 2 we reflected on the development of the Bible. In this chapter we have considered interpretation of the Bible. We ought to have a good understanding of the origin and interpretation of the Bible, but we must go beyond mere understanding to the realization that in the Bible God speaks to us as a loving Father to his children (C 104).

When we pick up the Bible, God, who is not limited by time or space, speaks to us through the same words as those addressed to Abraham, to Moses, or to the prophets. When we pick up the Bible, Jesus speaks to us here and now, just as truly as he spoke to the apostles two thousand years ago (C 101-102).

Through the Bible, God can give us special insights that will help us in the unique set of circumstances that come with each new day. Words we have read many times in the past may touch us with new power when we are grieving at the death of a loved one, when we are confused and don't know where to turn, when we are looking for answers to life's questions.

Each time we open the Bible, we "dial God's number." We can select any other book from a library shelf, read it, and learn valuable information. All the while, however, the book's author is not aware of what we are doing. But when we pick up the Bible, God says "Hello."

God is right there for us with answers to today's problems. "Indeed, the word of God is living and effective...and able to discern reflections and thoughts of the heart" (Heb 4:12). The *Catechism of the Catholic Church* urges us to understand the literal meaning of Scripture, the meaning intended by the human authors. But it also invites us to seek out further spiritual meanings that can allow God to speak personally to us.

When we are discouraged, Jesus says to us, "Come to me, all you who labor and are burdened, and I will give you rest" (Mt 11:28). When we are fearful, Jesus tells us, "Peace be with you" (Jn 20:19). When we are lonely, Jesus assures us, "I am with you always" (Mt 28:20).

God's words in the Bible invite a response. We respond in *prayer:* We read God's words, then talk to God as we would to any friend. We respond through our *life choices:* We read until we come to a phrase that challenges us to a decision, then make a resolution based on what God has spoken to us. There is no other book that allows this kind of communication with God. "Indeed, the word of God *is* living and effective!"

Questions for Discussion and Reflection

What is your understanding of literary forms? How many kinds of literary forms can you identify in the daily newspaper? How many in the Bible? How does each literary form in the newspaper and in the Bible convey truth? What are the differences between the contextual and the fundamentalist approaches to the Bible? What is the difference between historical and true? Have you ever thought of interpreting the Old Testament in the light of Jesus Christ? Does this invite you to rethink the way you've understood certain Old Testament passages? In what ways is the Bible a Catholic book? What does it mean to say: "When you pick up the Bible, you dial God's number"?

Activities

Call a friend on the telephone, just to enjoy a pleasant conversation. Then, with that experience fresh in your mind, pick up your Bible and enjoy a pleasant visit with Jesus.

PART II

THE OLD
TESTAMENT

CHAPTER FOUR

First Steps in the Old Testament: Adam to Moses

Wayne and Rita listened as their children chattered all the way home from a Christmas visit to Rita's parents. The children repeated stories Grandpa had told them about the old days and questioned their parents about elderly relatives.

Intrigued by their children's interest in the past, Wayne and Rita decided to look into their family history. They asked their parents to tape-record reminiscences. They began to trace their family tree. They took the children to visit churches where family members had been baptized and country graveyards where relatives were buried. Parents and children alike were fascinated by old newspaper articles and courthouse records of land transactions.

Eventually, Rita and Wayne traced their origins back to Germany. They discovered that their ancestors had left Europe in 1849 to escape religious persecution, endured a difficult transatlantic voyage, floated by raft down the Ohio River, and finally settled in Kentucky.

By investigating their past, they gained a new appreciation of their Catholic faith and of America as a land of opportunity. They acquired new insights into the meaning of family. They talked about the values their ancestors had treasured and what those values meant to them. Their family tree took on new life because it was now firmly rooted in the past.

The Roots of Our Spiritual Family

In a rapidly changing world, people are looking for the stability and assurance that come from having roots. We who are Catholic have roots that go much deeper than courthouse records or old gravestones. We can trace our spiritual ancestry back to ancient traditions found in the Old Testament.

If we see the books of the Old Testament as records of our own family history, we will discover a key that unlocks some of the greatest treasures of Scripture. They are not just stories from the distant past, lists of names, and ancient laws and regulations. They are our family history, the names of our ancestors in the faith, the details of how our family used to live. We then look into the Old Testament with the same enthusiasm anyone might feel looking into old family treasures.

Reading the Old Testament

One of the purposes of this book is to help people *read* the Bible by offering them a guided tour with background information and selected passages for the books of the Bible. The information and selections will be limited to keep this work at a reasonable size. Readers can get more detailed explanations for individual passages in Bible commentaries. (See Bibliography.)

We begin with an introduction to the Pentateuch, then move on to the books of the Bible, following the order given in the *New Revised Standard Version of the Bible.*

The Pentateuch

The editors who constructed the Pentateuch, the first five books of the Bible, about five hundred and fifty years before Christ, wanted to give the Israelites stability and assurance. Their people had been uprooted and exiled by the Babylonians. Those who returned were tempted to abandon God for pagan deities. They were attracted by pagan myths which claimed that evil and chaos guided human destiny.

The editors wanted to turn the Israelites from such errors to the solid traditions handed down from Abraham and Moses. They recorded the oft-told stories about their ancestors who had followed God's will. They taught that God existed, that God had created all good things, and that evil was not a divinity but the consequence of sinful choices made by human beings.

We are faced with temptations like those challenging the ancient Israelites. We are tempted to discredit our faith as old fashioned, to worship the false gods of materialism, lust, and secular humanism, to fear that evil has the power to crush what is good, loving, and beautiful.

The Pentateuch proclaims to us, as it has to previous generations, that one true God exists, that good will overcome evil, that we can safely walk along the paths chosen by our ancestors. The Pentateuch is relevant for us today because it records our family past and, under divine inspiration, answers the most basic questions in life.

The Book of Genesis: 1–11

Genesis is a book wherein the Israelites recall their family origins in the patriarchs Abraham, Isaac, and Jacob, then go far beyond them to the origins of the universe and the meaning of life itself. Now, open your Bible and read *Genesis 1:1–2:4.*

This section of Genesis is from the Priestly tradition, and it may have been used in Temple worship. It presumes the Jewish understanding of the world as a flat structure elevated by columns above the oceans, and the sky as an inverted bowl with windows to let in rain and snow. There is a repetition of phrases designed to make memorization easier: "And God said," "And it was so," "And God saw that it was good," "And there was evening and there was morning." The seven-day structure is poetic, designed to teach the sacredness of the Lord's day, for even God rested after six days of work!

The structure also provides an interlocking of the days, another memory aid. Day one, when God creates light, is connected to day four, when God creates the sun, moon, and stars. Day two, when God creates the dome of the sky separating the rainwaters from the waters below, links with day five, when God creates the birds that fly beneath the sky and the fish that swim in the sea. Day three, when God causes dry land to appear and creates plants, is related to day six, when God creates animals and humans that live on the land and eat the plants.

Special attention is given to the creation of human beings. God says, "Let us make humankind in our image." The meaning of this phrase is debated by scholars. One opinion is that "let us" may be a plural of majesty, a solemn declaration of God's intent to do something special.

"In our image" probably refers to the fact that people have dominion over the earth as representatives of God and are called to care for the world God has given to us.

In contrast to the pagan myths of the time, this creation account teaches that there is only one God who creates all things. Creation does not come from the battles of gods of good and evil who are only a part of nature.

The message holds true for us today. The universe does not come from nothing. Its organization could not happen by accident from the random clashing of atoms. God exists. God created this universe. We human beings are not accidents but creatures of worth, because we are God's own representatives on earth. The first chapter of Genesis does not provide a scientific account of creation (this was unknown at the time Genesis was composed), but it does teach religious truth in language that brims with power and beauty.

The Catholic Church teaches that Genesis is not in conflict with modern scientific theories of creation, including those that allow a place for evolution, as long as these do not deny the existence of God and the fact that all things find their origin in God. Genesis is concerned with religious questions, the *why* of creation. Science is concerned with what is observable, the *how* of creation. It is possible that God may have created the universe over eons and that in God's providence, some evolution might have occurred in the creatures God made. Genesis teaches that in whatever way the universe came into being, it came from the love and wisdom of God.

Read *Genesis 2:4–3:24*. This section contains a second account of creation drawn from the Yahwist source. There are some inconsistencies in the two accounts. For example, human beings are created after animals in the first but before animals in the second. The final editors of Genesis obviously were not concerned with such differences, and this fact alone shows that they were not attempting to present a scientific description of creation. They included both accounts because each had long been treasured in the community and each emphasized particular religious truths.

The ancients wondered, as we do today, why the world includes sin, suffering, pain, and death. The second account of creation, in colorful language full of symbols and insight into the human condition, addresses these issues. It weaves a story not just about the first humans on earth but about us.

God has given us life in a world that could be a paradise. We are free, intelligent beings invited to walk hand in hand with a loving God. We are given the possibility of faithful commitment in marriage and of sharing with God in the creation of new life. We are to use our freedom well, choosing what God declares to be good and avoiding what God declares to be evil. But the first human beings ate from "the tree of knowledge of good and evil." Tempted by the devil (represented by a serpent, a common pagan symbol), they said to God: "You can't tell us what to do. We will decide what is good and what is evil." Through their choice, sin came into the world and built a wall between us and God. We became liable to suffering and death, to strife in human relationships, to fatigue and boredom in our work, to pain in such human functions as childbirth. What could have been paradise became a world where we sink into death and despair, into a helplessness where salvation can be found only in God, who even at the worst of times promises that the serpent's head can be crushed and evil overcome.

The rest of Genesis 4–11 is a commentary on the truth that sin tends to increase its hold on human beings. Like Cain, people stoop even to murdering members of their human family. We are trapped in a flood of evil from which only God can rescue us. We become alienated from God, from ourselves, and from one another until the whole earth seems a Tower of Babel.

Abraham: Genesis 12–25

The first eleven chapters of Genesis show humankind moving away from God. But at the end of Chapter 11, a man is introduced who will turn people back to God. That man is Abram, son of Terah, who in about 1900 B.C. migrated with his family from Ur (present-day Iraq) to Haran (a city near the present-day Turkish-Syrian border). After Terah's death, Abram heard God calling him to a new home and promising to make of him a great nation. Abram promptly obeyed, taking his wife, Sarai, his nephew, Lot, and his whole household to the land of Canaan (present-day Israel). In subsequent visions, God renewed the promises in the form of a covenant, changed Abram's name to Abraham and Sarai's name to Sarah, then blessed them with a son, Isaac.

Genesis 12–25 contains many colorful stories about Abraham and his family. Scholars debate the historical actuality of these stories, but there is no doubt that Genesis establishes Abraham as a model of faith, as the ancestor of the Israelite people, and as the one to whom God promised the land later claimed by the Israelites.

Now read *Genesis 12:1-9, Genesis 15:1–17:27, Genesis 21:1-8,* and *Genesis 22:1-19.* In these passages, Abraham's faith in God is constantly emphasized. The covenant ceremony in which animals were cut up was practiced in the Middle East. Participants walked between the pieces of the divided animals to show that they expected the same fate if ever they broke their promises. The story of Abraham's being called by God to sacrifice his son points out the depth of Abraham's faith. It also showed the Israelites (living among pagans who practiced human sacrifice) that God wanted the sacrifice of animals instead of human beings.

Before Abraham died, his son Isaac married Rebekah, a grandniece of Abraham and, therefore, according to the customs of the times, a suitable bride for Isaac. It was through Isaac that God's promise to Abraham would be fulfilled.

Isaac, Jacob, and Jacob's Sons: Genesis 25–36

Isaac and Rebekah had twin sons, Jacob and Esau (Gen 25:19-34). They became rivals, and Jacob deceived his elderly father, Isaac, into giving him the blessing due to Esau. A number of other stories are told about Jacob, many of them dealing with his craftiness. Some of the stories are based on folklore. They reshape old myths and legends, giving popular explanations for place names and the origin of various traditions.

Jacob went to Haran to find a wife and ended up marrying the two daughters of his uncle, Laban. (Polygamy, the taking of many wives, was common among ancient peoples and was practiced by Israelite kings until the fifth century B.C.) His wives and their maidservants became the mothers of Jacob's twelve sons, forerunners of the twelve tribes of Israel. Two separate accounts (Gen 32:29 and Gen 35:10) explain that Jacob's name was changed by God to Israel, which became the name of the people who descended from him. Eventually, Jacob returned with his family to Canaan and was reconciled with Esau.

Read *Genesis 25:19-34, Genesis 27:1-45, Genesis 33:1-20,* and *Genesis 35:9-15.* These passages relate key moments in Jacob's life and show how God remained faithful to the promises made to Jacob's grandfather, Abraham. The story of how Jacob deceived his aged father, Isaac, into giving him a blessing meant for Esau shows that God can use even the misdeeds of sinners to accomplish divine purposes. This does not mean that God desires those misdeeds, but that God is able to redirect them to bring about good—in this case, the fulfillment of God's covenant with Abraham. (See Gen 35:9-12.) There is a lesson in this: God can bring good out of misfortune, even from our own past failures, if we turn to God with faith and trust.

Joseph: Genesis 37–50

The story of Joseph, which concludes Genesis, teaches the same lesson. Joseph relies on God in the worst of circumstances, and God turns disaster into triumph again and again.

When Joseph is sold into slavery by his brothers, he becomes a successful steward. When he resists advances of his master's wife, he is falsely accused and thrown into prison, which becomes a most unlikely steppingstone to authority in Egypt. Worldwide famine, however, becomes an opportunity for Joseph to display his administrative abilities and to be rejoined to his brothers and his father, Jacob.

Because Jacob is reunited with Joseph, he dies a happy man. His burial by Joseph in the land of Canaan is yet another sign that his family will one day return from Egypt to the Promised Land.

Read *Genesis 45:1-28*. This passage paints a beautiful picture of the emotional reunion of Joseph and his brothers and of Jacob's receiving the incredible news that Joseph was alive.

You may want to read the whole Joseph story. It is interesting, fast paced, hard to put down. It leaves us with the family of Israel in Egypt where yet another tragedy, harsh slavery, will be turned by God into freedom and new life.

The Book of Exodus: 1–18

Genesis concludes with the death of Joseph in Egypt about 1750 B.C. Five hundred years lapsed between Joseph's death and the events described in the next book of the Bible, Exodus. In those five hundred years, the descendants of Abraham became slaves. Ancient records speak of those descendants as "Habiru," a nomadic people put to work on Egyptian building projects. (From *Habiru* comes the term *Hebrew,* another name for the Israelites.)

The Book of Exodus describes the slavery of the Israelites and their deliverance under the leadership of Moses. The Israelites had lost their identity, but when God appeared to Moses as "the God of Abraham, the God of Isaac, and the God of Jacob" (Ex 3:6), a process was begun that would lead the Hebrews back to their destiny as the People of God.

Apparently, there were several migrations of Habiru into Egypt and several occasions when some of them fled from the bonds of Egypt. The Bible focuses on the Exodus led by Moses. Most scholars place the events of this Exodus during the reign of Ramses II and date the Exodus at about 1250 B.C. Many scholars suppose the number of those led by Moses out of Egypt to be relatively small, no more than a few thousand. But as the story of the Exodus was retold time and time again, it took on epic proportions. The number of those who escaped began to approach the population of Israel at its peak. The events of the Exodus were enlarged until they became miraculous manifestations of God's power and protection: the plagues, the parting of the sea, the pillar of fire.

What is the historical core behind the Exodus? One possible scenario follows. A great leader, Moses, experienced the presence of God in prayer (the burning bush). He discerned God's will that Israel should be free. Taking advantage of natural events that caused disruption (Nile flooding; frogs deposited by floods; gnats and flies feeding on dead frogs, spreading pestilence and disease; hail; locust plagues; desert sandstorms; perhaps the death of Pharaoh's son), Moses led a band of Israelites to an area known as the Sea of Reeds (not "Red Sea," seemingly a mistranslation of the Hebrew original). The Israelites crossed it successfully, but the Egyptians in their war chariots were bogged down. Many were lost, and the Israelites fled into the desert, where they wandered for forty years before entering the Promised Land under the leadership of Moses' lieutenant, Joshua.

But why not take the Exodus story at face value? Why not assume, as some fundamentalist interpretations do, that the Book of Exodus is history in the modern sense?

First of all, we do not deny God's ability to perform any of the miracles in the Exodus story. God is God and *can* do the miraculous. But when we look at the Exodus material, we are led to believe that the biblical authors intended to write not modern history but an epic presentation exalting God's glory and ridiculing God's enemies. These writers assembled from ancient sources a story that is truly memorable, extols

God's power, and recalls the national origins of Israel as mere history cannot.

We might compare Exodus to the Johnny Horton country song, "The Battle of New Orleans." The song has a real basis in history, but it is written as an epic song, with imagination and humor. Yes, there was a battle of New Orleans in 1814-1815, and General Jackson did defeat the British (the song helps people remember these facts better than history classes could). But the fabulous elements of the song (alligators are used as cannons when artillery overheats!) were never meant by the songwriter to be taken as history. Similarly, the authors of Exodus never intended that all the details of their story should be taken as history.

There are clues within the story that lead us to interpret the literary form as epic rather than history. First, why would Pharaoh allow Moses to keep coming back with threats and demands? Why not throw Moses in prison or have him executed? Second, Exodus 12:37 speaks of 600,000 men leaving Egypt; this would suggest a departure of several million people. But earlier the story mentions only two midwives for all the Hebrews! Third, there are inconsistencies that cannot be historical. As an example, "all the livestock of the Egyptians died" in the fifth plague (the pestilence), but the livestock are killed again by the hail and yet again in the death of the firstborn. Fourth, there is the incongruity of a God who would wreak havoc on one people in favor of another, not stopping even at the slaughter of innocent children. Such a God is not easily identified with the God revealed by Jesus Christ.

Again, we do not deny the possibility of miracles. God is all-powerful and is not limited by the laws of nature. But because of the literary form and epic makeup of the Book of Exodus, we cannot arrive at definite conclusions about the precise character of the miracles described there. Exodus gives us the essential historical core of an Israelite escape from Egypt under the leadership of Moses. Exodus teaches important religious lessons: God cares about people and is on the side of freedom. Beyond such basic facts there is much room for speculation, and the Catholic Church has not made dogmatic statements about these issues.

Read *Exodus 1* to experience the misery and hopelessness of Israelite slavery in Egypt. Read *Exodus 14* to sense the joy of freedom. Think of Jewish children, seven hundred years later, sitting around their grandfather: "Tell us again, Grandpa, how God led Moses and the Israelites through the sea!"

The Covenant at Mount Sinai: Exodus 19–40

The people Moses led from Egypt were a tattered group of refugees. They argued with Moses, complained about their hardships, and at times even wanted to return to Egypt.

But the Lord was to form these refugees into the People of God. At Mount Sinai, God made a covenant with the Hebrews that is centered on the Ten Commandments. The Israelites were to keep these commandments as their part of the covenant. God's part of the covenant was the divine promise to be their God, to protect them, and to guide them to the land promised to Abraham.

The Ten Commandments are given in Exodus 20:1-17 (and again in a slightly different form in Deuteronomy 5:1-21). The tradition of counting them as ten comes from Exodus 34:28. The manner of numbering them varies. Catholics count Exodus 20:1-6 as one commandment and Exodus 20:17 as two.

The Bible speaks of the Ten Commandments as coming from the hand of God (Ex 34:1) and from the hand of Moses (Ex 34:28). These traditions point out that the very existence of the Israelite nation depended upon its allegiance to God. They show that Moses was chosen by God to establish the legal tradition of Israel and to form a people who would worship the true God. They designate Moses as the religious leader who designed the Ark of the Covenant, a portable chest that contained the Ten Commandments and was the throne where God would meet Israel. Moses, then, was the leader who put Israel in touch with God.

For these reasons, many of Israel's later laws, liturgical regulations, and ideals for Temple construction and worship were gathered in the Book of Exodus as coming with the Ten Commandments from God through Moses. The editors who, seven hundred years after Sinai, put together the Book of Exodus from its various sources realized that all of Israel's laws could be summed up in the covenant at Sinai.

They realized as well that Israel's history could be summed up in the events of the Exodus. That is why they included the story of the Golden Calf (Ex 32–34) among the lists of laws and regulations. Just as the Israelites in the desert were prone to ignore God, so their descendants would repeat their failures, even to the making of more golden calves. (See 1 Kings 12:26-32.) Just as God forgave the Israelites when they sought pardon, so down through the centuries God would forgive repentant sinners, calling them back to covenant faithfulness.

What do these chapters from Exodus say to us today? They tell us that God wants to be close to us (Ex 33:12-13). God wants us to observe the commandments because they keep us in his presence. These chapters teach us how to be truly free. God was the one who led the Israelites out of slavery. When God gave them the Ten Commandments, it was to keep them free from a worse bondage—slavery to sin. If we observe the commandments today, we will enjoy the full range of human freedom without being trapped in the chains of sin.

We can learn even from the chapters that list laws and regulations we no longer follow. They remind us of the commitment of our spiritual ancestors to right living and dedicated worship. They encourage us to give the best of our obedience and worship to God, "The LORD, the LORD, a God merciful and gracious, slow to anger, and abounding in steadfast love and faithfulness" (Ex 34:6).

Read *Exodus 20:1-17,* which describes how God gives the commandments to the Israelites. Read *Exodus 24:1-8,* where the Israelites accept the terms of the covenant and Moses leads them in a ceremony of acceptance. In this ceremony, the altar is a sign of God's presence, and blood is a symbol of life. When Moses takes the sacrificial blood, splashes half on the altar and sprinkles half on the people, he testifies to the union existing between God and the Israelites. Read *Exodus 32:1-20* and *Exodus 34:1-9* for the story of the Golden Calf and the renewal of the covenant. Read *Exodus 38:1-8* for a sample of the worship legislation contained in Exodus. Note the attention to details, vivid testimony to the Israelite desire to worship God worthily.

The Book of Leviticus: "Be Holy as I Am Holy"

The Book of Leviticus derives its name from *Levi* because it consists mainly of ritual laws prescribed for priests of the tribe of Levi. These laws are presented as coming from Moses, and some may have originated with Moses during the Exodus. But most seem to reflect later times and customs. They were placed into the Pentateuch about 550 B.C.

Modern readers may find the regulations and rituals of Leviticus to be tedious reading. But we can derive much profit from the book if we see it as a document setting forth the ideals and goals of Old Testament conduct, as the pattern our ancestors followed in their veneration of God.

Read *Leviticus 19:1-19.* Here we find the central theme of Leviticus, "You shall be holy, for I the LORD your God am holy." Here we learn that fulfilling our obligations to others is connected to the fulfillment of our obligations to God. We find some of the Ten Commandments restated, and we read the beautiful directive to love our neighbor as ourself. We discover regulations we might characterize as quaint, such as the mandate not to wear garments woven with two different kinds of thread. Scholars debate the origin of such regulations. Sometimes the regulations were ritual in nature. At other times they were practical; for example, Jewish regulations against eating pork may have developed because so many people who ate pork were afflicted with trichinosis. What began as a taboo against potentially dangerous food gradually took on religious overtones.

Read *Leviticus 23,* which mandates the observance of the Sabbath and five Jewish holy days—Passover, Pentecost, New Year's Day, the Day of Atonement, and the Feast of Booths. The purpose of the Sabbath and these holy days was to help the Jews remember the most basic truth: "I am the LORD your God" (Lev 23:43).

Leviticus can help us remember that the Lord *is* our God and that we must order our lives according to the patterns given us by God. We must be holy because God is holy.

The Book of Numbers

Numbers takes its name from the account of two censuses of the Hebrews and from lists of items and persons described in the book. It portrays the forty years spent by the Israelites in the desert and ends with them ready to enter the Promised Land. Its reports, lists, stories, and traditions were handed down by the Israelites for centuries before being edited into their present form. By their arrangement of these materials, the final editors of Numbers encouraged the Israelites of 550 B.C. to see themselves as a holy community, organized by the will of God, called to follow God's law.

You may wish to skim through the lists in Chapters 1–3 to become acquainted with this type of literature. Read *Numbers 20* to get a sense of the passage of forty years in the desert. Note the death of Moses' sister, Miriam, the complaining of the Israelites about the lack of basic necessities like water, the harassment endured from hostile neighbors, and the death of Moses' brother, Aaron.

Read *Numbers 22–24*. Here we find a legend (possibly developed from historical antecedents) designed to teach a religious truth. As the Israelites drew near the Promised Land, their presence worried the King of Moab. He tried to hire a prophet, Balaam, to curse them. But, as the legend relates, Balaam is guided by God and so can only bless the Israelites. There is a great deal of humor in the story, especially in a somewhat disconnected fable about a talking donkey. Read *Numbers 22:22-35* to see how this fable teaches the religious truth that Israel is under God's protection.

The Book of Deuteronomy

Deuteronomy means "second law," or "copy of the law." The name is appropriate because the Book of Deuteronomy is a restating of much that is found elsewhere in the Pentateuch. It is presented in the form of a sermon delivered by Moses to the Israelites shortly before they enter the Promised Land.

Moses reviews the events of the Exodus from Egypt and of the forty years in the desert. He restates the laws, including the Ten Commandments (Deut 5:1-21) by which Israel is to be governed. He lists blessings that will come upon the Israelites if they obey God and warns them of curses that will afflict them if they disobey. After Joshua is commissioned by God as Moses' successor, Moses blesses the tribes, climbs Mount Nebo to view the Promised Land, and dies there.

The Book of Deuteronomy ends, as the Israelites prepare to enter the Promised Land, with a eulogy for Moses, who "was unequaled for all the signs and wonders the LORD sent him to perform in the land of Egypt...and for all the mighty deeds and all the terrifying displays of power that Moses performed in the sight of all Israel" (Deut 34:11-12).

Because Deuteronomy presents Moses as an orator addressing the people of Israel, fundamentalists interpret the book as a speech actually delivered by Moses. However, the language, style, and references to later historical events make this unlikely. Unlikely also is the notion of a man one hundred and twenty years old delivering a sermon as long as the Book of Deuteronomy to hundreds of thousands of people. Rather, the setting of Deuteronomy may be a literary device. Moses is put on center stage as a historical person speaking to later ages in much the same way as the characters in a play speak to an audience.

It is certainly possible that parts of Deuteronomy and other portions of the Pentateuch find their origin in Moses. But the Book of Deuteronomy in its present form was probably written by Israelite religious leaders at the time of the Babylonian exile. Jerusalem had been destroyed, tens of thousands of Jews slaughtered, and thousands more dragged across the desert to Babylon. At this desperate hour in Jewish history, the authors of Deuteronomy placed Moses before the Israelites. The setting was the assembly of his people before they entered the Promised Land, but the real audience was the battered band of those who survived the exile. The message was clear. There is only one true God. God is faithful. God alone is to be worshiped and adored. Obey God and you will thrive. Disobey God and you will be destroyed.

This message is the foundation of what has been called the Deuteronomist theology. The authors of Deuteronomy looked back at Jewish history and saw a pattern. God is always faithful. When Israel obeyed God, things went well; when Israel disobeyed, things went badly. As for the future, kings and armies could not save Israel. Only God could. And obedience to God would be the only way to receive salvation from God.

The Book of Deuteronomy is composed almost entirely from the Deuteronomist tradition. The Deuteronomist tradition is found elsewhere in the Pentateuch only in a few scattered verses. But it is the source of Joshua, Judges, 1 and 2 Samuel, and 1 and 2 Kings. It is also an important influence in the composition of other books in the Bible. The Book of Deuteronomy had a great impact on Judaism and on Christianity. It is quoted or referred to about two hundred times in the New Testament.

The theology of the Book of Deuteronomy is limited. Its authors were people of their own times, and they did not have the fullness of Revelation granted through Jesus Christ. They, along with many other Old Testament authors, did not make distinctions between God's causing something and allowing something. Since God is all-powerful, they believed that God had to be the cause of everything, including suffering. And if God caused something bad to happen, God must have had a good reason. Usually, that reason was punishment for sin. So if people suffered, it was because they had sinned.

But this theology posits too close a connection between sin and suffering. It is true that we should obey God, and our world would be a far better place if all people did. (Imagine how wonderful our world could be if all merely kept the Ten Commandments!) But because so many do disobey God, the world is far from what God wants it to be. In the world as it is, innocent people can be hurt directly and indirectly by the sins of others. Obedience does not always guarantee prosperity, and suffering is not always the result of personal disobedience.

The main problem with the Deuteronomist theology, then, is that it leads people to believe that personal suffering is always the result of personal sin. This mistaken notion was questioned in some Old Testament books like Job, and it was refuted once and for all by the teaching and life of Jesus Christ, the innocent victim of the sins of others. In reading Deuteronomy, we are challenged to formulate our own philosophy of suffering, going beyond the limitations of the Old Testament to the fullness of Revelation found in Jesus.

Read *Deuteronomy 1:1-8,* where the author sets the stage for Moses to speak to the Israelites, not just those preparing to enter the Promised Land but those of every age. Read *Deuteronomy 5:1–6:9* for a repeat of the Sinai Covenant *(Horeb* is another word for Sinai). Here also is a Deuteronomist view of Moses, a statement that prosperity is the reward for fidelity and the first declaration of the "Great Commandment." Read *Deuteronomy 30,* a chapter which summarizes the Deuteronomist theology. Note how the first ten verses are addressed to exiles at Babylon.

The Pentateuch: A Unit

The Pentateuch, as we have noted, was called by the Jews the *Torah* and was considered a unit by them. Genesis relates the origins of God's people. Exodus recounts the story of the birth of the Israelite nation. Leviticus stresses the holy nature of God's people. Numbers describes the organization of the nation. Deuteronomy shows the spirit of love and obedience that should characterize God's people. Together these books form the constitution of the Jews, our ancestors in faith.

Questions for Discussion and Reflection

How much do you know about your own family tree and roots? How far back can you trace your family history? Do you have family keepsakes? What are your favorite family traditions (observance of holidays, certain foods for special days, and so forth)? Have you ever thought of the Old Testament as a record of *your* family tree and roots; history, keepsakes, and traditions? Does this help you to see some value even in the lists of names, regulations, and blueprints that are found in the Pentateuch and elsewhere in the Old Testament?

Have you ever thought of the Ten Commandments as intended by God to keep us truly free? Consider how our world is held in bonds by sin. How would our world change if today everyone would observe the Ten Commandments?

Modern specialists in astronomy, physics, and microbiology have affirmed that the vastness of the universe and the complexity of its smallest components lead to belief in God. It makes sense to say that our universe with its one hundred billion galaxies could come from an eternal, all-powerful Being, for $E=mc^2$. But it makes no sense to say that everything could come from nothing. The human body is made up of approximately 75 trillion cells, each cell composed of more than a trillion atoms. Such complexity, described in books like *The Hidden Face of God* by Gerald Schroeder and *More Than Meets the Eye* by Dr. Richard Swenson, testifies that human life cannot have evolved by mere chance. How have the findings of science strengthened your faith in God?

The Bible teaches religious truths which are reinforced by recent scientific studies. Gerald Schroeder points out amazing parallels between the six days of creation and science's understanding of the pattern of expansion following the Big Bang. Other scientists, observing how Genesis mentions light before the creation of stars, explain that the first product of the Big Bang was intense radiation, which in everyday language may be described as light. In this sense, light really did come before the stars. Have you studied such parallels between the Bible and science? Is it possible that God inspired these parallels to "catch our attention" as our knowledge of the universe grows more sophisticated?

Activities

Go outside on a clear night and look at the sky. There are more than 100 billion stars in our Milky Way galaxy and over 100 billion galaxies in the universe. The distances involved in space are unimaginable. Just to travel by present-day spaceships to the nearest star in our galaxy would take 100,000 years. Even at the speed of light (186,282 miles per second), it would take about 30 billion years to travel from one end of the universe to the other. Ask yourself: Could all this come from nothing? Consider Genesis 1:31: "God saw everything that he had made, and indeed, it was very good." Praise God for the magnificence of the universe. Thank God that we have forever to explore the beauty of creation.

CHAPTER FIVE

The Historical Books:
Joshua to the Exile

M emory is one of the most important building blocks of life. What we are and what we will be depend largely on what we have been and on our remembrances of the past, on our *story*.

The same is true of nations. Each can be understood only in the light of its *history*. Indeed, awareness of the past can be essential for the survival of a nation. When Abraham Lincoln was trying to guide America through the terrible crisis of civil war, he focused on its history: "Fourscore and seven years ago our fathers brought forth on this continent, a new nation, conceived in Liberty."

What is true of individuals and nations is true also of the Jewish and Christian religions. They can be fully understood only in the light of their past. Judaism originated from historical events that formed the Jews as a people and gave them a mission. Christianity finds its roots in the history of Judaism and in later events relating to the life, death, and resurrection of Jesus Christ. Judaism and Christianity are built on the foundation of the past.

Therefore, the historical books of the Old Testament are significant. But they are not modern history. Ancient historians did not have video recorders, telephones, and printing presses. They did not achieve the accuracy we expect from modern historians. Their purposes were different from those of modern historians.

Salvation History

In 1948 the Pontifical Biblical Commission, the scriptural teaching office for the Catholic Church, stated that history in the Bible is not history in the modern sense of the word. Rather, it is history as people of ancient times understood and wrote it.

Biblical history is *first* the telling and *later* the writing down of the collective memory of families, tribes, and nations. Often such history cannot reproduce the past exactly and turns to imaginative reconstruction called folklore. Biblical history focuses on relationships between God and people, and for this reason it is called salvation history.

Salvation history may be defined as the story of the encounter of God and human beings. It tells how God has entered into our world and invites us to attend to the reality of God's presence and providence.

In this chapter we will spotlight the spiritual messages of salvation history, most often found in broad religious themes rather than in specific moral directives. We will also be attentive to the main events and personalities of Israel's history, which offer the framework for a better understanding of all Scripture.

Such books as the Psalms and the works of the prophets are more intelligible when we can place them in the context of their own historical circumstances. Psalm 137, for example, will speak to us with more power and poignancy when we realize that it was written by a Jewish exile during the Babylonian captivity.

The development of doctrine is more easily understood when we are familiar with Old Testament history. If we are able to distinguish older books from newer ones, we will not be surprised to find that the older ones have no clear notion of eternal life, and we will be able to see how God gradually led people to a more complete knowledge of the divine plan as they became more open to God's wisdom and inspiration.

The Deuteronomist History

Scripture scholars tend to regard the Books of Joshua, Judges, 1 and 2 Samuel, and 1 and 2 Kings as arising from the same theological viewpoint as the Book of Deuteronomy. They categorize these six books as the Deuteronomist history. The books are a compilation of oral and written accounts, including popular stories, folklore, eyewitness biographies, annals of kings, folk tales, official documents, tax reports, and other sources. For the most part, these sources were not fused into a smooth narrative. Instead, the sources were taken as found, then arranged to illustrate Deuteronomist theological principles. As a result, these books sometimes contain sudden transitions, duplications, and contradictory accounts.

Many scholars theorize that the Deuteronomist history was first composed from its various sources about 620 B.C. It was updated and edited into its present form about 550 B.C., during the time of the Babylonian exile. It covers events from the death of Moses (1210 B.C.) to the Babylonian exile (550 B.C.).

Why was the Deuteronomist history written? The Jews of 550 B.C. were aware of God's promises to make them a chosen people. But after the glory days of David and Solomon, the Israelite people had not fared well. Split into separate kingdoms by civil war, they never achieved the greatness they hoped for. The northern kingdom of Israel was destroyed by Assyria in 721 B.C., and the southern kingdom of Judah was destroyed by Babylon in 587 B.C. The survivors wondered why. Was their God the one true God? If so, why had God allowed them to be reduced to such misery? Were they still God's people? What did the future hold for them? The Deuteronomist history was intended to answer such questions.

It affirmed that there is only one true God. God was faithful to the covenant made with the Israelites, but all too often the Israelites were not faithful in return. The evils that fell upon them were seen as punishments for their disobedience, but if they would repent, they would experience God's forgiveness. The Israelites of 550 B.C. were still God's people; their future depended upon how well they could learn the lessons taught by the past. Obedience to the covenant would bring blessings. Disobedience would bring further ruin.

As explained in chapter 4, we must recognize the limitations of the Deuteronomist theology. It is true that obedience is rewarded and disobedience punished, but we know from the teachings of Jesus that God's Final Judgment occurs only after death. We know also from Jesus that suffering is not necessarily God's punishment for personal sins.

Another weakness in the Deuteronomist theology may be found in its approach to God as the cause of all things. Deuteronomist authors did not understand the difference between God's causing something and God's allowing something. As a result, they sometimes saw God as causing a sinful decision and punishing that same decision. An example

57

of this is 2 Samuel 24, where God is said to have prompted David to carry out a census of the Israelites and then to have punished David and the Israelites for the same census! This passage illustrates the fact that God's inspiration of biblical authors does not remove their limitations. We see in 2 Samuel 24 the faulty theology of its author, and we are spurred on to find a better understanding of divine causality in the light of the entire Bible, especially the light flowing from the teaching of Jesus.

Having acknowledged the weaknesses of the Deuteronomist's theology, we can learn much from its focus on the preeminence of God and the value of obedience. The Deuteronomist history teaches us to put God first in our lives and to see every choice as an opportunity to respond to God's will.

The Book of Joshua

The Book of Joshua is named for its hero, Joshua, the successor of Moses. It tells how Joshua led the Hebrews across the Jordan River into the Promised Land, conquered its inhabitants, and divided the land among the tribes of Israel.

The main purpose of the Book of Joshua is to show God's faithfulness in delivering the Promised Land to the Israelites. The impression given by the book is that they formed a mighty army that conquered all the inhabitants of Canaan and took possession of the land. However, the Book of Judges paints a different picture. It shows how the Israelite tribes had to struggle mightily to establish a foothold in the Promised Land.

This latter picture is probably closer to historical reality. The Book of Joshua almost certainly contains an idealized picture of the conquest of the Promised Land, condensing into a few years events that actually took several centuries. The basic fact of the Hebrew invasion of Palestine and the gradual conquest of its inhabitants is the historical core behind the Book of Joshua. Along with that historical core are many stories, such as the storming of Jericho, which cannot be verified by archaeology and should be categorized as folklore. The purpose of the authors was to teach theological lessons, not history in the modern sense.

Realizing that the Book of Joshua is not history in the modern sense can help us resolve one of the main problems in Joshua and other books of the Old Testament. This problem is the often repeated statement that

God ordered the wholesale annihilation of those who opposed the Jewish people.

Note that the holy wars, with their presumption of God's command to slaughter men, women, and children, were recorded about seven hundred years after they supposedly occurred, at a time when the Jewish people were desperately trying to survive. Therefore, many of the holy wars, wherein enemies were placed under the ban (condemned to death), may have been a literary device rather than a historical fact. The holy wars as reported in Joshua and elsewhere may have actually been a warning to the Jews of 550 B.C.

These Jews, for example, were tempted to intermarry with foreigners and to accept their pagan gods. The editors of the Deuteronomist history remembered the tales of conquest by Joshua and his successors. They recalled especially the folklore that glorified God with stories of complete victory for the Jews and the complete eradication of their enemies. They saw both victory and eradication as coming directly from the hand of God. They retold these stories to warn the Jews of 550 B.C. to be wary of paganism. Their warning may be restated like this: "Stay away from pagans. Our ancestors did. In fact, they had strict orders from God to kill every last one of them. The least we can do is avoid them!"

When we look at Jesus, we see a further reason for such an interpretation. Jesus never advocated the massacre of human beings. We cannot imagine Jesus telling Joshua to put innocent men, women, and children to the sword. We ought not then feel compelled to believe that God gave such orders in Old Testament times. Most probably, slaughters like those described in Joshua occurred less frequently than reported. When they did occur, they were due to the mistaken perceptions and sinfulness of human beings rather than to a direct command from God.

We are not doubting the inspiration of Scripture when we question whether God actually commissioned the holy wars and the systematic slaughter of innocent people. We are saying that the Bible is accurately recording the perceptions of Israelites of long ago, but that those perceptions were wrong. The inspired message, the one intended by the inspired authors, is not that God orders the destruction of pagans, but that the readers of the Bible should not be ensnared in paganism.

We moderns have read messages similar to those of the Deuteronomist into our own history. Not long ago, Americans saw the Indian wars of the nineteenth century as a divinely commissioned annihilation of savages to make way for civilized people. Only recently have we rethought our history and reached the understanding that God could not have countenanced the slaughter of so many innocents by people on both sides of the conflict. Reading the historical books of the Old Testament can be an occasion for us to look for those times when we rashly presume that God is on our side, whether in international conflicts or in everyday disagreements with relatives, neighbors, or coworkers.

Read *Joshua 3* for a description of the entry into the Promised Land. Scholars observe that the Jordan River is occasionally dammed up by landslides and that such an event might have allowed the Israelites to cross on dry land. Whatever the historical reality, the story would have shown the Israelites that God was with Joshua as God had been with Moses at the crossing of the Sea of Reeds forty years before.

Read *Joshua 6* for the account of the destruction of Jericho. (You may wish to refer back to *Joshua 2* for background material on Rahab.) Read *Joshua 24* for a report of Joshua's last days, his renewal of the covenant, and his death and burial.

The Book of Judges

Many nations look back to a frontier period, a time of conquest and settlement when rugged individuals overcame great obstacles to create a home for themselves and family. For the Israelites, that frontier period was the time of the Judges, approximately one hundred and fifty years between the death of Joshua and the career of Samuel the prophet.

The judges were not legal experts, but heroes and heroines who rescued the people of Israel from difficult situations. The Book of Judges is dominated by the Deuteronomist principle that disobedience brings misfortune and obedience wins God's favor. According to the Book of Judges, when the Israelites turned away from God, "the anger of the LORD was kindled against Israel, and he gave them over to plunderers....Whenever they marched out, the hand of the LORD was against them to bring misfortune" (2:14-15). When the Israelites repented, God "raised up judges for them" and "delivered them from the hand of their enemies all the days of the judge; for the LORD would be moved to pity by their groaning because of those who persecuted and oppressed them" (2:18).

The period of the Judges was at best a harsh and ruthless time when the Israelites and their pagan neighbors engaged in bloody struggles for survival. The stories contained in the Book of Judges may be based on historical events, although some of them, especially those dealing with Samson, are colored by folklore and legend. In Judges, the reader will find tales of intrigue and assassination (Judg 3:15-30), deceit and murder (Judg 4), war (Judg 6–8), treason and fratricide (Judg 9), rash vows (Judg 11), civil conflict (Judg 12), vandalism, treachery, and suicide (Judg 13–16). There is an appendix of stories about the tribes of Dan and Benjamin (Chapters 17–21) even more gruesome than those in Chapters 1–16. The entire book paints a macabre picture of humanity at its worst and of what happens to people when they turn away from God.

What can we learn from this book? Perhaps the most important lesson of Judges is that humanity needs salvation. Left to itself, humanity degenerates into a frightful caricature of what we ought to be. We see such lessons repeated in recent history, in those nations of the twentieth century that attempted to construct a godless society and ended up instead in war and self-destruction. In the Book of Judges, we see our need for God.

Read *Judges 15–16* for the last two chapters in the story of Samson. In them, we observe how lust, pride, and disobedience can turn strength to weakness and bury the world's pleasure, power, and possessions under a pile of rubble.

The Book of Ruth

Placed after the Book of Judges is a narrative that is not part of the Deuteronomist history. The Book of Ruth is a short story that may have a historical foundation. It teaches in beautiful fashion the virtues of love, loyalty, and devotion. The book is situated after Judges because its action takes place "in the days when the judges ruled" (Ruth 1:1) and because it supplies details about the great-grandparents of King David, thus providing a bridge between the period of the Judges and the era of Israel's kingship. The virtues reflected in this book provide a refreshing contrast to the degradation of Judges and the human weaknesses so evident in the books that follow.

There are many opinions about the literary form and time of composition of the Book of Ruth. Such issues need not be resolved for us to learn the lessons God inspired the author to share: love, loyalty, and devotion to God and family.

Read *Ruth 1–4*. The story is short and enchanting. Ruth's expression of devotion to her mother-in-law, Naomi, is sometimes read in wedding ceremonies and may be used to express commitment to family members at any time.

1 and 2 Samuel

The First and Second Books of Samuel take their name from the prophet Samuel, whose lifetime saw the end of the period of the Judges and the beginning of Israel's kingship. The books originate from a number of sources, including ancient stories about the Ark of the Covenant, several narratives about Samuel, Saul, and David, and a masterfully written family history of David (2 Sam 9–20). In the opinion of many scholars, 1 and 2 Samuel were created from these sources about 620 B.C. and edited into their present form about 550 B.C.

The First and Second Books of Samuel are not a continuous history describing events in a systematic way. Rather, they are collections of stories about various episodes and personalities. The books were written primarily to illustrate the theology of the Deuteronomist and, therefore, should be classified as salvation history. But they contain much reliable historical data, especially as the events described approach the time of King David's reign, when a court was established and records of many kinds were kept.

The books begin with the story of Samuel's birth. Samuel was dedicated to the service of the Lord by his parents and as a young boy lived at a shrine in Shiloh, about twenty miles north of what is now Jerusalem. Eli was priest at Shiloh but because of his advanced years, his wicked sons were ministering at the shrine and abusing their privileges. According to the First Book of Samuel, it was for their crimes that God promised affliction for Eli's family. At the death of Eli and his sons, Samuel became the spiritual leader of Israel at a time when the Ark was a symbol of religious unity for the tribes and the basis of many old stories (1 Sam 1–7).

It fell to Samuel's lot to anoint Israel's first king, Saul. The kingship had a blemished history, and there were factions for and against the monarchy. Those who read 1 Samuel in its entirety will notice evidence of both factions, and there are several conflicting stories about Saul's anointing (1 Sam 8–12).

Saul was successful in his early years as king. He became a focal point for cooperation among the tribes and formed a powerful army that defeated many enemies of Israel. But, Scripture tells us, Saul began to disobey God. He became mentally unbalanced and lashed out at those closest to him, even his armorbearer and son-in-law, David. David had to flee, becoming leader of an armed band that roamed about Palestine until the death of Saul in a battle against the Philistines at Mount Gilboa, southwest of the Sea of Galilee (1 Sam 13–31).

Read *1 Samuel 3* for a story about the call of Samuel the prophet. Read *1 Samuel 9:1–10:1* for a promonarchic narrative of Saul's anointing by Samuel, and *1 Samuel 10:17-24* for an account that viewed the anointing of a king as a rejection of God. Read *1 Samuel 17:1-11,32-51* for the famous story of David and Goliath. Read *1 Samuel 31* for the tragedy of Saul's death.

Saul's passing opened the way for David, who was asked to assume the kingship over the tribe of Judah. The other tribes, however, followed Saul's son Ishbaal, and for seven years there was war between Ishbaal's army, led by Abner, and David's soldiers, led by Joab. After a quarrel with Ishbaal, Abner pledged his loyalty to David. He was murdered by Joab, however, and Ishbaal was assassinated. The tribes of Israel then claimed David as king (2 Sam 1:1–5:5).

David quickly conquered the city of Jerusalem and turned it into his capital. He brought the Ark of the Covenant into Jerusalem, thus making the city the religious and political center for all Israel. David's armies succeeded in routing the Philistines and other enemies of the Jews, including Edom, Moab, and Ammon to the south and east and Aram-Damascus to the north. David now exerted considerable control over an area some two hundred miles long and eighty miles wide. He strengthened his armies, created governmental structures, and set up trade with foreign countries. He built a palace in Jerusalem and made elaborate preparations for the construction of a temple. In about forty years he turned a dispirited, disorganized people into a nation (2 Sam 5:6–10:19).

But David's career was not without its tragedies. The Deuteronomist editor of 2 Samuel traces them to David's sins of adultery with Bathsheba and of the murder of Bathsheba's husband, Uriah (2 Sam 11–12). Subsequently, David's son Amnon raped his half-sister, Tamar, then was killed by Absolom, Tamar's full brother (2 Sam 13). Although Absolom fled into exile for a time, he was reconciled with David and then led a revolt which ended in his death. Later, David's victories over various enemies of Israel consolidated his power (2 Sam 14–24).

Subsequent generations would look back on David as the greatest of Israelite kings. His accomplishments were, indeed, remarkable. He sinned, but when confronted by the prophet Nathan, he repented with sincerity and humility. Nathan promised David that by God's power his kingdom would endure forever (2 Sam 7:8-17). This prophecy would offer hope to Israel in times of defeat, as the Jews began to look for a messiah, a savior, who would spring from the family of David and restore Israel's fortunes. Their hopes for a messiah were to be fulfilled in Jesus Christ and the establishment of his eternal kingdom.

Read *2 Samuel 5* for an account of David's assuming the kingship, his capture of Jerusalem, and his victories over the Philistines. Read *2 Samuel 11:1–12:15* for the dramatic story of David's sins and subsequent repentance. Read *2 Samuel 18:1-17* for details of Absolom's death at the hands of David's soldiers.

1 and 2 Kings

Like 1 and 2 Samuel, 1 and 2 Kings came from a number of sources. (See 1 Kings 11:41 and 1 Kings 14:19.) They first appeared about 620 B.C. and were edited into their present form about 550 B.C. They tell the story of the Israelite monarchy from the death of David (961 B.C.) through the destruction of Jerusalem (587 B.C.). They are written from the Deuteronomist's viewpoint and report the lives of the kings of Israel and Judah in terms of their obedience or disobedience to God. Obedient kings (unfortunately a small minority) brought good to the Jews. Disobedient kings brought calamity, from civil war at home to exile in Babylon.

The First Book of Kings opens with the details of Solomon's ascendancy to the throne. Thanks to the scheming of his mother, Bathsheba, Solomon was named by the elderly David as his successor. After David's death, Solomon moved quickly to consolidate his power by executing potential rivals, including his brother Adonijah, the old general Joab, and Shemei, a former nemesis of David (1 Kings 1–2).

Solomon proved to be an enlightened ruler for many years. He organized the kingdom of Israel into twelve districts and built a magnificent Temple for worship and an even more magnificent palace for himself. He expanded the size of his army and developed a powerful chariot corps. He built fortress cities throughout his kingdom and established agricultural settlements south of Jerusalem. His kingdom became a hub for trade between Asia and Africa, a center for education and art, and a nation renowned for its power, wealth, and influence (1 Kings 3–10).

But power, wealth, and fame have been the downfall of many rulers, and they proved to be the downfall of Solomon. He sought to solidify his power through alliances sealed by marriages to foreigners. In an attempt to please his many foreign wives, he built temples to their pagan gods. In his greed for wealth, he overtaxed his people, especially the northern tribes. In his quest for fame as a builder, he drafted his own subjects as forced laborers. Eventually, resentment smoldered to the point where civil unrest began to surface. By the time of Solomon's death around 922 B.C., tension within the borders of his kingdom had reached a critical level (1 Kings 11).

Solomon was succeeded by his son, Rehoboam. When the northern tribes asked for relief from the burdens Solomon had placed upon them, Rehoboam promised only more oppression. With that, the northern tribes seceded from Judah in 922 B.C. and appointed a man named Jeroboam as their leader. Jeroboam quickly set up religious shrines at Bethel and in Dan to further separate his people from Jerusalem. There was little Rehoboam could do to stop the rebellion as his army was outnumbered. The unity forged by David collapsed, and the era of the divided kingdoms, Israel in the north, Judah in the south, began (1 Kings 12–14).

The division ushered in an epoch of decline. The two kingdoms warred with each other and both were attacked by neighboring nations. In the fifth year of Rehoboam's reign, Egypt attacked Jerusalem, raided the Temple treasures (1 Kings 14:25-28), and devastated many fortified cities of Judah and Israel. Leadership in the north and the south was dismal. Most kings were faithless to the covenant, a fact noted by the Deuteronomist editors of 1 and 2 Kings who, in relating the lives of the kings, focus on their fidelity or infidelity to the Lord (1 Kings 15–16).

A series of stories about prophets begins in 1 Kings 17. Prophets were those who spoke for God. From the time of Samuel there were groups of prophets in Israel who organized themselves for worship; many were believed to have special powers. True prophets were seen by later ages to have been called by God to oppose wicked kings. Perhaps this is why the reign of the Israelite king, Ahab, sets the stage for a cycle of stories about the prophet Elijah.

Ahab reigned over Israel about 870 B.C. to 850 B.C. He married a Sidonian princess, Jezebel, and built altars to the pagan god Baal in the

Israelite capital of Samaria. For this sin and for crimes of injustice and greed, he was opposed by Elijah. The conflict reached its climax in a contest between Elijah and 850 pagan prophets at Mount Carmel. Jezebel was enraged when Elijah slaughtered these prophets, and Elijah had to flee for his life. Strengthened by an encounter with the Lord, however, Elijah continued his prophetic mission and anointed a successor, Elisha. Ahab, meanwhile, won two victories over Ben-hadad, king of Aram (Syria), then was killed in a third battle (1 Kings 17–22).

The stories about Elijah and other prophets in 1 and 2 Kings seem to be based on historical events. But they also contain legends and fables designed to teach religious messages: God cares for loyal believers (1 Kings 17 and 19); those who worship pagan gods deserve death (1 Kings 18); obedience to God is rewarded and disobedience is punished (1 Kings 20–22; 2 Kings 1–8).

Read *1 Kings 3* for stories of Solomon's wisdom and *1 Kings 11* for the account of his last years. Read *1 Kings 12* for details of the secession of Israel from Judah. Read *1 Kings 21* for the dramatic tale of Ahab's treachery and God's judgment on him.

The first thirteen chapters of 2 Kings relate stories and legends about Elijah and Elisha as well as a number of historical events occurring during their lifetimes. These include a temporary alliance of Israel, Judah, and Edom in a successful military campaign against Moab (2 Kings 3), an Israelite victory over the Arameans (2 Kings 7), the slaughter in 842 B.C. of Jezebel and of Ahab's entire family by the army general Jehu (2 Kings 9–10), and other political intrigues in Israel and Judah (2 Kings 1–13).

After the death of Elisha, there were more years of decline, civil unrest, and war involving Israel, Judah, Aram (Syria), Edom, Moab, and Ammon. In about 783 B.C. King Amaziah of Judah was assassinated by political foes, and his sixteen-year-old son Azariah (also known as Uzziah) succeeded him. Surprisingly, this young man proved to be an able ruler. During his long reign, a renaissance occurred in Judah, paralleled by one in Israel under King Jeroboam II (786-746 B.C.). Judah expanded its borders as far south and Israel its borders as far north as in the days of David. Cities were built and fortified; trade was promoted; agriculture and forestry were expanded. Both kingdoms enjoyed years of wealth and prosperity (2 Kings 14:1–15:7).

Unfortunately, injustice, greed, and immorality also flourished, especially in the north. Prophets like Amos and Hosea castigated the rich and powerful, foretelling destruction for Samaria. Their prophecies were soon fulfilled. After Jeroboam's death, chaos reigned in Israel; four of its next five kings were assassinated, and in 734 B.C. the powerful empire of Assyria began a series of assaults against Israel that ended in the complete destruction of Samaria in 721 B.C. The Assyrian monarch, Sargon II, sent almost thirty thousand Israelites into exile in Mesopotamia (present-day Iraq) and resettled other conquered nations in Israel. These intermarried with Israelites who had been left behind and formed the mixed-blood people later known as the Samaritans (2 Kings 15:8–17:41).

When Assyria was attacking Israel, Ahaz, then king of Judah, paid tribute to Assyria. His successor, Hezekiah (715-687 B.C.), decided to withhold tribute and to rebel against Assyria. He fortified Jerusalem and other cities, led the people in a religious revival under the guidance of Isaiah the prophet, and tried to form alliances with other states. In 701 B.C. the Assyrians, under King Sennacherib, moved against Judah. They pillaged the countryside around Jerusalem, then laid siege to the city. Jerusalem appeared to be doomed, when suddenly Sennacherib's army was decimated by "the angel of the LORD" (2 Kings 19:35), perhaps a severe plague. The Assyrians returned home, and Jerusalem was spared. But much of Judah had been laid waste, with thousands of citizens killed or captured, and Hezekiah had to resume payment of tribute to Assyria until his death in 687 B.C. (2 Kings 18–20).

Hezekiah's son Manasseh, in his forty-five-year reign, also paid tribute to Assyria. He provided troops for Assyria and worshiped pagan gods. His son, Amon, continued these practices until he was murdered after only two years on the throne. In what must have seemed a prelude to disaster, he was succeeded in 640 B.C. by his eight-year-old son, Josiah. But Assyria had begun to lose control over its subjects. Freed from fear of Assyria, Josiah in 621 B.C. led Judah in religious reforms and expanded its borders to the north, west, and south. Nineveh, the capital of Assyria, fell to Babylon in 612 B.C., but when Babylon pushed west, it was opposed by Egypt. In 609 B.C. Josiah decided to intercept the Egyptian army at Megiddo. He was badly wounded and died at Jerusalem a short time later (2 Kings 21:1–23:30).

The next four kings of Judah were caught in the web of Egyptian-Babylonian entanglements. Ignoring the advice of Jeremiah the prophet, they sided with Egypt. In 597 B.C. Nebuchadnezzar, the Babylonian king, took control of Jerusalem. He sent King Jehoiachin and many leading citizens into exile and installed Zedekiah as a puppet king. When Zedekiah foolishly rebelled against Babylon in 589 B.C., Nebuchadnezzar attacked Judah with a huge army, destroyed its chief cities, and mounted a siege against Jerusalem. After almost two years of incredible hardship, Jerusalem fell in 587 B.C. The Babylonian army ransacked the city, deported thousands of its survivors to Babylonia, then burned Jerusalem. The nation created by Saul, David, and Solomon was dead (2 Kings 23:31–25:29).

In 600 B.C. about a quarter of a million people lived in Judah. Many fled to escape the Babylonian invasion, taking refuge as far away as Egypt, where a sizable Jewish community settled. Tens of thousands of Jews perished in battle, starved to death, or succumbed to disease. Perhaps twenty thousand were deported to Babylonia. The ruined condition of the country led to more emigration, and by 550 B.C. there were less than fifty thousand people living in what was once Judah.

Those deported to Babylon had to endure a forced march of almost a thousand miles. The survivors were treated decently enough after they arrived in Babylonia. They were permitted to live in Jewish communities and allowed to farm or engage in commerce. Because Nebuchadnezzar had deported the most educated, skilled, and influential citizens of Judah, the Jews of Babylon were a capable group, and some achieved success and wealth. Many were interested in their Jewish heritage, and intellectual and religious leaders began to collect ancient writings into portions of what we now know as the Old Testament.

Read *2 Kings 2* for legends about Elijah and Elisha. It is unlikely that these events occurred as recorded, but they are meant to teach respect for prophets. In particular, the story about the boys and the bears may not be in keeping with our modern sensibilities, but it is just the sort of story a grandparent might relate to a naughty little boy who sasses his elders. We can hear the grandparent's warning: "You mustn't talk like that. Let me tell you what happened when some bad boys called the prophet Elisha a baldhead." Read *2 Kings 17* for the destruction of Israel by Assyria and *2 Kings 25* for the fall of Jerusalem.

Modern readers can learn a great deal more than historical facts from the books of Samuel and Kings. In the careers of Samuel, Saul, David, and their successors, we see how disobedience to God results in calamity. We learn how the abuse of power is destructive of society and of individuals. We are reminded that unbridled lust can tear apart families and wreck lives. By attending to these lessons, we can spare ourselves misfortune and misery.

Questions for Discussion and Reflection

The Deuteronomist theology states that good is rewarded and evil is punished. To what extent is this theology true? In what ways is it incomplete? If it is true that suffering has come into our world as the result of sin, is it also true that the suffering of a specific individual must be the result of personal sin? Why or why not? The Deuteronomist theology and the teaching of the prophets blamed many of Israel's troubles on the fact that the government, business, and social life of the nation had become godless. Is our country becoming godless in government, business, and social life? How many of our modern television shows reflect a sincere and humble belief in God? Do TV families pray or consider the will of God in making decisions? Should they? To what extent does godlessness in the media affect the thinking of our nation? What can you do about this in your home, family, and circle of friends?

Activities

Compare the early years of Israel with those of our own nation. For example, in the United States, there was a frontier period, cultivation of land already occupied by others, a union of thirteen states, the founding of a nation, a civil war involving north and south, and so on. Compare some of our nation's heroes and heroines with those of ancient Israel. Draw any other parallels that will help you to understand the history of Israel and our own history.

CHAPTER SIX

The Historical Books:
The Postexilic Period

S hortly after the destruction of Jerusalem, the Babylonian empire began to crumble. King Nebuchadnezzar's death in 562 B.C. brought rapid decline. In 539 B.C. Cyrus, king of Persia (present-day Iran), defeated the Babylonian army at the Tigris River and entered Babylon almost without resistance.

For the Jews, Cyrus seemed a messenger sent from God. His method of dealing with conquered nations was the reverse of the brutal policies of Assyria and Babylonia; he treated subjects well in order to win their loyalty. In 538 B.C. he issued an edict allowing the Jewish people to return to Jerusalem. He commissioned them to rebuild the Temple, provided funds, and restored the sacred vessels looted by Nebuchadnezzar.

Soon a small band of Jews led by a Judean prince, Sheshbazzar, set out on the long journey to Jerusalem. The Jews had been in exile for almost fifty years, so most of those who went to Jerusalem had been born in Babylonia. They no doubt were excited by the prospect of going to Israel but had little idea of how enormous a task lay before them. They found Jerusalem in ruins, desolate and overgrown after five decades of neglect. They were confronted by unfriendly people who lived in the region, including the Samaritans. Beset by problems on every side, they were able only to lay foundations for a new Temple.

About eighteen years later another band of Jews, under the leadership of Zerubbabel, a member of the family of David, returned to Judah. Spurred on by the prophets Haggai and Zechariah, Zerubbabel directed the Jews in rebuilding the Temple, which was completed and dedicated in 515 B.C.

After the dedication, the Jewish community in Judah must have had a very difficult time. In 445 B.C. some residents reported to government officials at the Persian stronghold of Susa: "The survivors there in the province who escaped captivity are in great trouble and shame; the wall of Jerusalem is broken down, and its gates have been destroyed by fire" (Neh 1:3). Nehemiah, the recipient of this report, was a high official in the government of Artaxerxes, then king of Persia. He requested permission of the king to rebuild the walls of Jerusalem and was sent there as governor with a military escort and another band of Babylonian Jews.

Nehemiah realized that the Jewish community could survive only if it had security. So he quickly organized the people into groups, assigning each group a portion of the wall to be rebuilt. When Samaritans and others hostile to the Jews threatened violence, Nehemiah had the workers arm themselves, exchanging shifts as stone masons and guards. In fifty-two days the walls were rebuilt, and Jerusalem's inhabitants were safe from their foes.

Nehemiah then concerned himself with forming the people into a real community. He had a tenth of the country people move into Jerusalem and insisted that the wealthy stop oppressing the poor. Having fulfilled a twelve-year term as governor, he went to Susa and sought reappointment. Returning to Jerusalem, he made arrangements for the support of the Temple and its priests, restored the Sabbath observance, and forbade intermarriage with pagans.

In 398 B.C., Ezra, a priest and scribe skilled in the Law of Moses, was sent from Babylon to Jerusalem by King Artaxerxes II. Ezra was commissioned to administer justice in Judah, to see to the proper care of the Temple, and to instruct the people in the law. Upon arriving, Ezra assembled the Jewish community. For two days he read and explained the law, most likely portions of the Pentateuch, and the Jews then celebrated the Feast of Booths. Next, Ezra addressed the problem of intermarriages with pagans and convinced the Jews to abandon such marriages.

Nehemiah and Ezra were the two leading figures in the restoration, as the period of reconstruction and renewal after the Babylonian exile is called. Nehemiah made it possible for the Jews to reestablish themselves as a nation, and Ezra formed the Jewish community into the people of the law. Without these two, there might have been no Jewish community in the first century B.C. to await the coming of a savior.

The Chronicler

Much of the history of postexilic Judaism is known from the works of an inspired writer called the Chronicler. (The Chronicler may possibly have been a group of writers but will be referred to here in the singular.) He is believed to have lived in the fourth century B.C. and to have intended his writings for the Jewish community of the restoration. He used as sources parts of the Pentateuch and Deuteronomist's history as well as many other volumes that he cites. His works include 1 and 2 Chronicles, Ezra, and Nehemiah and are classified as idealized salvation history.

The First and Second Books of Chronicles cover the same span of years as the Pentateuch and Deuteronomist's history, but the Chronicler had a special purpose: to strengthen the Jews of fourth-century Judah in their love for God's law and to teach them that obedience to God was their only hope for survival.

The Chronicler emphasized God's greatness and underscored God's intervention in history. He placed the heroic deeds of past Israelite leaders in the spotlight, ignoring their weaknesses. In even stronger terms than the Deuteronomist, he taught that virtue is rewarded and sin punished. He accentuated the primacy of the Jerusalem Temple.

The Chronicler wanted to say to the remnant, the Jewish community of the restoration: "Remember what God has done for you. Look at the great heroes of our past. See how evil has always been punished and good rewarded. Realize that the Temple must be the focal point of our lives." He painted an idealized picture of the past in order to give the Jews an ideal for the future. That is why his works are called idealized salvation history.

1 and 2 Chronicles

The First Book of Chronicles summarizes human history from creation to the time of the exile by the use of genealogical tables (1 Chr 1:1–9:34). The remainder of the book contains selected material from the life of David; it places special emphasis on David's relationship to temple worship and spells out long lists of temple functionaries and supplies in order to highlight the Jerusalem Temple (1 Chr 9:35–29:30).

The Second Book of Chronicles opens with an idealized view of Solomon's reign and his construction of the Temple (2 Chr 1–9). It mentions the rebellion of the northern tribes, then focuses on the southern kingdom of Judah from Jeroboam through the fall of Jerusalem (2 Chr 10–36). Much of the material is taken from 1 and 2 Kings, adapted to fit the special purposes of the Chronicler.

Read *1 Chronicles 12* for an example of the Chronicler's style. Note the lists of names and numbers, the idealization of the army, and the portrayal of *all* Israel supporting David as king. Read *2 Chronicles 14* for a legend about an invasion of "a million men and three hundred chariots" from Ethiopia; this tale (which may have some basis in a raid by a band of nomads) is meant to show God's power and should not be taken as history.

Ezra and Nehemiah

The historical events behind the books of Ezra and Nehemiah have been outlined above according to a chronology devised by Scripture scholars. In writing these books, the Chronicler used memoirs of Ezra and Nehemiah but arranged some of the material out of sequence, possibly for theological reasons. Both books begin with the rebuilding of material structures, then move on to reformation of the community.

The stories told in Ezra and Nehemiah, especially the first person memoirs, are lively and interesting. Ezra and Nehemiah offer much accurate historical information, verifiable from other written sources and from archaeological studies. But their primary purpose was theological, and, like 1 and 2 Chronicles, they are best described as idealized salvation history.

Ezra and Nehemiah show God as active in human history, providentially sending Cyrus to deliver the Jews from exile. These books point out the centrality of Temple worship and allude to the Davidic ancestry of Sheshbazzar and Zerubbabel, thus keeping alive among the Jewish community a hope that a messiah would come from David's family. Ezra and Nehemiah demand that Jews be holy, free from pagan influence (especially from intermarriage with pagans), and faithful to the law.

The Book of Ezra opens with Cyrus' proclamation allowing the exiles to return to Jerusalem, then describes the efforts at reconstruction under Sheshbazzar and Zerubbabel (Ezra 1–6). The second part of the book describes the mission of Ezra in 398 B.C., especially his denunciation of mixed marriages (Ezra 7–10).

The Book of Nehemiah recounts Nehemiah's feat of rebuilding Jerusalem's walls and his census of the people (Neh 1–7). It describes Ezra's promulgation of the law (Neh 8–10), then presents Temple records, lists of names, and an account of the dedication of the city walls. It concludes with Nehemiah's efforts to eliminate abuses in worship, Sabbath observance, and intermarriages (Neh 11–13).

Read *Ezra 1*, which cites Cyrus' decree and describes the exiles' preparations to return to Jerusalem. Read *Ezra 6:14-22*, which relates the rebuilding and rededication of the Temple as well as the celebration of Passover.

Read *Nehemiah 4* for a vivid picture of the trials undergone by the Jews in rebuilding Jerusalem's walls. Read *Nehemiah 8:1-12* to learn how Ezra taught God's law to the people of Jerusalem. (Nehemiah's name has been inserted in the passage for editorial reasons, but his mission was completed before that of Ezra.)

Modern readers can best profit from 1 and 2 Chronicles, Ezra, and Nehemiah by being attentive to the spiritual purposes of the Chronicler. We can imitate the Chronicler's reverence for God. His attention to God's activity in history can make us more mindful of God's providence. We can admire the Chronicler's love for his ancestors, even as we admit their weaknesses. While we must amend his primitive notions of reward and punishment, we can emulate his enthusiasm for duty and obedience. His devotion to the Temple can inspire us to worship God with all our heart.

From Ezra to the Maccabees

We know little about the Jewish community from the time of Ezra to that of the religious persecutions of 167 B.C. We do know that in God's providence, the walls of stone erected by Nehemiah and the law promulgated by Ezra gave Judaism the stability and strength it needed to survive several centuries of change and chaos.

The Persians continued to rule their vast empire through much of the fourth century. But in 336 B.C. a twenty-year-old prince from Macedonia (modern Greece) named Alexander the Great began one of the most spectacular military campaigns in history. When his father was assassinated, Alexander took control of the Macedonian army and set out to conquer the world. After subduing the Greek states, he defeated the Persian army, then moved through Judah and Samaria and vanquished

Egypt. He bypassed Jerusalem, destroyed Samaria, and left the entire area under his control. Next, he swept eastward in a march that ended with the defeat of a powerful Indian army. Alexander now turned toward home but died of a fever in Babylon at the age of thirty-two.

After his death, Alexander's generals began to fight over his empire. Antigonus of Asia Minor had designs on Judah and the other countries on the eastern Mediterranean, as did Ptolemy Lagi of Egypt. Judah (now known as Judea) passed back and forth between the two until Antigonus' defeat at the battle of Ipsus (Asia Minor) in 301 B.C. In the peace treaty after this battle, Judea was awarded to another of Alexander's generals, Seleucus Nicator, who had partial control over an area from Greece to India. However, Ptolemy of Egypt claimed Palestine (Judea, Samaria, and Galilee), and for more than a century the area would be fought over by the successors of Ptolemy, called Ptolemies, and those of Seleucus, known as Seleucids.

Alexander the Great had left his mark on both Ptolemies and Seleucids. That mark was Hellenism (from *Hellen,* meaning "Greek"), the spread of Greek culture, language, art, philosophy, and religion in the lands he had conquered. Subsequently, civil leaders tried to *Hellenize* their followers as a way of achieving unity. Many Jews saw Hellenism as a threat to their religion and nation, and soon divisions arose among those Jews who rejected Hellenism and those who accepted it.

In 198 B.C. the Seleucids gained the upper hand over the Ptolemies, but soon a new Mediterranean power, Rome, forced them to abandon much of their territory outside Syria and Palestine. For about thirty years the Seleucids, pressured by Rome, allowed the Jews a measure of self-rule under the authority of the high priest.

But in 167 B.C., the Seleucid ruler, Antiochus IV (also called Antiochus Epiphanes), in an effort to unify his subjects by forcing them to accept Hellenism, proscribed Judaism. Jewish practices such as circumcision, Sabbath observance, and dietary restrictions were outlawed. A statue of the Greek god Zeus was set up in the Jerusalem Temple and all Jews were ordered to worship Zeus. Those who refused were mercilessly persecuted; men, women, and children were tortured and put to death.

When Antiochus' representative came to the Jewish village of Modein, about twenty miles from Jerusalem, a priest named Mattathias killed him and started a revolt. With his five sons, he fled into the nearby hills and was soon joined by many other Jewish patriots, including the

Hasideans, forerunners of the Pharisees. Mattathias appointed his son Judas Maccabeus as military leader of these patriots. After his father's death in 166 B.C., Judas led a successful guerrilla campaign against the Seleucid overlords. Time after time Judas made surprise attacks on the Syrian armies, inflicting heavy casualties. In December 164 B.C., Judas moved into Jerusalem and rededicated the Temple, an event since celebrated by Jews at the Feast of Hanukkah.

Soon after this, Antiochus Epiphanes died, and the Syrian capital of Antioch became a hotbed of intrigue as different parties vied for the throne. Judas continued to fight for Jewish independence, even forming an alliance with Rome. In 161 B.C. he achieved one of his greatest victories in wiping out an army led by the Syrian general, Nicanor. But that same year Judas was killed and his troops routed by a much larger army under Bacchides, yet another Syrian general. The guerrilla forces went into hiding, gradually building up strength under the leadership of Judas' brother Jonathan.

In 156 B.C. Jonathan led his men in attacks against Syria, and, after vicious fighting, Bacchides decided to negotiate. Jonathan moved to Jerusalem as political and religious leader of his people. When conspiracies continued in the Syrian high command, Jonathan skillfully won one concession after another. But in 143 B.C. he was murdered by a Syrian general, Trypho, and was replaced by Jonathan's brother Simon.

The next year Simon won political independence for Judea and was recognized by his people as high priest and civil ruler. Thus began a new dynasty, called Hasmonean after a tribal name of the old priest Mattathias. Simon presided over Judea until 134 B.C., when he was assassinated by his son-in-law, Ptolemy, an agent of the Syrians. Simon's son, John Hyrcanus, assumed the high priesthood and was besieged by the Syrians in Jerusalem. The siege ended in less than a year when the Syrian government collapsed.

John Hyrcanus quickly expanded Jewish borders, taking over Samaria to the north and Idumea to the south. His death in 104 B.C. was followed by years of confusion as the Hellenistic aristocratic class, the Sadducees, struggled with the Pharisees, a religious sect devoted to strict observance of Jewish laws. In 90 B.C. a civil war broke out, and tens of thousands lost their lives in nine years of conflict as the Pharisees tried to overthrow Alexander Janneus, high priest and king. Eventually, Janneus and the Sadducees prevailed. In a victory celebration, Janneus is said to have banqueted with his concubines and viewed the crucifixion of eight hundred Pharisees who had to watch from their crosses while their wives and children were slaughtered. In the years that followed, Janneus extended the borders of Judea almost to the limits of David's kingdom. He died in 76 B.C. and was succeeded as ruler by his widow, Salome Alexandra; his son Hyrcanus II became high priest.

Nine years of prosperity followed, but when Salome died, her younger son Aristobulus rebelled against Hyrcanus. The resulting conflict was settled only when the Roman army, under Pompey, entered into the struggle, besieging Jerusalem, which was under the control of Aristobulus. In 63 B.C. Jerusalem's walls were breached and Judea became a Roman vassal state. Sporadic civil strife and battles with Rome continued until an Idumean named Herod, with support of Roman authorities, assumed control after a bloody campaign against Judea and Jerusalem. In 37 B.C. Herod was recognized by the Romans as King of Judea, Samaria, Galilee, Perea, and Idumea.

With the support of the Romans and with revenues from taxes during a time of prosperity, Herod embarked on an extensive construction program. He fortified and restored Jerusalem, built a lavish palace, and erected a Temple that was one of the architectural wonders of the age. He rebuilt Samaria and constructed new fortresses and cities throughout his realm. He organized his government into an efficient police state, but was resented by many of his Jewish subjects, who considered him a foreign pretender to the throne. He was cruel and ruthless in putting down opposition, so paranoid about threats to his power that he executed, among many others, his own wife, his mother-in-law, and three of his own sons. He died about 4 B.C., not long after the birth of Jesus Christ. (See page 120 which explains the date of the birth of Christ.)

Religious Historical Novels

The turbulent centuries following the exile were the background for three books found after Nehemiah in our present-day Catholic Bible—Tobit, Judith, and Esther. While placed among the historical books, these works are more properly classified as religious historical novels.

Historical novels are books that tell stories about fictitious characters placed in the context of actual historical events. Such works can help us understand the past because, by allowing us to experience historical events through the eyes and minds of participants, they can evoke an awareness of life long ago and an empathy for people of times past in a way that scholarly history cannot.

Religious historical novels put the spotlight on supernatural issues and spiritual messages, and in this lies the special value of Tobit, Judith, and Esther. These books also feature a timelessness that derives from their authors' practice of joining one epoch to another. For example, in the Book of Esther, the hero Mordecai is said to have been deported to Babylon in 597 B.C., but is still living during the reign of Xerxes of Persia (485-464 B.C.). In the Book of Judith, Nebuchadnezzar (who was king of Babylon during the fall of Jerusalem) is said to be the king of Assyria and to wage war on Judah after the return from exile! This timelessness and many other features of these writings point out the authors' intent to transcend history, not to create scholarly documents.

Tobit

Tobit, according to many scholars, was written in the second century B.C. for Jews struggling with the question of whether they could adapt to the Greek customs of the world around them. It is a fascinating story about Tobit, a faithful Jewish exile in Assyria. Tobit worships God and cares for neighbors even at the risk of his own life. Worn out by trials and the burden of blindness, he begs God for death, then sends his son Tobiah to Media to collect a large sum of money. In Media, Sarah, a young woman, is also praying for death because she has been married seven times, and each time a demon has killed her husband on the wedding night. God sends the angel Raphael to accompany Tobiah on his journey. Raphael guides Tobiah safely to his destination, brings about a successful marriage between Tobiah and Sarah, acquires the money, then heals Tobit of his blindness.

The story is meant to teach that good Jews should remain faithful to the laws and traditions of their ancestors. Thus, Tobit exemplifies the virtues of reverence for God, devotion to temple worship, love of family, charity, prayer, almsgiving, and fasting. Tobiah and Sarah display faith, piety, and married love. The instructions given by Tobit and by Raphael are actually intended for all who read the book. In the setting of the story, they acquire a special charm and interest. Even today, we can profit from the beautiful ideals exemplified in the actors and dialogue of this book.

Read *Tobit 4* for Tobit's instructions to his son to prepare him for the journey to Media. They may be seen also as instructions to prepare any reader for the journey of life. You may want to read the whole story as well as the stories of Judith and Esther which follow. They are brief, absorbing, and enjoyable.

Judith

In this colorful story, Nebuchadnezzar, presented as king of Assyria, sends his general, Holofernes, to lead 132,000 soldiers to attack Judah. These enemies represent all the forces hostile to God's people, and they besiege the Jews at Bethulia, an imaginary city said to be north of Jerusalem. When the situation seems hopeless for the Jews, Judith (her name means "Jewess") enters the enemy camp, beguiles Holofernes with her beauty, gets him drunk at a private banquet in his tent, then cuts off his head. The army panics when the headless body of its leader is discovered. The soldiers flee, only to be pursued and slaughtered by the Jews.

This story was most probably written before or during the Maccabean period to give hope to Jews who were undergoing persecution from the Seleucid dynasty. The lesson of the story is that God can deliver faithful believers from the worst of times if they put their trust in God's power and observe the law. We who read the book in different historical circumstances can still benefit from its insistence that we put faith in God.

Read *Judith 8* for an introduction to the heroine of this story. Note how she encourages the people to be faithful to the law and to realize God's power to deliver them. These words spoke directly to the situation of Jews persecuted by the Seleucids for observing the law.

Esther

This book, named after its heroine, may best be understood as a melodrama designed to give Jewish people an opportunity to celebrate their survival through the ages. The author, an unknown Jew writing after the fourth century B.C., tells the story as an explanation for the Feast of Purim.

The tale is set in the time of King Ahasuerus (Xerxes I, 485-464 B.C.) of Persia. Ahasuerus is displeased with Queen Vashti and replaces her with the beautiful Jewess, Esther (both women are unknown to history). Mordecai, a devout Jew and Esther's uncle, displeases the evil Haman, a high official of Ahasuerus, and Haman plots to have Mordecai and all Jews in the empire executed in a single day. The plot is foiled when Esther intercedes for her people. Haman is hanged on the very same gallows he had prepared for Mordecai. Mordecai is elevated to Haman's former position. The Jews are allowed to slaughter 75,000 of their enemies.

It sounds gruesome, but it is just a story. Down through history, it has been the reason for many a party at the springtime Feast of Purim, an occasion for revelry and the dramatization of the Esther story, with cheers for Mordecai and jeers for Haman.

Jews celebrate their survival and God's providential care with the story of Esther and the Feast of Purim. We who are Christian may read Esther as a reminder of the protection we have received from God. We can see the story as a foreshadowing of Christ's victory over the devil. We can rejoice at how Christ has turned the tables on Satan by overcoming evil on the gallows of the cross. We can celebrate Christ's victory over the powers of sin and death and the downfall of demons allied with Satan. This interpretation was not intended by the author, of course, but it is one we may add to give *us* a reason to party!

Read *Esther 7* for the overthrow of Haman. Read *Esther 9:20-28* for the linking of the Esther story with the Feast of Purim.

1 Maccabees

The title for 1 and 2 Maccabees comes from the name given to the leader of the Jewish anti-Seleucid guerrilla forces, Judas Maccabeus. Maccabeus means "hammer," and came to be applied also to Judas' family and followers.

The First Book of Maccabees was written in Hebrew by a Palestinian Jew about 100 B.C. It provides much reliable historical information, including records of Jewish defeats and victories. The author cites a number of official documents and is quite accurate in giving dates and Palestinian locations. The First Book of Maccabees is, nonetheless, salvation history and is most concerned with the religious life of the Jewish people and their relationship to God.

The First Book of Maccabees opens with a brief review of Alexander the Great's life, then moves into the reign of Antiochus Epiphanes and his persecution of the Jews (1 Macc 1). It next describes the revolt begun by Mattathias and the battles waged by Judas Maccabeus against Seleucid oppressors. The high point of Judas' career, the rededication of the Temple, is followed by his death in battle (2–8). The book then relates the career of Judas' brother and successor, Jonathan, including his successful efforts against the Seleucids and their Hellenizing Jewish allies. Unfortunately, Jonathan puts his trust in a Syrian general, Trypho, and is murdered by him (9–12). Finally, 1 Maccabees tells how Simon, the last of Mattathias' sons, achieves independence for Judea and becomes high priest and civil ruler. After Simon's assassination, he is succeeded by his son, John Hyrcanus. The book ends with a summary of John's reign (13–16).

Read *1 Maccabees* 2 for the beginning of the Maccabean revolt under Mattathias. Read *1 Maccabees 4* for an account of several of Judas' victories and his rededication of the Jerusalem Temple. Read *1 Maccabees 16* for the death of the last Maccabee brother and the start of a new era under John Hyrcanus.

Modern readers of 1 Maccabees may learn a great deal about second-century B.C. Palestine. But we should also look to the spiritual lessons offered here. We may not endure persecutions as the Jews did, but like them we are faced with a choice. They had to decide to accept the principles of Hellenism or those of the God of Abraham. We must decide to accept the principles of a secular society or those of Jesus Christ.

2 Maccabees

The Second Book of Maccabees is not a sequel to 1 Maccabees. It was written around 100 B.C. by a different author in another language (Greek) at a separate location, possibly Alexandria, Egypt. It has a narrower focus, covering the events from the final years of Onias the high priest, about 180 B.C., to Judas' defeat of Nicanor in 161 B.C. Rather than relating historical facts, it tends to offer theological interpretations for historical events. It embellishes these events with legendary details, edifying speeches, and grisly descriptions of persecutions and divine punishments. It tends to blame treasonous Hellenizing Jews for the sufferings befalling those loyal to the Torah. Its purpose is to elicit sympathy for victims of persecution, to convince readers of God's providential care even at the worst of times, to designate the Jerusalem Temple as the proper site for orthodox worship, and to present the concepts of eternal reward and punishment.

The Second Book of Maccabees begins with several letters relating to the Jerusalem Temple and the Feast of Hanukkah, including the author's preface explaining that he is summarizing another work, that of Jason of Cyrene (1–2). There follows an account of assaults on the Temple during the time of Onias, the high priest (2 Macc 3). Next, the persecution of the Jews and profanation of the Temple by Hellenizing apostates and Seleucid rulers are described (4–7). The rest of the book deals with the campaigns of Judas Maccabeus against the Seleucid armies and their allies (8–15).

Read *2 Maccabees 2:19-32* for the author's preface. Note how this book was produced at the cost of "sweat and loss of sleep" and how the author good-naturedly alludes to the length of his remarks. Read *2 Maccabees 7,* an example of how the author portrays the grisly details of a martyrdom under the Seleucids. Whatever the historical content behind this story, it carefully teaches in the speeches of the martyrs that death is better than breaking the law because God bestows eternal life on those who are faithful to the end. Read *2 Maccabees 12:38-46,* which demonstrates the Jewish practice, at least a century before Christ, of praying for the dead. This passage is the scriptural basis for Catholic doctrines of purgatory and prayer for the deceased.

As we read 2 Maccabees, we are encouraged to love God's law and house of worship. We reflect on our belief in eternal life. We learn that when we pray for the deceased, we are one with heroic spiritual ancestors like Judas Maccabeus and part of a tradition that stretches back more than two thousand years.

The Historical Books: A Reflection

As they study the historical books of the Old Testament, many people are dismayed at what they read. In these books they find every possible sin, every human weakness, every tragedy, every failure. They expect more truth and beauty in the story of the encounter of God and humanity.

But the Old Testament tells it like it is. The Old Testament does present the truth and beauty springing from the creative love and everlasting fidelity of God. It does present truth and beauty in the responses of great believers like Abraham and Ruth. But it does not give a retouched portrait. It shows that humankind without God is prone to disaster and decay. The historical books demonstrate our need for salvation. They teach us that salvation must come from God, that any Savior must be divine.

Questions for Discussion and Reflection

Of all the men and women you have met in your study of Old Testament historical books, who are your favorites? Why? If you could choose one era from Old Testament history to live in, which would it be? Why? Would you prefer that era to now? Were there any "good old days" in the Old Testament?

In the last two chapters we have studied the events of thirteen hundred years. Can you list at least one key event and one key person from Jewish history for each of the thirteen centuries before Christ?

Can you name from memory the historical books? Can you give one practical lesson from each book for readers of today? Do you think that your study of the historical books will help you gain more from the readings at Mass? Will this study help you grow spiritually? In what ways?

Activities

Construct a family tree, listing the best of the spiritual ancestors you have met in the historical books of the Old Testament. For each individual in your family tree, list one quality or virtue of that person you would like to possess. Then spend a few minutes in prayer. Thank God for the good qualities of our spiritual ancestors, and ask God to help you imitate these qualities in your everyday life.

CHAPTER SEVEN
The Wisdom Books

H aste makes waste." "A word to the wise is sufficient." "Do unto others as you would have them do unto you." Such proverbs are part of the wisdom that guides us through life.

Wisdom may be expressed in many other forms, all of which help us determine values and discover meaning. Drama like *A Man for All Seasons* demonstrates courage and integrity. The song "Amazing Grace" reminds us of God's mercy. Proverbs counsel us in everyday decisions. Wry wit like "The slowest line at the checkout counter is always the one you join" keeps us from taking life's foibles too seriously. Poetry like Elizabeth Barrett Browning's "How Do I Love Thee?" teaches that human relationships are more precious than gold. Reflections on the past, like the PBS television series *The Civil War,* display the heroism of predecessors. *Poor Richard's Almanac* and other collections of sayings keep us in touch with time-tested truth.

People of the Old Testament revered wisdom and preserved the insights of sages in seven works known as the Wisdom Books. In them we find drama, the Book of *Job;* songs, the Book of *Psalms;* a Book of *Proverbs;* the wry wit of *Ecclesiastes;* the love poetry of the *Song of Solomon;* reflections on the past, the *Wisdom* of Solomon; and an almanac of sayings, the Book of *Sirach.*

The Content of Wisdom Literature

There were many Wisdom traditions in the ancient world. Israel's sages studied these traditions and learned from them. Jewish wisdom, however, was unique in the way it reflected a distinctive belief in God and in a moral order based on God's will.

Old Testament Wisdom Literature differs from the Pentateuch and Historical Books in that its authors deal more with personal matters than with religious issues like the covenant. These authors look at life from the viewpoint of the individual rather than of the nation. They discuss such things as good manners, moral behavior, business, marriage, family, the home, social life, and human relationships. They look into the questions that trouble us as individuals: the meaning of pain and suffering, good and evil, wealth and poverty, life and death.

The Form of Wisdom Literature

The Wisdom Books tend to follow patterns of Jewish poetry, depending on the balance of thoughts rather than on rhyme. Among the most common patterns are repetition, contrast, and construction.

In *repetition,* similar ideas are expressed in different words:

O LORD, do not rebuke me in your anger,
  or discipline me in your wrath (Ps 6:2).

In *contrast,* dissimilar ideas are compared:

Hatred stirs up strife,
  but love covers all offenses (Prov 10:12).

In *construction,* ideas are built upon one another:

Set me as a seal upon your heart,
  as a seal upon your arm;
  for love is strong as death,
  passion fierce as the grave.
Its flashes are flashes of fire,
  a raging flame.
Many waters cannot quench love,
  neither can floods drown it (Song 8:6-7).

Once we are aware of these patterns, we can enjoy the flow and balance of ideas that make up Hebrew poetry. We can more readily understand and appreciate Wisdom Literature.

The Origin and Development of Wisdom Literature

Wisdom traditions existed in Egypt and Mesopotamia before the Exodus. Israelites probably knew of them and used proverbs to teach youth as far back as the time of the Judges. During the era of the kings, there were court scribes who collected sayings and established schools. The Wisdom tradition continued throughout Old Testament history, and the Wisdom of Solomon was the last Old Testament work to be written.

King David is said to be the composer of many of the Psalms, and King Solomon is named as the author of Proverbs, Ecclesiastes, Song of Solomon, and parts of the Wisdom of Solomon. While David may have written some of the Psalms attributed to him, and Solomon may have written proverbs and instructions, neither actually authored the books attributed to them. It was common in the ancient world to assign authorship of a work to a famous person to give that work special prestige.

Job

An elderly lady in the cancer wing of a hospital was crying. The chaplain asked what was troubling her. She replied that a friend had said that if she would pray with faith, she would be healed. Her friend, far from comforting her, laid a burden of guilt on her. "I'm not being healed," she reasoned, "so I must not have faith."

The old notion that God will bless us only if we are good enough and that all suffering is punishment from God for *not* being good enough is still around. And it does a great deal of harm, as it did in Old Testament times.

The Book of Job was written by an inspired poet who saw the error of equating suffering with divine punishment. Its date of composition is uncertain, but many scholars place it around the time of the Exile.

The story begins with a prose narrative about Job, an enormously wealthy chieftain who lived blamelessly before God. But one day Satan (not the devil, but a sort of devil's advocate) challenged God to test Job, saying that if God deprived him of his great wealth, he would certainly curse God. Job is subsequently stripped of wealth, family, and health, yet bears it all patiently.

The scene then changes, and the book turns from prose to poetry as it relates how three of Job's friends, Eliphaz, Bildad, and Zophar, come to console him. When they arrive, Job becomes very *impatient* and bewails his fate. His friends then engage in a poetic dialogue with Job in three cycles of speeches. Each accuses Job on the grounds that his sufferings prove him to be guilty of sin. Job, however, denies any guilt and demands that God explain why he must suffer. Then a young man, Elihu, makes his appearance to defend God. His speech closes with the remark that God "does not regard any who are wise in their own conceit" (37:24).

Then the curtains part and God stands front and center on the stage. Speaking "out of the whirlwind," God confronts Job: "Who are you to question me? Could you create the universe? Do you govern the stars? Are you master of life? Can you control the power of untamed animals?"

Job is overwhelmed. "I know that you can do all things," he whispers to God. "...I have uttered what I did not understand....I had heard of you by the hearing of the ear, but now my eye sees you; therefore I despise myself, and repent in dust and ashes" (42:2-6).

A return to prose signals the last act. God reproves Job's three friends, no doubt to their surprise and dismay: "...for you have not spoken of me what is right, as my servant Job has" (Job 42:7). God commands them to offer sacrifices of reparation and to ask for Job's prayers! Then God blesses Job by restoring his possessions twofold and by giving him a new family.

Read *Job 31:35-37,* Job's plea to God for an answer. Read *Job 38:1– 42:6.* God's long speech may be representative of how the author of Job reflected on the wonder of creation, and through it came to experience the Creator.

There are two important morals to the story. First, we ought not attempt to bring God down to our level by offering simplistic answers to life's greatest problems. To presume, on the one hand, as Job's friends did, that suffering must be punishment from God is an insult to the Lord. To presume, on the other hand, as Job did, that we can understand all the riddles of life is foolish. Second, when we are suffering, all the logic in the world will not help. Only an encounter with the Lord and the awareness that God is close to us in our pain can bring us peace. When we can say to God, "Now my eye sees you," we may not understand all the reasons for our pain, but we can accept it.

The Book of Job is a drama. But behind it, no doubt, is a real story of anguish and suffering. Its author may have been stricken with a mortal illness. His friends may have suggested that if he would pray with faith, all would be well. Then the author felt God's presence in some powerful way, perhaps through a near-death experience, and this encounter brought him peace.

People who have had a near-death experience testify to receiving from it a peace beyond expectations. Friends may ask them, "How can you say that life is good when you have a terminal illness? How can you say that God is present when there is so much suffering in the world?" They respond simply, "I can't explain it. I just *know* that God is near and that all will be well." Such experiences of God transcend language. Even the greatest poetry, like that of the Book of Job, can give only the faintest hint of Ultimate Reality. But as a frightened child finds peace in a mother's arms, so those who encounter God find peace.

The Book of Job encourages us to seek God in prayer. It helps us realize that while there are no easy answers to the problem of suffering, there *is* an answer. It is the faith-realization that God is near and that we can entrust ourselves to God's loving arms. When we pray with Job, "I have uttered what I did not understand, but now my eye sees you," we are on a journey that will lead us to Jesus. "My God, my God, why have you forsaken me?" (Mk 15:34). "Father, into your hands I commend my spirit" (Lk 23:46). We are on the pathway from pain to peace.

Psalms

The Book of Psalms is a collection of 150 prayers in the form of Hebrew poetry. Compiled after the Exile from earlier collections, it is grouped into five books in imitation of the Pentateuch.

The Psalms were written at various times. The oldest go back at least to David's reign, and the most recent to the fourth century B.C. More than half the Psalms are attributed to David. It is unlikely that he wrote all of these, but he is the founder of the Jewish psalm tradition and no doubt wrote some Psalms. Other Psalms are attributed to individuals like Moses or to groups such as the Korahites, possibly song leaders at the Temple.

Many Psalms have introductory notations mentioning an author, the type of accompaniment, a recommended melody, historical references, and other information.

The Psalms address every human emotion and situation and vary in style, length, and approach. Some were meant for community prayer, especially in the Temple; others were intended for individual use. Scholars offer many classifications of Psalms. Among them are: praise (104), personal lament (51), collective lament (90), trust (23), thanksgiving (98), royal (20), liturgy (134), procession (122), history (78), messianic (2), and wisdom (1).

The Psalms were written more than two thousand years ago for Jews. Yet they have been prayed by believers of every age, nation, and culture, and remain popular today. They give us words to express the varied emotions we bring to God. The Psalms are for the most part general in tone and so allow us to fit our particular circumstances into their framework. They join us to the community of believers who have prayed them down through the centuries. They allow us to stand before God not as isolated individuals but as members of a family that prays with us and for us today.

A good way to make the Psalms our own is to read through them all, keeping a list of those most appealing for prayer and reflection. When we pray the Psalms, it is often helpful to adapt them to our own situation. For example, Psalm 23 will have one meaning if we use it before setting out on a long journey, and another if we pray it while waiting for the results of a medical test.

The Psalms can be powerful intercessory prayers, especially when we pray them for another as if we were that other person. In praying Psalm 6, for instance, we may not be feeling the distress and anguish verbalized in the Psalm, but we may know a friend who is experiencing great sorrow; we may pray Psalm 6 in the name of that friend, who through our prayer, can be touched by God's grace.

The Psalms, of course, antedate the teaching of Jesus, and they have limitations. Some reflect a spirit of vengeance: "O God, break the teeth in their mouths" (Ps 58:6), and a spirit of cruelty: "O daughter Babylon, you devastator, / happy shall they be who pay you back… / who take your little ones / and dash them against the rock!" (Ps 137:8-9). Some of the most wonderful Psalms, like Psalm 139, have passages that may not be in keeping with the forgiveness of mercy of Christ (verses 19-22). We may skip over inappropriate Psalms and passages in our prayer, focusing instead on those that reflect the sentiments of our heart and best imitate the prayer of Jesus.

Read *Psalm 1,* which mirrors themes common in the other Wisdom Books. Read *Psalm 90,* a moody reflection on the brevity of life and a good example of a community lament. Read *Psalm 104,* a beautiful song praising God the Creator. Read *Psalm 150,* a grand hymn of praise that closes the Book of Psalms.

Proverbs

The Book of Proverbs takes its name from its first verse: "The proverbs of Solomon, son of David." Solomon was not the actual author of Proverbs, which was compiled from numerous earlier collections of wise sayings. He is, however, the "patron" of the Jewish Wisdom tradition.

Some parts of the Book of Proverbs go back to ancient Egyptian and Mesopotamian sayings which were adapted by Jewish sages to instruct young people. Other parts come from collections made by teachers to educate students at the royal court or at their own schools. In about 500 B.C., these and other sayings were edited into the Book of Proverbs by an unknown sage.

Much of the book consists of the recitation of sayings and proverbs which are connected only loosely, if at all. There are a few sections that develop topics in an orderly fashion, for example, the "Ode to a Capable Wife" (Prov 31:10-31). Many of the proverbs deal with secular wisdom and mundane details of everyday life, but underlying every proverb is the foundation of religious belief: "The fear of the LORD is the beginning of knowledge" (Prov 1:7).

Read *Proverbs 1:1-7* for the introduction. Read *Proverbs 15* as a sampler. You may wish to search for the three Hebrew poetical structures mentioned above; for example, verse 1 uses contrast, verse 3 uses construction, and verse 10 uses repetition. Browse through the book; you will find many of the proverbs witty and memorable.

Ecclesiastes

One of the most striking features of the Bible is its honesty in facing the unpleasant side of life. There are times in life when we feel confused, discouraged, even hopeless. The Book of Ecclesiastes is about such times. It shows that our fears, doubts, apprehensions, and dark feelings do not cut us off from God.

Ecclesiastes was written about three hundred years before Christ by a Jewish sage called Qoheleth, which means "teacher." Qoheleth was apparently an older man who had spent most of his years instructing others. As the years went by he began to see human existence as foolish and futile. Life seemed to have little meaning because it led inevitably to the tomb. Even the longest human lifetime passed by swiftly, and in the grave, he thought, all were the same: dead and gone.

Qoheleth rejected the easy answers of earlier generations. The good did not always find happiness, and the wicked were not always punished. Around and around life seemed to go, heading nowhere. All the good things—knowledge, love, wealth, friendship—passed away. The more the old man thought about it, the more depressed he became.

Qoheleth's reflections are much like ours when we become despondent. We see something one way, then another. One moment an idea makes sense; the next moment it doesn't. Traditional wisdom seems to offer a solution but then is rejected. Contradictory thoughts and feelings wash over us like waves against the shore. The problems seem to outweigh the solutions.

But while Ecclesiastes is hardly cheerful reading, it is thought-provoking. It teaches that we human beings cannot achieve lasting happiness or find real meaning when left to our own resources. The best advice Qoheleth could give to his readers was to lead a moral, balanced life, without expecting too much happiness. Ultimately, Ecclesiastes is a book of questions waiting for answers.

Fortunately, those answers are supplied by Jesus Christ. In this we discover the real value of Ecclesiastes: It demonstrates our need for the wisdom only Christ can give.

Read *Ecclesiastes 3,* which includes the famous reflection on time and which points out so many of the questions to be answered by Jesus. For example, Qoheleth notes that God "has put a sense of past and future" into our hearts, but Qoheleth cannot explain why. Jesus, however, can. Jesus shows us that God has put a sense of past and future into our hearts because we are made to live forever.

If you really want to become depressed (!), read *Ecclesiastes 12:1-8,* which closes the reflections of Qoheleth with a memorable poem about old age and with his oft-repeated refrain, "Vanity of vanities...all is vanity!" Verses 9-14 seem to be an epilogue added by another writer who has learned from Qoheleth not to post easy answers to hard questions. He does add what seems to him to be the best advice to problems posed by Qoheleth: "Fear God, and keep his commandments; for that is the whole duty of everyone" (12:13).

Song of Solomon

The title of this book comes from its first verse, "The Song of Songs, which is Solomon's." (In some Bibles, this book is called the "Song of Songs.") The book seems to be a collection of love poems that have been loosely organized to depict the courtship and marriage of a young country couple. In spite of obstacles, they seek each other. Even the fantasy of a proposal from King Solomon himself cannot destroy their love, which is as "strong as death" and which "many waters cannot quench" (Song 8:6-7).

The book's language and style date it to a time after the Exile. Its reference to Solomon means only that the work belongs among those books credited to him as Israel's first sage.

The Song of Solomon has been praised by many through the centuries for its vivid imagery and passionate language. But there are many opinions as to how it ought to be interpreted. Some view the work as a parable portraying the love of God for people. Others see it as an inspired poem showing the beauty of human marital love.

Perhaps the best way to read the Song of Solomon is to see it as a love poem that also reminds us of God's love for us. However, one person's poetry is another person's poison. A young man today would hardly attempt to praise his beloved with the words, "Your hair is like a flock of goats" (Song 6:5). We might not use its language of love, but we can learn to appreciate the poetry and passion of the Song of Solomon. We can learn that human marital love is good, so good that it becomes in the Bible a symbol of God's love for us.

Read *Song of Solomon 2* for a sample of its poetry. Be attentive to any footnotes for explanations of vocabulary and imagery. Read *Song of Solomon 8:6-7* for a beautiful hymn in praise of human love. These lines can exemplify the two ways of using the Song of Solomon: A married couple might speak them to each other to express love, or any of us might make of them a prayer to God who *is* Love.

The Wisdom of Solomon

The title fits this book, a treatise on divine wisdom. (In some Bibles, it is called simply the Book of Wisdom.) Most Catholic scholars agree, based on its content and style, that it was written about 50 B.C. by a Jew living in Alexandria, Egypt. The author wrote in Greek and quoted the Septuagint version of the Old Testament.

The last century before Christ was a time of turmoil for Jews in Palestine and elsewhere. Early in that century a bitter civil war pitted Pharisees in Judea against the Hellenizing high priest, Alexander Janneus, and his Sadducee allies. Alexander won the war; subsequently, he and his successors tended to mingle Hebrew traditions with Greek philosophies and ideals.

At this time Jews in Egypt probably outnumbered those in Palestine. In a cosmopolitan city like Alexandria, they were confronted with all kinds of pagan religions. They were tempted to abandon the old ways for modern ideas flowing from the Greek culture that seemed to be taking over the world, even their beloved Jerusalem.

In this milieu, an unknown Jew acquainted with Greek culture and fluent in the Greek language was inspired by God to write the Wisdom of Solomon. He wanted to show the Jewish people that true wisdom is found in God's revelation, not in pagan religions or pagan philosophies.

His book may be divided into three sections. The first section deals with divine wisdom and its relationship to human destiny in life and after death. This material offers the clearest Old Testament teaching on the reality of eternal life (Wis 1:1–6:21). The second section puts Solomon in the pulpit to praise wisdom and to pray for wisdom (6:22–9:18). The third section shows the place of God's wisdom in guiding the people of the Old Testament. It focuses especially on God's providential care for the Jews during the Exodus. It contrasts God's concern for the Israelites with God's punishment of the Egyptians, thus warning the people of Alexandria that they should not abandon Jewish traditions for the Greek ideas then fashionable in Egypt and elsewhere (10:1–19:22).

The Wisdom of Solomon is not directly quoted by New Testament authors, but it clearly influenced their thinking. Note, for example, how Wisdom 2:12-20 is reflected in Matthew 27:39-43.

Read *Wisdom of Solomon 9,* a beautiful prayer for wisdom. Read *Wisdom of Solomon 10:15-21,* a prologue introducing the long treatise on the Exodus.

Sirach (Ecclesiasticus)

This book takes its name from its author, "Jesus, son of Eleazar, son of Sirach" (Sir 50:27). He was a sage who probably lived and wrote in Jerusalem, producing this work in Hebrew about 180 B.C. In 132 B.C.

his grandson, then in Egypt, translated the book into Greek, adding a foreword that is not part of the inspired text. The Greek text became part of the Alexandrian list and was accepted later by the Catholic Church so enthusiastically that it became known as "Ecclesiasticus," the "Church Book." (It is still designated by this name in some Catholic Bibles.)

Sirach is a lengthy collection of sayings and proverbs arranged according to content. Subjects treated include duties to God and family, friendship, use of wealth, moderation in speech, training of children, table etiquette, sickness, and health.

Sirach's style is concise and colorful. The proverbs are witty and wise. The advice given is full of common sense. Sirach counsels reverence for God, love for family and friends, and other virtues designed to help people lead useful, happy lives. Sirach seems unaware of the reality of eternal life, but he counsels acceptance of God's will in all things, including death. He opens our hearts to that revelation of God's will made known through Jesus, that we should have eternal life.

Sirach offers beautiful meditations on God's majesty and mercy (18:1-14) and on God's creative power (39:12-35). Perhaps his most magnificent verses are those praising the works of God in nature (42:15–43:33). Finally, he shows that wisdom is not a lifeless, abstract ideal. It finds expression in the actions of the great people of the Old Testament. Sirach applauds them and commends them as models to be imitated (44:1–50:24).

Read *Sirach 42:15–43:33,* the praise of God's works in nature. You may want to scan this book, choosing sections that are of special interest to you.

The Wisdom Literature: Epilogue

One of the great insights of the Wisdom Books is that "to fear the LORD is the beginning of wisdom" (Sir 1:14). This fear is not fright, but awe and reverence. When human beings build their lives on the foundation of reverence for God and obedience to God's guidance, they will make the most of the days allotted them on this earth.

The Wisdom Books teach us how to build our lives on time-tested principles that flow from the inspiration of God. They touch upon our personal hopes and fears, our everyday existence, our relationships with people and with God. They advise us to avoid simplistic answers. They offer patterns for a lifetime of prayer. They point out the beauty of human love. They prepare us for Christ's revelation of eternal life. They are like the advice of loving grandparents who have been through much and who want to share their experience with us. No wonder Sirach proclaims:

> All wisdom is from the LORD
>> and with him it remains forever....
> The fear of the LORD delights the heart,
>> and gives gladness and joy and long life....
> To fear the LORD is the beginning of wisdom (1:1,11,14).

Questions for Discussion and Reflection

What is your favorite saying from Proverbs? from Sirach? What is your favorite Psalm? If you could go back in time and visit with one of the authors of the Wisdom Books, would you prefer to talk with the author of Ecclesiastes or the author of Sirach? Why?

Activities

You have studied *Sirach 42:15–43:33.* Now use this same passage for prayer. As you "call to mind the works of the Lord," make your reading of this passage a poem of praise to God.

Read *Psalm 6,* a prayer for times of distress. Think of someone you know who is experiencing distress (perhaps a serious illness, the death of a loved one, or the loss of a job). Pray this Psalm as if you were that person, offering your prayers for that person.

Pray *Psalm 117.* As you do, think of how you are one with all generations of believers, Jewish and Christian, who have prayed these words for over twenty-five hundred years. Think of how you are one with believers throughout the world today, and pray in their name as you thank God for the blessings poured out upon us.

CHAPTER EIGHT
The Prophetic Books

M any people think of the Old Testament prophets as those who did nothing but foretell the future. They imagine the prophets to have been crystal-ball gazers who spent most of their time predicting details of Christ's life for the benefit of future generations.

But the word *prophet* means "someone who speaks for another." Old Testament prophets were those who spoke for God to their contemporaries. They were mainly concerned with current events and their own situations.

The kings and priests often failed in their role as spiritual leaders. When they did, God inspired prophets to speak out, to remind people of the covenant and call them to repentance. The prophets threatened evil leaders, warned sinners, consoled the suffering, advised rulers, and taught morality.

The prophets, however, did not completely ignore the future. They had a view of what it should be, and some of them foretold that God would send a Messiah (meaning "anointed one") who would be a savior for God's people. Most often, they seemed to place hope for such a savior in their immediate future.

But in God's plan, their messages about the immediate future could foreshadow the distant future. The prophecy in Isaiah 40:3-5, "In the desert prepare the way of the LORD," foretold that God would lead the Israelites back home from exile in Babylon. In the New Testament, Luke saw this prophecy as prefiguring the coming of Christ, and John the Baptist as the one who prepared the way of the Lord (Lk 3:4).

Some prophecies were fulfilled in ways the prophet might never have imagined. For example, Nathan's prophecy that David's house would endure forever (2 Sam 7:16) was thought by many Israelites to show that God would restore Israel to worldly power. But God had something far greater in mind. Luke 1:32-33 views the kingdom that will endure forever as the spiritual kingdom of Jesus Christ. New Testament writers, looking back, could see things in God's inspired word that would not have been evident to Old Testament readers.

Reading the Prophets

A guiding principle in reading the prophets is to remember that they were preachers, not scientists, lawyers, or theologians. Their aim was to persuade people to act. They used all the means that preachers employ. They focused on the imagination. They used figures of speech: similes, metaphors, parables, paradoxes, exaggerations, and puns. At times they acted out messages from God.

For the most part, the prophetic books are compilations of sermons, poems, conversations, and historical notes. In ancient times people did not have the technology to record such material exactly. So we find bits and pieces of one prophetic utterance joined to others from different times and places. A sermon admonishing people for their sins is placed next to words of comfort. Such abrupt changes in the train of thought can be disconcerting for readers. Good Bible commentaries can be helpful because they offer explanations of the historical situations behind each prophecy as well as interpretations of difficult words and phrases.

Isaiah

The Book of Isaiah was composed by a number of authors. The first thirty-nine chapters originate from the prophet Isaiah, whose ministry was centered in Jerusalem during the years 742-701 B.C. Isaiah 1:1 says that he prophesied "in the days of Uzziah, Jotham, Ahaz and Hezekiah, kings of Judah." These "days" were troubled times, marked by the constant threat of attack from Assyria. When Assyria moved against Samaria in 734 B.C., Ahaz made an alliance with Assyria. But the next king of Judah, Hezekiah, rebelled against Assyria. In 701 B.C. the Assyrian army besieged Jerusalem, only to be turned back by "the angel of the LORD" (Isa 37:36), perhaps the bubonic plague.

Many of Isaiah's sermons and writings can be traced to these historical events. His preaching, however, was based on his vision of God: "Holy, holy, holy is the LORD of hosts; the whole earth is full of his glory" (Isa 6:3). In every situation, Isaiah believed, we must be obedient to the all-holy God. "If you do not stand firm in faith, you shall not stand at all" (Isa 7:9). Isaiah saw little hope in alliances with Assyria, Egypt, or any other nation. Instead, he seemed to advocate a simple way of life, away from the current of international politics and warfare. In retrospect, he was correct. The more Judah tried to play the game of politics, the more it was driven toward its final confrontation with Babylon in 587 B.C., long after Isaiah's death.

Chapters 24–27 seem to be a collection of oracles (prophetic sayings) by several authors from postexilic times. Chapters 36–39 are a historical appendix taken largely from 2 Kings 18–20. Other segments of Isaiah 1–39 may have been composed by different writers.

Read *Isaiah 6:1-8* for the call of the prophet. Note the emphasis on God's holiness and awesome power. Read *Isaiah 7:10-16.* This prophecy relates Isaiah's assurance that Judah, under King Ahaz, need not fear the alliance of Israel and Damascus. But it is a prophecy with a deeper meaning, understood by Matthew's Gospel as the virgin birth of Jesus Christ (Mt 1:22-23). Read *Isaiah 11:1-11,* a vision of peace and justice to be brought about by the coming of a Messiah, a child sprung from Jesse (King David's father).

Chapters 40–55 of the Book of Isaiah were written by a great poet near the end of the Babylonian captivity (587-539 B.C.). The author saw Cyrus, King of Persia, as one anointed by God to bring deliverance to the Jews in Babylon. He believed that the one true God was in control of human history and would return the Jews to their home: "In the wilderness prepare the way of the LORD!" (Isa 40:3). He portrayed Israel as a servant whose suffering would bring redemption to the nations. In these "Suffering Servant" songs, the poet foreshadowed a deeper reality, the salvation given to the world through the suffering and death of Jesus Christ.

Read *Isaiah 53,* the last of the four Suffering Servant songs. You may wish to study these verses by relating them to the passion and death of Christ. This prophecy finds its fulfillment only in Jesus.

Chapters 56–66 contain poems and writings by unknown prophets who wrote in the spirit of Isaiah late in the sixth century B.C. These chapters sound a note of hope that all people can find salvation and peace in the God of Israel.

Read *Isaiah 65:17-25* for a vision of "new heavens and a new earth," a vision of peace and security that can be fully realized only in the new life of heaven.

Modern readers can learn much from the Book of Isaiah. We are taught to bow down before the holiness of God. We are drawn to Jesus Christ as our Messiah, the Suffering Servant who saves us from sin. We are encouraged to look to God as the source of peace and hope for the world.

Jeremiah

Jeremiah was born of a priestly family in Anathoth, a small town north of Jerusalem, about 650 B.C. He was called to the prophetic vocation in the thirteenth year of Josiah, 626 B.C. (Jer 1:2). He supported the religious reforms under Josiah and experienced the prosperous years of that great king's reign. But Judah was caught in the conflict between Egypt and Babylon, and Josiah was killed in battle in 609 B.C. Jeremiah saw the foolishness of taking sides and the hopelessness of doing battle with Babylon. He spoke out against the wicked successors of Josiah, especially Jehoiakim (609-598 B.C.).

This brought Jeremiah persecution from every quarter. His relatives plotted against him (Jer 11:18–12:6). He was scourged and imprisoned (Jer 20:1-2). He lived through the first siege of Jerusalem by Babylon in 597 B.C. During the second siege, he was arrested as a traitor and dropped into a cistern to die. He was rescued and, after the destruction of Jerusalem in 587 B.C., was allowed by the Babylonians to remain in the city. Later, however, he was taken to Egypt by Jews who had assassinated the governor left behind by the Babylonians. Legend says that Jeremiah was murdered in Egypt by his own people.

Jeremiah suffered a great deal, and he expresses his pain in passages called the confessions of Jeremiah (11:18–12:6; 15:10-21; 17:14-18; 18:18-23; 20:7-18). He complained bitterly to God about his fate but felt compelled to continue his mission in spite of the opposition he encountered. There is much biographical information about Jeremiah throughout his book, and we know more about him than about any other prophet.

Jeremiah is one of the longest books of the Bible. The prophet dictated a large part of it to his secretary, Baruch (36:32). But this and other parts of the book were somehow separated and reassembled by editors long after the Exile. Oracles and sermons from various periods were also mixed and placed out of sequence. As a result, studying the book can be difficult, and readers are advised to consult a commentary or Bible footnotes in order to fit sermons into the proper historical context.

Jeremiah proclaimed God's faithfulness to the people of Judah. He attacked their infidelity and warned them of terrible punishment for their sins. But when that punishment came and Jerusalem was destroyed, Jeremiah offered the hope of a New Covenant from God, who said to the people, "I have loved you with an everlasting love" (31:3).

Read *Jeremiah 20:1-18,* which includes the last of the confessions of Jeremiah. The prophet shouts out his anguish and pain, and wavers between hope and despair, wanting to remain silent, yet compelled to speak out. Read *Jeremiah 32:26-35* for a warning about the imminent destruction of Jerusalem. Read *Jeremiah 31:31-34* for the beautiful promise of a New Covenant.

Jeremiah teaches us the virtues of fidelity and perseverance. He shows that great people can experience moments of despair and share their feelings honestly with God. Jeremiah's life, with its pain and persecution, foreshadows the life of Christ and teaches us to bear suffering courageously. Jeremiah reminds us that even in the worst of times there is hope, because God is forever faithful.

Lamentations

This book is a collection of five poems lamenting the destruction of Jerusalem. It was written during the Babylonian Exile by an unknown author or authors who had witnessed the destruction of Jerusalem. The five poems are bitter outpourings of grief but are carefully composed. The first four poems are acrostic: Each verse begins with the successive letters of the Hebrew alphabet.

The Book of Lamentations reflects the prevalent theology of the time, namely, that God caused the destruction of Jerusalem as punishment for sin. Today, we would say that the sins of the people led inevitably to the ruin of Jerusalem and that God allowed this to happen. But Lamentations recognized that the defeat of the Jews was not a defeat for God. It gave hope to the survivors that by repentance and by hope in God, Israel could survive.

Read *Lamentations 2:8-13* for a sense of the horror of Jerusalem's destruction. Read *Lamentations 3:17-33* to hear a note of hope in the midst of affliction.

We who read Lamentations today are given a dramatic picture of the suffering caused by war. We learn from these poems the importance of expressing our grief. We find reason to hope that God can deliver us from any affliction.

Baruch

The opening words of this book attribute it to Baruch, secretary of the prophet Jeremiah. It seems, however, to have been written by more than one author. Intended for Jews who lived outside Palestine, it was put into its present form as late as 200 B.C. It was originally written in Hebrew, translated into Greek, and accepted as part of the Alexandrian list.

After a brief introduction, Baruch contains a prayer of repentance, a poem praising the wisdom of the Law of Moses, a lament for Jerusalem, a song of hope for its restoration, and a long diatribe against idols in the form of a letter ascribed to Jeremiah.

Read *Baruch 5* for the feelings of those many Jews who lived far from Jerusalem but remained faithful to the law, loyal to the ideal of temple worship, and hopeful that Jerusalem would one day be restored to its former greatness.

Today we can read Baruch for insights into the hearts and minds of postexilic Jews. We can make their prayers our own (for example, Bar 3:1-8). From Baruch we can learn to disdain the materialism and other false idols of our own age.

Ezekiel

The Book of Ezekiel is named for its author, a priest who was deported from Jerusalem to Babylon in 597 B.C. There, in a dramatic vision, he received from God the call to be a prophet. At first he warned his hearers about Jerusalem's coming destruction. Then after Jerusalem fell, he encouraged the Jews in Babylon to turn to God for mercy and to trust that Jerusalem would eventually be restored.

Ezekiel was a colorful character. He acted out many of his messages in dramatic ways. He reported strange visions. His metaphors—Israel and Judah the prostitutes, Tyre the ship, and Egypt the crocodile—were vivid and sometimes coarse. His hopes for the future were expressed in blueprints, lists, and measurements. But behind all was Ezekiel's emphasis on the majesty of God and on the importance of liturgy and worship.

The Book of Ezekiel begins with the call of the prophet (1–3), followed by a description of Ezekiel's efforts to prepare the Jews in Babylon for the coming destruction of Jerusalem (4–24). After a series of prophecies against foreign nations (25–33), the book offers a message of hope to the Jews who had heard the news of Jerusalem's fall (33–48). The prophet Ezekiel is the source of much of the material, but it was arranged and adapted by later editors.

Read *Ezekiel 1* for the prophet's vision of God's holiness. This may have come in a dream, and Ezekiel is trying to express in vivid language what is beyond human understanding. Read *Ezekiel 37:1-14* for the famous vision of the dry bones, a symbol of the restoration of Jerusalem.

We can best profit from Ezekiel by focusing on its main messages, especially the splendor of God and the importance of reverent worship.

Daniel

The Book of Daniel is placed among the prophetic works but is actually a collection of stories and apocalyptic messages. It is named for its hero, who is said to live among the exiles in Babylon. The book was composed in three languages—Hebrew, Aramaic, and Greek—by several different authors. It was put into its present form about 165 B.C. to give hope to Jews during the terrible persecution of Antiochus Epiphanes.

The stories about Daniel were meant to show how God protects those who are faithful. They place their hero in semihistorical situations described with a good deal of artistic license. In these stories Daniel is represented as a victim of persecution, just as the Jews of 165 B.C. were victims of persecution. As God delivered Daniel, so God would deliver the Jews of 165 B.C. (And God did deliver them, when the Maccabees threw off the yoke of Syrian oppression.)

There were other messages that were meant to encourage the Jews of 165 B.C. as well. These were apocalyptic in nature—a literary form that was common from 200 B.C. to A.D. 200. Characterized by figurative language, visions, symbols, numbers, heavenly messengers, and battles between good and evil, it promises ultimate victory to God.

The stories in Daniel are among the best known in the Bible. The three young men in the fiery furnace, Daniel in the lions' den, and the handwriting on the wall are entertaining and instructive. The apocalyptic material, however, is more difficult and is best studied with the help of a good commentary.

Read *Daniel 6* for the lively story of Daniel in the lions' den. Read *Daniel 12:1-3* for a sample of apocalyptic writing. This passage gives a clear teaching of resurrection and life after death.

Modern readers can enjoy the stories in Daniel and easily draw the lessons intended by the authors: trust in God and fidelity to God's commandments.

Hosea

The Book of Hosea is a prophecy that springs from the personal experience of Hosea ben Beeri, a native of Israel who lived during the last years of the northern kingdom. Hosea married Gomer, a woman who proved to be unfaithful to him. In spite of her infidelity, Hosea never stopped loving her and eventually won her back. He saw in his own situation a pattern for the relationship between God and Israel.

God was a faithful spouse to Israel, but Israel was like Gomer, a prostitute who went after the false gods and fickle promises of foreign nations. God was always ready to take Israel back, and Israel, like Gomer, could return to the faithful marriage of the Covenant. Unfortunately, Israel, which imitated Gomer in her infidelity, would not imitate her repentance.

Hosea grew up during the reign of Jeroboam II (786-746 B.C.), an era of prosperity marred by idolatry, immorality, injustice, and oppression of the poor. After Jeroboam II came a series of ineffective kings who wavered back and forth in alliances with Assyria and Egypt. Their inept blundering ended in war with Assyria, the destruction of Samaria, and the obliteration of the northern kingdom. Hosea apparently escaped this holocaust, fleeing to Jerusalem, where his writings were later collected and edited.

Read *Hosea 2:16-23*. (Some Bibles number these verses differently.) God calls back Israel as Hosea had called back Gomer. Read *Hosea 11* for another image of God's love, that of a parent for a beloved child.

The Book of Hosea still speaks of God's tender love for us and of God's readiness to forgive our sins.

Joel

Joel, the son of Pethuel, is named as the author of this prophetic book, but the Bible does not mention him elsewhere. According to many

Catholic scholars, Joel probably lived in Jerusalem and wrote this prophecy about 400 B.C.

Joel's prophecy was occasioned by a terrible plague of locusts, which devastated Judah's crops and made life miserable for the nation (see, for example, Joel 1:4,16-18). Joel told the people of Judah to fast and pray for relief. He promised that God would take pity on Judah and restore their fortunes.

Joel saw the plague of locusts as symbolic of the Day of the Lord, a day when God would judge all the nations. In apocalyptic language, Joel promised that God would bring salvation to the faithful.

Read *Joel 2:23-32* (in some Bibles, *Joel 2:23–3:5*) where the prophet promises an outpouring of God's spirit. Saint Peter, in his sermon at Pentecost, saw this as a prophecy of the coming of the Holy Spirit upon the apostles (Acts 2:17-21).

Joel looked at natural events and drew spiritual lessons from them. We can learn from him to see God at work in the world. His prophecy of the outpouring of God's spirit reminds us to pray that the Holy Spirit will touch the hearts of all people.

Amos

Amos was a shepherd and tree trimmer from Tekoa, a town ten miles south of Jerusalem. He was called by God to prophesy in Israel during the reign of Jeroboam II (786-746 B.C.). This was a time of prosperity for both Israel and Judah, but it was also a time when the rich oppressed the poor.

A member of the working class, Amos would naturally have sympathized with the poor. His book shows that he had a fine command of language, poetic imagery, and current events. As a shepherd and agricultural worker, he used symbols he had experienced in farm and field: laden wagons, roaring lions, flocks plundered by wild beasts. He must have been a strange figure, a shepherd-farmer from the south proclaiming the word of the Lord before shrines in the northern kingdom.

Amos began his prophecy by calling down God's judgment on the nations surrounding Israel. No doubt this won the applause of his hearers. But he was really drawing a circle of doom around the northern kingdom. He proceeded to attack its luxuries and its crimes in colorful, outspoken language. Israel's women were like "cows of Bashan" (4:1); its men were complacent and spoiled, eating and drinking to excess and anointing themselves with expensive oil (6:4-8). Amos wanted God's judgment to fall upon these men and women in a way that would allow them no escape, "as if someone fled from a lion, and was met by a bear" (5:19). Israel would be utterly destroyed and the house of Jeroboam cut down.

Such language infuriated the leaders of Israel, and Amaziah, the high priest at the shrine of Bethel, ordered Amos to go back home to Judah. Apparently, Amos did so, but not before leveling a final curse upon Amaziah and Israel (Am 7).

Read *Amos 5:7–6:8,* listing punishments prophesied by Amos for Israel. Note the fiery language and powerful imagery.

Modern readers will find in Amos a fire-and-brimstone preacher against complacency, injustice, and neglect of the poor. This book reminds us that our Final Judgment will be based on our treatment of others. (See Mt 25:31-46.)

Obadiah

The prophecy of Obadiah is the shortest book of the Old Testament. It is a statement that God will punish Edom for its hostility to Judah. Edom was the territory south of Judah, and its inhabitants were said to be descendants of Esau. The hostility that existed between Edom and Judah was traced by the Jews to the uneasy relationship between Esau and his brother Jacob.

After Jerusalem was destroyed by the Babylonians, the inhabitants of Edom moved northward and were a constant threat to the Jews who returned after the Exile. The prophecy of Obadiah is dated by most scholars to the years after the destruction of Jerusalem. Nothing is known about Obadiah himself.

The prophecy condemns Edom for its treachery against Judah and foretells its downfall. (After 450 B.C. Edom was overrun by tribal warriors from Arabia.)

Read *Obadiah.* Our look into this brief prophecy can be a lesson that God is the ruler of all nations.

Jonah

People who have any familiarity with the Old Testament have heard of Jonah, the prophet swallowed by a great fish. Many fundamentalist interpreters take the Book of Jonah as history, but many modern Bible scholars see it as a cleverly written parable.

The book is not a collection of sermons like most other prophetic works. Instead, it tells the story of "Jonah son of Amittai," names taken from 2 Kings 14:25. The action begins when God calls Jonah to preach in Nineveh, the capital of the evil empire, Assyria. Jonah wants no part of Assyria and boards a ship headed in the opposite direction, but God sends a great storm that threatens destruction. The pagan sailors pray to their gods while Jonah sleeps. Finally, the sailors cast lots to find out who is responsible for the storm. Jonah is pointed out, and he pleads guilty to running from the Lord. He asks the sailors to throw him overboard. Reluctantly, with a prayer, they do so, and the storm immediately ceases.

In "the heart of the seas" (Jon 2:3), Jonah is swallowed by a huge fish that carries him on a three-day journey to Assyria, where it spits him upon the shore. This time Jonah decides to obey God and warns Nineveh of impending destruction. Incredibly, the king and the entire city (including the animals) fast and do penance. Jonah, however, sulks and complains to God about pardoning the people of Nineveh. God simply asks Jonah, "Is it right for you to be angry?"

Jonah continues to sulk and decides to keep an eye on Nineveh, perhaps in the hope that God will have a change of heart and wipe it out. Instead, God considerately raises a gourd plant to shade Jonah from the sun but then sends a worm to kill the plant. When Jonah finds himself uncomfortably hot, he complains that he would be better off "to die than to live." God again asks him if he has reason to be angry. Jonah replies that he does have reason to be angry, "angry enough to die." God then poses a final, ironic question (here paraphrased): "Jonah, how can you be so upset about a plant and not expect me to care about the people of Nineveh, or even the cattle?" (4:1-11).

Why do scholars regard this book as a parable instead of history? The conversion of Nineveh is unknown to history and is not mentioned elsewhere in the Old Testament. Assyria, of course, wiped out Israel in 721 B.C. and gave no evidence of ever worshiping the true God. The story is full of fabulous elements, such as the storm, the fish, the gourd, the worm, and the exaggerated size of Nineveh ("a three day's walk across"). The literary style is marked by irony, satire, and humor.

Jesus refers to Jonah in his teaching (Mt 12:39-41; Lk 11:29-32), but this does not mean that Jonah must be a historical person. After all, preachers today refer to the prodigal son and good Samaritan without implying that they are real historical persons.

The Jews who returned from exile in Babylon were persecuted by the foreign nations around them. They, in turn, responded with hatred and isolationism. Marriages with foreigners were prohibited. Samaritans were shunned. Many Jews felt that they alone were the people of God. After all they had endured, such an attitude was understandable. But it did not go unchallenged.

This is where the Book of Jonah fits in. It portrays Jonah as a spoiled, petulant child who wants everything his way. Jonah disobeys God. He sleeps in the boat while pagans pray. He complains when sinners repent because he wants to see them punished. He wants God to pamper him with shade but to pour down fire and brimstone on his enemies.

The person who first told the story of Jonah may have done it from the steps of the rebuilt Temple in Jerusalem. We can picture people listening to this humorous tale, laughing at the peevish prophet, and then suddenly being faced with the question: "Dear God, am *I* just like Jonah?"

And that's the point for us today. When we read this inspired book, we must ask ourselves, *Am I just like Jonah? Do I wish punishment on my enemies? Am I racist or selfishly nationalistic?*

Read *Jonah 1-4*. The "Psalm of Thanksgiving" in the second chapter is a later addition by an editor. Omit this Psalm to enjoy the story as it was originally told.

Micah

"The word of the LORD that came to Micah of Moresheth in the days of Kings Jotham, Ahaz, and Hezekiah of Judah, which he saw concerning Samaria and Jerusalem."

These words introduce the Book of Micah, point to its time of composition, summarize its content, and tell us all we really know about the prophet Micah. He began to prophesy during the reign of Jotham of Judah (742-735 B.C.), when Judah and Israel were nearing the end of an era of great prosperity. Micah saw that injustice and exploitation of the poor were leading both Jerusalem and Samaria to destruction.

Moresheth was a small town about twenty miles southwest of Jerusalem, and no doubt Micah knew many humble people who had suffered harsh treatment at the hands of the powerful (Mic 2). He, like his contemporary, Isaiah, was appalled at the corruption of the civil and religious leaders (Mic 3). He knew that such crimes would lead to the destruction of Samaria (1:6-8). He could foresee such a fate even for Jerusalem (1:9).

The Book of Micah is organized into two sets of threats (1–3; 6:1–7:7) and two sets of promises (4–5; 7:8-20). Many scholars believe that this arrangement came from later editors, who also added some material after Micah's death.

Read *Micah 5:1-4* for the promise of a shepherd-ruler from the family of David. In Matthew 2:6, this promise is seen as being fulfilled by the coming of Christ. Read *Micah 6:1-8* for an example of a dramatic style of prophecy: God puts Israel on trial, reminding her of the blessings of the Exodus. A humbled Israel finally realizes that God does not want sacrifices, especially not the human sacrifice of pagan religions. Instead, God calls for justice, goodness, and a closer walk with God.

Micah reminds us of God's concern for the poor. He teaches us to honor God with upright lives as well as proper worship.

Nahum

Assyria was the scourge of the Middle East for three hundred years. This nation of pitiless warriors plundered lands from Egypt to India. It specialized in terrorism. Cities were leveled and burned; enemy soldiers impaled alive on posts; headless corpses of men, women, and children piled high; mounds of skulls left outside the rubble of city walls. Survivors were dragged naked from one place to another for sale as slaves or worse.

It is no surprise that when Nineveh, the capital of this awful empire, began to collapse under the pounding of the siege engines of Babylon and Persia, shouts of joy were heard throughout the world. "The book of the vision of Nahum of Elkosh" is one such shout. It may seem like a song of revenge to us, but it echoes the Jewish belief that savagery must be punished by God. Nahum saw God's sentence in the final destruction of Nineveh in 612 B.C. He saw hope for Jerusalem in God's care. Unfortunately, the destruction of Jerusalem by Babylon was not far off. Hope would have to be maintained through the hard times of the Babylonian Exile.

Nahum is regarded by scholars as one of the most talented poets of the Old Testament. Even in translation, his words have a dramatic power and riveting presence:

The crack of whip, the rumble of wheel,
  galloping horse and bounding chariots!
Horsemen charging,
  flashing sword and glittering spear,
  piles of dead,
  heaps of corpses (Nah 3:2-3).

Read *Nahum 2,* a poetic description of the fall of Nineveh. This passage teaches that the greatest of earth's glories, if not built on the foundation of God's word, will surely pass away.

Habakkuk

The Book of Habakkuk addresses questions as old as time. Why does God allow evil? Why do the innocent suffer at the hands of the wicked? Habakkuk was a prophet in Judah. His mission took place sometime after the fall of Assyria in 612 B.C. and before the destruction of Jerusalem in 587 B.C.

He could see that Babylon (Chaldea), which had wiped out Nineveh, would soon be on the move toward Judah. He dreaded the evil and agony of war, and so he put God on trial.

First, Habakkuk cries out to God about the misery and violence all around. Why? (1:2-5). God answers that Babylon has been raised up to punish the wicked (1:5-11). Habakkuk seems unsatisfied and questions God about the continuing oppression of the innocent by the wicked (1:12–2:1). God counters with the answer, "But the righteous live by their faith," and continues with a condemnation of the unjust and idolatrous (2:2-20). The book closes with a canticle of praise, possibly added by an editor.

Read *Habakkuk 1:12–2:4,* Habakkuk's complaint to God that evil seems to conquer good, and God's response.

Habakkuk might not have realized the full implications of his statement that the righteous live by their faith. We, who have been enlightened by Jesus, however, know that while the righteous may suffer evil treatment, as Jesus did, they will live...forever!

Zephaniah

Zephaniah lived during the reign of King Josiah of Judah (640-609 B.C.). Josiah's father, Amon, and grandfather, Manasseh, had worshiped pagan gods and allied themselves with Assyria by paying tribute and furnishing troops. Amon was assassinated in 640 when Josiah was only eight years old. Reformers then guided the young king, supported by Zephaniah and other spiritual leaders.

Zephaniah raged against the pagan worship of the evil kings, warning of a day of the Lord. This day would be one of judgment and punishment (Zeph 1). He condemned the nations who oppressed the Jews and tried to thwart God's purposes (Zeph 2). He reproached Jerusalem for its crimes but promised that a remnant would remain faithful and would find restoration and peace (Zeph 3).

Read *Zephaniah 3:14-20,* a beautiful prophecy of a day when God would be close to faithful people. Phrases from this oracle are repeated in Luke 1. When we read these verses, we think of Jesus as the Lord God in our midst.

Zephaniah teaches the absolute necessity of righteousness and fidelity. He foretells the coming of Jesus, the supreme teacher of righteousness.

Haggai

The prophets who warned that Jerusalem would be destroyed for its infidelity were sadly on the mark. Jerusalem was devastated by the Babylonians in 587 B.C., and thousands of survivors were exiled to Babylonia. Then Cyrus the Persian conquered Babylon in 539 B.C. and invited the Jews to return to Jerusalem. When many of them did, they were overwhelmed by problems. They started to rebuild the Temple but were able only to lay the foundation.

Around 520 B.C. a second band of Jews, under the leadership of Zerubbabel, a Davidic prince, left Babylon for Jerusalem. Soon after this group's arrival, God's word came to Haggai the prophet. As a result, Haggai encouraged Zerubbabel, the governor, and Joshua, the high priest, to rebuild the Temple. He cajoled and exhorted (1:1–2:9), and excluded those whose offerings were unclean (2:10-14). Haggai promised God's richest blessings (2:15-23). Work began anew, and in 515 B.C. the new Temple was completed.

Read *Haggai 2:1-9* to hear the prophet encouraging Zerubbabel, Joshua, and the Jewish people.

We find in the Book of Haggai the motivation and encouragement we need to face difficult tasks.

Zechariah

The Book of Zechariah is a two-part work. The first section (1–8) originates from the prophet Zechariah who, along with Haggai, encouraged the Jews of 520 B.C. to rebuild the Temple. The second section (9–14) was written by unknown authors at least two hundred years later.

Whereas Haggai spoke in plain language, Zechariah communicated primarily through prophetic visions. He taught the need for kindness, compassion, and social justice. He foresaw a better day of peaceful prosperity for Jerusalem.

The second part of Zechariah consists of prophecies, allegories, and visions, many of them difficult to understand. The main thrust of this section is the hope that God will save the Jewish people by sending a savior. There is a strong apocalyptic flavor in these chapters, which may reflect persecutions under Egyptian and Seleucid overlords.

Read *Zechariah 8:1-8*, an oracle of God's love for Jerusalem and a vision of peace. Read *Zechariah 9:9-10*, a messianic prophecy. All four gospels see this prophecy fulfilled by Christ's entrance into Jerusalem on Palm Sunday.

Modern readers will find this book as difficult as any in the Old Testament. Its messianic passages, however, speak with clarity because they have been fulfilled in Jesus Christ.

Malachi

Malachi means "my messenger," and some scholars think that Malachi is a title rather than a proper name. The author composed his work sometime after the rebuilding of the Temple in 515 B.C. and before the mission of Nehemiah in 445 B.C.

At this time the Jewish community in the Jerusalem area had grown stagnant. The hopes of the prophets Haggai and Zechariah had not been realized. The priests of the rebuilt Temple were community leaders but were lax in their duties. Family life was at a low ebb because Jewish men were divorcing their wives and marrying foreigners. Such abuses, the author of Malachi realized, would lead to the disintegration of the community. Inspired by God, he created this prophecy to recall the people to covenant faithfulness.

The author relied heavily upon the literary tool of dialogue. God and the prophet enter into conversation with the people of Judah and their priests. God accuses them of worshiping insincerely, of breaking faith with marriage partners, and of injustice. God promises to send "my messenger to prepare the way before me" (3:1). On the day of the Lord, God will punish the guilty and reward the faithful.

Apparently, the Book of Malachi helped Nehemiah and Ezra in their work of reforming the Jewish community. There was a sincere effort under these leaders to strengthen the family bonds that would help ensure fidelity to God's covenant. If anything, the trend after 450 B.C. was toward an excessive nationalism which had to be balanced by the realization that God loves all people. We see this realization in the Book of Jonah and even in Malachi, where God says, "my name is great among the nations" (1:11).

Read *Malachi 2:10–3:1,* a powerful dialogue against the breakup of the family, and God's promise that a messenger will prepare the way for the Lord's coming. Read the last two verses of *Malachi (4:4-5* in some Bibles, *3:23-24* in others). These are the closing words of the Old Testament. The "messenger" of Malachi 3:1 and the "Elijah" of these verses were interpreted by New Testament writers as referring to John the Baptist.

We know that John prepared the way for Jesus Christ. The offering by all the nations spoken of in Malachi 1:11 has often been interpreted as referring to the Eucharist, and we can share in that offering today. Malachi was not the final book of the Old Testament to be written, but it is placed last of the forty-six books. Fittingly so. It looks back to the "covenant of our ancestors" (2:10). It looks ahead to the fulfillment of that covenant. It does, indeed, prepare the way for Christ.

The Prophets: Looking Ahead

The prophets spoke primarily to their contemporaries. But they had a view of the future, one of hope in God. Amos prayed that God would raise up the fallen hut of David (9:11). Hosea foretold a new marriage relationship between God and the Israelites (3:16-25). Isaiah looked forward to the coming of Immanuel (7–9). Micah spoke of a new David to come out of Bethlehem (5:1-4). Jeremiah proclaimed a new covenant (31). Malachi promised one who would prepare the way (3).

In the long run, the prophets succeeded in their mission as those who spoke for God. Israel never completely abandoned God. Israel never abandoned hope in the coming of a Messiah. There were always those who remained faithful to God, a faithful remnant. When the Messiah, Jesus Christ, came, he found Israelites who were ready to accept him and believe in him.

Questions for Discussion and Reflection

If you could interview one of the prophets, which one would it be? Why? What questions would you ask?

Formerly, Christians tended to believe that the prophets had a clear prophetic view of the details of Christ's life (like seeing them in a crystal ball). Now, scholars prefer to speak of messianism, a hope for God's intervention in history through a savior. Christians believe that such a hope could be fulfilled only by Jesus Christ and that it was indeed fulfilled by him. Have you modified your ideas about Old Testament prophecy through your reading of this study and of the prophets? If so, how?

Are there prophets today? In what sense? Are *you* a prophet? Should you be?

The question is sometimes asked: "Why did God establish the Old Testament laws and feasts, then suddenly change plans with Jesus?" God did not suddenly change plans. God had one plan for our salvation: The Old Covenant led to the New and was completed by it (see Mt 5:17). Can you explain this from your study of the Old Testament?

Activities

Write down as many of the sins denounced by the prophets as you can recall. Then write down these sins as they are found in our society today (for example, worship of false gods may be found in our world as excessive materialism). In prayer, ask for God's forgiveness for our world; ask that all people may imitate God's justice and righteousness.

Then write down reasons for hope you have seen in reading the prophets. Write down how these reasons for hope still exist in our world today (for example, God's definitive intervention in history through Jesus Christ). Pray to God, asking that we and our world may be led to hope in God's promises and grace.

113

PART III

THE NEW
TESTAMENT

CHAPTER NINE

The Gospels

L ook behind us," said Joseph. "The sun is shining on Mount Hermon." Mary and Jesus turned around to gaze at the snowcapped peak, some sixty miles north. They were leaving Nazareth, a little town in the district of Galilee, to join a caravan bound for Jerusalem and the Passover celebration.

"We're about halfway between Hermon and Jerusalem," continued Joseph. "Day after tomorrow, we'll be at the Temple!" The caravan of 150 men, women, and children, assorted beasts of burden, and a stray dog or two moved southward down the ridge road. Galilee was glorious in the spring. Fields of barley and wheat, soon to be harvested, glistened in the morning sunlight. Gardens with onions, leeks, peppers, and other vegetables were everywhere. Meadows shimmered with brightly colored wildflowers. Fig trees, vineyards, and olive groves dotted the hillsides. The early figs would be ready in a month or two. Summer would bring grapes and more figs. Autumn would mean the olive harvest and the thanksgiving Feast of Booths. Then it would be time to ready the soil for another planting.

By noon they were in Samaritan territory. "Are we in any danger?" asked Mary. "I don't think so," replied Joseph. "We are a large group, and lately there have been few problems." At times the Samaritans, who worshiped God on Mount Gerizim, would harass travelers bound for the Jerusalem Temple. But most often Galileans could traverse the territory safely. After all, the Jews of strict observance in Jerusalem looked down on Galileans too, for their northern territory held pagan towns and temples.

"When tensions are high between us and the Samaritans," explained Joseph, "our people take the road down along the Jordan and pass through Jericho on the way to Jerusalem. But it's much hotter down there, and bandits often lurk in the forests and rocks." He then pointed toward the west: "There lies the Plain of Sharon, and on the other side, running along the Great Sea, is the road to Egypt. Caravans from the Far East travel that road often, and so have many armies down through the centuries...."

Evening brought them to the city of Sebaste. "It used to be called Samaria, like the territory," Joseph explained to Jesus, "but when King Herod rebuilt it, he named it in honor of the Roman emperor: Sebaste comes from the Greek for Augustus. He made land grants to six thousand Roman soldiers in this region. When David was king, all this belonged to him. But after Solomon died, the northern tribes separated from Judah. Later the Assyrians conquered Samaria and brought in foreign people to live here. Jews and Samaritans have been quarreling ever since."

Jesus gazed thoughtfully at the splendid new city but said nothing. The pilgrims had brought their own food and water, and after a simple meal, they settled down for the night outside the city walls.

Sunrise found them on the rocky road skirting Mount Gerizim. Thirty miles to their right was the Great Sea, the Mediterranean. Twenty miles to their left lay the Jordan River. From its origins on Mount Hermon, it flowed about twenty-five miles into the Sea of Galilee. Already six hundred and seventy feet below sea level there, it dropped another six hundred feet as it traversed the sixty miles to the Dead Sea. Joseph told Jesus about how David's son, Absolom, had pursued David through the Jordan wilderness and then met defeat and death at the hands of Joab. The area was now known as Perea and was under the control of Herod Antipas.

The land around them seemed drier and less fertile than the soil of Galilee, but grainfields waved in the hot wind and there were many flocks of goats and sheep. Late on the evening of the second day, they camped at a place called the Ascent of Lebonah. Men, women, and children chattered excitedly. The next day they would be in Jerusalem.

At dawn the travelers hurried through a breakfast of bread and dried fruit, then took to the road. Joseph, Mary, and Jesus prayed the psalm of pilgrims bound for Jerusalem: "I was glad when they said to me, 'Let us go to the house of the LORD'" (Ps 122:1). "I can hardly wait to see the Temple again," said Mary to Jesus. "They say that Solomon's Temple was magnificent, but it was destroyed by the Babylonians. When our people returned to Jerusalem from Babylon, they built another. Then Herod demolished that Temple to build one more grand than Solomon's. The work is still going on."

As they entered Judea, they noticed that the hills were more rugged than in Samaria. Yet olive trees, vineyards, and terraced gardens clung tenaciously to the hillsides. To their left, heat waves rose from the Judean wilderness and the cliffs that plunged down to the Dead Sea.

The pilgrims moved to the side of the road as a small band of Roman cavalrymen cantered toward Samaria. "When did the Romans conquer our land?" asked Jesus. "My father Jacob was a little boy," replied Joseph, "so it was almost seventy years ago. Herod was appointed King of Judea before I was born, but he had to capture Jerusalem from Antigonus, the last of the Hasmoneans. There was a terrible war, and much of Jerusalem was destroyed. Herod executed many of his foes and confiscated their lands. He raised taxes and built palaces, fortresses, and cities. Some people called him 'Herod the Great' because of all the construction done while he was king, but he was a cruel man who killed his wife and many of his children. He died shortly after you were born while we were in Egypt. The Romans appointed his sons to succeed him—Herod Antipas for Galilee, Philip for the territory northeast of Galilee, and Archelaus for Judea, Samaria, and Idumea. But Archelaus was as cruel as his father, and there were riots and civil war. Thousands died, and the Romans crucified two thousand rebels. Last year the Romans deposed Archelaus and appointed a Roman governor."

"My cousins Zechariah and Elizabeth said that life was terrible during those years," added Mary. "Thanks be to God, things are quieter now."

"But there are still problems," cautioned Joseph. "The Zealots, the freedom fighters, keep making raids on Roman supply lines. Many Jews support them, and they believe God will never allow our people to be destroyed by the Romans."

"I am afraid of where all this could lead," said Mary. "Our people are divided. The Sadducees are wealthy. They like Greek customs and collaborate with the Romans. The Pharisees don't trust anyone who doesn't interpret the law as they see it. The Romans are ready for war. It's a very dangerous situation." Joseph agreed. "And it's no wonder," he added, "that the Essenes have left the world to live in the desert down by the Dead Sea."

They walked quietly for a while. Then Mary said, "At least our priests and Levites still preside in the Temple." Joseph conceded, "That may be, but many of them act more like Greeks than Jews. We depend upon the Sanhedrin to make judgments in religious matters. Unfortunately, most of the seventy judges are Sadducees like the high priest, and like him, they live in luxury and collaborate with Rome. Annas, the high priest, was even appointed by the Romans!"

"Well," said Mary, "there are many good priests too, like my cousin Zechariah. If only he were the high priest!"

"Look," cried Jesus, who had run ahead. "We can see the Temple from here." The pilgrims hurried to the top of a little hill, and there in the distance, gleaming in the afternoon sunlight, were the walls of the city. Dominating the scene was the Temple, its gold ornamentation mirroring the sun's brightness. It sat in the middle of an immense courtyard, the Court of the Gentiles. In a remarkable feat of engineering, this courtyard had been built up from the valley east of Jerusalem. More than eight hundred feet wide and fourteen hundred feet long, it was surrounded by huge porches and storerooms, beautifully decorated with white marble columns. To the south, west, and north of the Temple lay the rest of Jerusalem.

"How many people live in Jerusalem?" asked Jesus, as the pilgrims pushed through the crowded streets toward the Temple. "At least fifty thousand within the walls, perhaps a hundred thousand in the area," replied Joseph, "but three or four times that many will be here for Passover."

When they arrived at the immense steps leading up to the Court of the Gentiles, Jesus, Mary, and Joseph prayed: "Our feet are standing within your gates, O Jerusalem" (Ps 122:2). Up the stairs they hurried to the Court. There stood the Temple, an awesome sight, all white marble and gold, the roof of its sanctuary rising 150 feet above the pavement. "My Father's house," whispered Jesus, "my Father's house."

The Birth of Jesus

Jesus Christ, who called God his Father, came into this world through a birth veiled in mystery. The story is told in the infancy narratives of the Gospels of Luke and Matthew. These narratives, rich in symbolism and Old Testament allusions, are meant to convey a truth that transcends history, that God became one of us in Jesus Christ.

Not long before the death of Herod the Great, according to the gospels, God sent the angel Gabriel to Mary, a young woman of Nazareth in Galilee. Gabriel announced that Mary, engaged to a carpenter named Joseph, would have a child, the Son of God, by the power of the Holy Spirit. When Mary consented, "the Word became flesh and lived among us" (Jn 1:14).

Mary was told by the angel that her cousins Elizabeth and Zechariah were expecting a son, though Elizabeth seemed past her childbearing years. Mary went to visit them at their home (believed to be Ain Karim, five miles west of Jerusalem). She stayed for about three months until their son, named John, was born. When Mary returned to Nazareth and Joseph discovered that she was pregnant, he decided to end the engagement quietly. But an angel explained to Joseph in a dream that Mary had conceived her child by the Holy Spirit, and Joseph took Mary as his wife.

Shortly thereafter they had to go to Bethlehem to register for a census mandated by the Roman emperor. While they were there, Mary gave birth to her son, named Jesus at his circumcision. When Jesus was presented at the Temple in Jerusalem, he was recognized as the Messiah by two elderly Jews, Simeon and Anna.

Later Jesus was honored with gifts by wise men from the East who had followed a star to his birthplace. Herod learned of Jesus' birth through the wise men and tried to get information on his whereabouts. But the wise men, warned in a dream that Herod actually wanted to kill the child, returned home secretly. Herod, in a rage, ordered the execution of all male boys two years old and under in the vicinity of Bethlehem. Jesus escaped because Mary and Joseph fled with him to Egypt, where they remained until Herod died.

The exact date of Jesus' birth is the subject of much speculation. According to the gospels, it occurred under the reign of Caesar Augustus (37 B.C. to A.D 14), "in the days of King Herod of Judea" (Lk 1:5), "while Quirinius was governor of Syria" (Lk 2:2). The Gospel of Luke mentions a census requiring Joseph to go to his ancestral town of Bethlehem for registration. While Joseph and Mary were there for the census, Jesus was born.

Herod died in 4 B.C., so Jesus must have been born before then. Quirinius began his term as governor of Syria in A.D. 6, but there is evidence that Quirinius served as a military leader in Syria from 10 B.C. to 6 B.C. Thus, there is good reason for dating the birth of Christ about

6 B.C. Some scholars arrive at the same year from an analysis of the story in the Gospel of Matthew about the wise men being guided by a star (Mt 2:1-11). These scholars believe that the star refers to conjunctions of Saturn and Jupiter, which occurred three times about 6 B.C. and can account for the movements of the star noted in the Gospel.

We celebrate Christ's birthday on December 25. This date was chosen in the fourth century so that the celebration of Christ's nativity might replace a pagan feast observed on that day. But the gospels do not give the exact day or month of Jesus' birth. Luke's Gospel says that shepherds were "living in the fields, keeping watch over their flocks by night" (Lk 2:8). Normally, shepherds in Judea kept their flocks out in the fields only during the warmer months, March through October. Therefore, it seems likely that Jesus' birth occurred during one of these months, around 6 B.C.

Readers may wonder how Christ could be born in 6 B.C. In the sixth century, a monk named Dionysius Exiguus tried to change the Roman method of calculating dates to one based on the birth of Christ. But he lacked precise historical data and apparently erred by six years in calculating the year of Christ's birth.

Whatever the exact date of Christ's birth may be, the infancy narratives of the Gospels of Matthew and Luke portray something beyond understanding, the mystery of the Incarnation, God becoming human. They hint that in the person of Jesus, the Old Covenant would be transformed into the New.

The Hidden Years

According to the Gospel of Matthew, Joseph, Mary, and Jesus settled in Nazareth after returning from Egypt (Mt 2:19-23). The next thing reported was a Passover trip to Jerusalem when Jesus was twelve years old. Few details are given, but it may have been much like the pilgrimage described above.

The Gospel of Luke indicates that Jesus was accidentally left behind by Mary and Joseph as they departed from Jerusalem. After searching everywhere, they found him in the Temple three days later. Mary asked, "Child, why have you treated us like this? Look, your father and I have been searching for you in great anxiety." Jesus answered with questions of his own: "Why were you searching for me? Did you not know that I must be in my Father's house?" (Lk 2:48-49).

Mary "treasured all these things in her heart" (Lk 2:51), for she knew that the Father of Jesus was her God, the God of her people, the God of the prophets and the Psalms, the God who had promised to send a Messiah—and now, the God who had sent the Messiah in the person of her Son, Jesus.

Jesus Begins His Public Ministry

Years passed. Mary and Joseph and Jesus lived in the village of Nazareth among relatives, neighbors, and friends. Jesus no doubt practiced the carpenter's trade he learned from Joseph. To all around them, they seemed an ordinary family.

Then, when Jesus was about the age of thirty (Lk 3:23), his cousin John, the son of Zechariah and Elizabeth, began to preach in the Judean wilderness. There was a power in his words that attracted huge crowds. He urged the people to repent of their sins and to live honest, upright lives. In the Jordan River, he baptized those who wished to reform, submerging them in water as a sign that their sins were to be washed away.

Many wondered if John, called the Baptist, might be the Messiah, but he answered them by saying, "I baptize you with water, but one who is more powerful than I is coming....He will baptize you with the Holy Spirit and fire" (Lk 3:16).

Jesus saw John's preaching as a sign that it was time to begin his own mission. He went to John for baptism. John objected that he himself should be baptized by Jesus, then complied at Jesus' insistence. As Jesus came out of the water, the Holy Spirit descended on him in the form of a dove, and a voice from heaven called out, "You are my Son, the Beloved; with you I am well pleased" (Mk 1:11).

Jesus then withdrew into the Judean wilderness for forty days of fasting and prayer. As a human being, Jesus needed to seek out his Father's way of accomplishing God's work. The gospels tell us that he was tempted by Satan to choose other ways. For example, the devil urged Jesus to use his miraculous powers for his own comfort, turning stones into bread. Then Satan tempted Jesus to seek fame, to leap from the Temple. Finally he offered Jesus earthly power, worldly dominance over the nations. Jesus resisted all these temptations, returned to Galilee, and began to teach.

It was about the year A.D. 26. (All subsequent dates are A.D. unless otherwise noted.) Herod Antipas and Philip still ruled the territories assigned to them after the death of Herod the Great. Judea, Samaria, and Idumea had remained under the control of Roman governors. In 26 a new governor took command; his name was Pontius Pilate.

Annas, the high priest when Jesus was twelve years old, had been succeeded by five of his sons. His son-in-law, Caiaphas, now held the office of high priest, but Annas still wielded a good deal of influence. They had no great love for Pilate but cooperated with him in the hope that they could avoid the catastrophe of civil war.

Such cooperation, however, was difficult, for Pilate was not always prudent. On one occasion, for example, he placed shields bearing the emperor's portrait in the Temple area, thus violating the Jewish law against graven images. The Jews raised such a complaint that Pilate had to remove the shields. Pilate could be harsh as well. He put down demonstrations with ferocity to keep the Jews under control. All the while, Zealots were everywhere, ready to plunge a dagger into an unwary Roman soldier or to stir up the crowds. Jerusalem seemed always on the verge of riot or civil war.

The Teaching of Jesus: His Parables

Jesus began his preaching with the words, "The time is fulfilled, and the kingdom of God has come near; repent, and believe in the good news" (Mk 1:15). The kingdom is the heart of Jesus' message, and it may best be understood as God's relationship with human beings. In many ways it parallels the idea of covenant in the Old Testament. When Jesus proclaimed that the kingdom of God was present in him, he was proclaiming a New Covenant.

Jesus spoke in concrete, down-to-earth language drawn from his experiences at Nazareth and Galilee. He did not teach in abstract lectures but in parables—colorful stories that illustrated important truths about God's kingdom and that described God's kingdom to his listeners.

The content of Jesus' parables may be summarized in the following statements. First, the kingdom of God, God's covenant with us, is present in Jesus. It is a treasure of supreme worth (Mt 13:44-46). Second, the kingdom is Good News, the Gospel, for it is God's loving forgiveness and new life offered to all through Jesus. Like an understanding father taking back a wayward son into the family, God welcomes sinners to new life (Lk 15:11-32). Third, we can receive God's gifts only if we are willing to share them with others. We must not imitate the servant who sought mercy from his master, then denied it to a fellow servant (Mt 18:23-35). Fourth, God is almighty, and the kingdom that God establishes through Jesus cannot be destroyed. Like a field that will surely produce a harvest, God's kingdom will prevail, for the weeds of sin and death cannot thwart God's designs (Mt 13:24-30). Fifth, God's invitation to new life here and to the eternal banquet of heaven calls for a response. We are like guests invited to a great wedding party, and we would be foolish not to accept the invitation (Mt 22:1-14).

We ought not miss the implications of this message. Jesus is saying that the hopes of Israel, and indeed of the human race, can be realized only through him. Jesus is answering the most basic questions of life. Does God exist? Of course! Does God care about us? More than we can imagine! With so much evil in our world, can goodness triumph? Absolutely! Why does this life fail to bring us complete happiness? Because we are made for God! What about death? It is birth to new life!

The Teaching of Jesus: *Abba* and *Amen*

In his parables, Jesus is saying that the hopes of the human race find their fulfillment in him. Jesus presents himself as more than just another Jewish prophet, more than a teacher, more than a social reformer. He comes bringing "a new teaching—with authority" (Mk 1:27). We find evidence of this throughout the gospels, but Scripture scholars note two words in particular used by Jesus to express his awareness of his unique role in history.

The first word is *Abba*. This is an Aramaic word for "father," which includes the intimacy and special relationship implied in our English "daddy." Jesus knew God as his Father in a way that was utterly unique. (See Mk 14:36.)

The second word is *Amen,* which is found frequently in the gospels. In some Bibles, like the *New Revised Standard Version*, it is translated as "truly." The phrase, "Amen (truly), I say to you," indicates that Jesus knew he held a singular position of authority. In Matthew 18:18, for example, Jesus used the word to make a declaration no ordinary human could reasonably make: "Truly I tell you, whatever you bind on earth will be bound in heaven, and whatever you loose on earth will be loosed in heaven."

The significance of Jesus' words was not lost to those who heard him. Huge crowds gathered to listen. Many were won over by his preaching and began to see him as the Messiah promised by the prophets.

The Teaching of Jesus: Father, Son, and Holy Spirit

Christians of today are so used to speaking of God as Father, Son, and Holy Spirit that we can forget that the Trinity was unknown before Christ. There were themes in the Old Testament that foreshadowed the Holy Spirit and the Son (see Num 11:29 and Wis 9:9, for example), but the Jews had no concept of the Trinity.

Jesus spoke of God as Father, Son, and Holy Spirit. His hearers probably had little idea of what he meant until after his Resurrection. Then they began to recall Jesus' teaching and expressed it in the New Testament. Several centuries later, the Catholic Church defined the Trinity as three divine Persons in one divine Nature.

Christ's revelation of God as a community of Father, Son, and Holy Spirit is central to our faith. God is not some distant, abstract power but a loving Family of three Persons, bound together in knowledge and love. "God is love" (1 Jn 4:16).

We are made in the image and likeness of God (Gen 1:27), and therefore, to be truly human means to be one who loves. Jesus taught that the first commandment is to love God with all our heart and the second to love our neighbor as ourselves. Because God is Love, everything depends on love (Mt 22:37-40).

The Miracles of Jesus

Those who were touched by the words of Jesus were even more impressed by what he did, especially by his miracles, astounding signs that had no natural explanation. Jesus healed; he gave sight to the blind and hearing to the deaf, he cured the paralyzed and the lame. Jesus exercised power over nature; he multiplied bread and fish to feed hungry crowds and calmed the raging sea. Jesus conquered death; he brought back to life the daughter of a Jewish official, a widow's son, and his friend Lazarus.

Miracles of healing that cannot be explained by any natural means still occur today. At Lourdes, for example, many have been thoroughly studied and documented by teams of physicians and scientists. Such miracles testify to the continuing power of Christ, and they draw immense crowds to Lourdes, just as the miracles of Jesus attracted huge numbers of people to him.

Most people who go to Lourdes do not receive miraculous physical healing, but almost all pilgrims seem to leave there touched in some way by the grace of God. Jesus did not heal most of the sick people of his time, and certainly he did not bring back to this life most of those who died. But his miracles touched people in marvelous ways and testified that the power of God was present in him.

Jesus' Power Over Satan

In New Testament times, people took for granted the existence of good spirits and evil spirits. The Catholic Church teaches that God created spiritual beings called angels. Some of them rebelled and are known as devils, or demons. They are personified in the Scriptures as Satan, Lucifer, or Beelzebub. Just as evil people persuade others to join them, so devils tempt people to win them over to their rebellion against God.

Satan, in tempting Jesus at the beginning of his mission, tried to convert Jesus to his ranks. Christ rejected Satan then, and he continued to exercise authority over demons. The gospels tell us that Jesus drove evil spirits from people on many occasions.

The power that Jesus showed in driving out demons was another sign of his unique authority. It caused many people to believe that Jesus was the promised Messiah.

Apostles and Disciples

Early in his public ministry, Jesus invited believers to follow him in a special way. These he called disciples (those who accept the teaching of a leader). From this group he "chose twelve of them, whom he also named apostles: Simon, whom he named Peter, and his brother Andrew, and James, and John, and Philip, and Bartholomew, and Matthew, and Thomas, and James son of Alphaeus, and Simon, who was called the Zealot, and Judas son of James, and Judas Iscariot, who became a traitor" (Lk 6:13-16).

The apostles were ordinary men who left all to follow Christ. They traveled with him, witnessed his miracles, and received special instructions from him. *Apostle* means "one who is sent," and the gospels report that at one point in his ministry, Christ sent the Twelve on a mission to proclaim the kingdom of God and heal the sick.

In the gospels, *disciples* may refer to the twelve apostles, or it may refer to the larger group of Jesus' followers. The Gospel of Luke states that Jesus sent seventy-two of his disciples ahead of him to the towns and villages he intended to visit (Lk 10:1). It is possible that this may refer to an intermediate group, less intimately connected to Jesus than the Twelve but more committed than those who simply listened to him. At any rate, Jesus did not choose his special followers from the aristocracy (Sadducees) or from those regarded as particularly devoted to the law (Pharisees). In fact, those he selected were scorned by both these groups, who felt that such ordinary people could have no special place in God's designs.

Jesus' Ministry: Location and Duration

The gospels show that Jesus preached in Galilee. He was rejected by his own townspeople in Nazareth, who seemed outraged that Jesus should think of himself as someone special. Leaving Nazareth behind, Jesus centered his Galilean ministry around the Sea of Galilee, a beautiful lake about twelve miles long and eight miles wide. He spent much time at Capernaum, an important town on the northwest shore. He visited Chorazin and Bethsaida, probably on the northern shore, and the territory of the Gadarenes on the southeast shore.

John's Gospel says that Jesus worked his first miracle, changing water into wine, at Cana, about ten miles north of Nazareth. He also healed a royal official's son there. Jesus raised a widow's son from the dead at Nain, five miles southeast of Nazareth. Jesus is said also to have journeyed to the region of Tyre and Sidon, north of Nazareth on the Mediterranean coast, and to Caesarea Philippi, twenty-five miles north of the Sea of Galilee.

John's Gospel indicates that Jesus went to Jerusalem three times for Passover celebrations during his public ministry. This means that Jesus' ministry lasted more than two years. The remarkable impact that Jesus had on so many people also suggests a ministry of at least two years.

The Response to Jesus

Jesus preached the Good News that God is loving and merciful and offers us an eternity of happiness. He worked miracles that revealed God's presence, mercy, and power. He demonstrated mastery over evil. It would seem inevitable that all would have accepted him as Messiah and Savior. But such was not the case.

It is true that large crowds flocked to Jesus, but they were looking for a Savior who would throw off the yoke of the hated Romans. They wanted an earthly kingdom, and Jesus had to resist their attempts to proclaim him king. At times he commanded people to keep quiet about miracles he had worked for them, to prevent the news from stirring up the crowds even more. He had to correct even the apostles for seeking a worldly kingdom.

Jesus' popularity alarmed the Sadducees, who were afraid that the crowds might riot or start a civil war, which would end in the destruction of Israel. The Zealots certainly noticed what was happening, and no doubt had hopes of recruiting Jesus and his followers to their cause, more so because one of the Twelve had been a Zealot.

Some of the aristocracy allied with King Herod Antipas feared Jesus. Herod had arrested John the Baptist soon after Jesus began his public ministry because John criticized Herod's marriage to his sister-in-law, Herodias. Eventually, Herodias succeeded in having John beheaded. Herod seems to have worried that Jesus was John back from the dead. He certainly saw Jesus as someone who might incite the crowds against him and against the Romans.

The Pharisees were enraged by the content of Jesus' teaching. Jesus refused to sanction their practice of keeping thousands of detailed regulations as a way to win God's favor. The Pharisees and scribes (specialists in Jewish law) accused Jesus and his apostles of breaking the law. They criticized Jesus for associating with sinners and daring to say that he could forgive sins. They downplayed his miracles and his power over demons by saying that he acted as an agent of Satan. In time they allied themselves with the Sadducees and the Herodians (supporters of King Herod Antipas) and began to plot against Jesus.

So Jesus was faced with huge crowds of people who misunderstood his message, with the rich and powerful who feared him, with subversives who hoped to use him to their advantage, and with the religiously influential who opposed his teaching. As his ministry continued he realized that his enemies were growing stronger in their resolve to destroy him. He began to warn his apostles that his foes planned to arrest him and put him to death. He said he would rise from the dead, but they seemed incapable of coming to grips with the idea of his death or the meaning of his Resurrection.

Jesus could have used his miraculous powers to crush any opposition, but he had come to bring God's mercy to all, even his enemies. He refused to use force against them and relied only on love to call them to repentance. Reflecting on the Suffering Servant prophecies of Isaiah, he must have seen himself as the "lamb that is led to the slaughter," to be "stricken for the transgression of my people" (Isa 53:7,8). He accepted the terrible truth that if he continued to love his enemies, he would have to love them even to death on a cross.

Finally, Jesus decided to go to Jerusalem, the stronghold of his enemies. He went at Passover time when the city was thronged with pilgrims. Accompanied by crowds of his followers, Jesus rode into the city on a donkey, not a war-horse, as if to show that he was not interested in an earthly kingdom. There he confronted his foes.

He drove from the Temple those who were changing money and marketing animals for sacrifices, extorting huge profits from the poor. This was a challenge to the priests, Levites, and Sadducees who benefited from those profits. He denounced the Pharisees, apparently in a final attempt to shock them into recognizing their hardness of heart. But they, along with the Sadducees and Herodians, only intensified their efforts to have Jesus killed.

The Crucifixion and Death of Jesus

Because of Jesus' popularity with the multitudes of pilgrims, his enemies could not risk arresting him publicly. Then Judas Iscariot, one of Jesus' apostles, went to the chief priest and offered to betray Jesus for thirty pieces of silver.

On the Thursday evening after his arrival in Jerusalem, Jesus shared a Passover meal with the Twelve. He told them of his love for them and for all. Taking bread and wine, he changed the bread into his body, soon to be broken, and the wine into his blood, soon to be shed.

Then Jesus went with his apostles to pray in a garden on the Mount of Olives east of the city walls. Shortly thereafter, soldiers led by Judas arrested Jesus, who was abandoned by his apostles, and took him to

Caiaphas and Annas. He was questioned, subjected to an unfair trial before the Sanhedrin, and sentenced to death.

But the Jewish leaders did not want to be blamed for Jesus' death, and they wanted him to undergo the humiliation of a Roman crucifixion. So they led him to Pontius Pilate, who was probably residing at the Fortress Antonia, adjoining the Temple area. There they accused him of treason. Pilate questioned Jesus and decided that he was innocent. After learning that Jesus was a Galilean, Pilate sent him to Herod Antipas, in Jerusalem for the Passover. Although Herod had long wanted to see Jesus, he mocked Jesus and sent him back to Pilate when he refused to answer questions. Pilate then had Jesus scourged to placate the Jewish leaders. Finally, he made an effort to release Jesus by offering freedom either for Jesus or for a notorious criminal, Barabbas. A mob, gathered by Jesus' enemies, chose Barabbas and demanded that Pilate execute Jesus. When Pilate still balked, they threatened to denounce him to the Roman emperor. At last, fearing such denunciation and seeing danger of a riot, Pilate gave in and condemned Jesus to death by crucifixion.

Jesus was forced to carry his own cross several hundred yards to a place outside the city walls called Golgotha, where he was crucified between two criminals. Nails were driven into his wrists and feet, and suspended from these nails, he suffered the horrors of crucifixion. The weight of his body caused him to sink down until constriction of chest muscles started to suffocate him. In order to breathe again, he had to pull himself up on the nails, which grated against bone and flesh. When he became too weak to stand the pain of the nails, he began to sink down again. And so, for at least three hours, in waves of unspeakable torment, Jesus endured his crucifixion.

In spite of his agony, Jesus was loving and compassionate to the last. He felt desolation and abandonment but showed concern for his mother, who was standing at the cross with a few faithful followers. He promised heaven to one of the criminals who turned to him as Lord. He forgave those who had crucified him. He then commended his spirit to his heavenly Father, and died. A Roman soldier thrust a spear into his side to guarantee the fact of his death.

The Burial of Jesus

Joseph of Arimathea, a member of the Sanhedrin but also an admirer of Jesus, asked Pilate for his body. Aided by the Pharisee Nicodemus, a secret follower of Jesus, Joseph of Arimathea placed the body of Jesus in a tomb and covered its entrance with a huge stone. Jesus' enemies, remembering his promise that he would rise from the dead, went to Pilate and asked for soldiers to guard the tomb. This was done, and a seal was placed on the stone blocking the entrance. Jesus' enemies were sure that they were rid of him forever.

The Resurrection

Jesus was crucified on a Friday. Thus the burial arranged by his friends was hastily done before the Sabbath rest. On the third day after his death, some women followers went to the tomb to anoint his body with spices. Astonished to find the stone rolled back and the tomb empty, they ran to tell his apostles, who were in hiding.

No one knew what to make of the empty tomb until Jesus appeared to his followers. He was risen and glorious, now Christ the Lord, no longer limited by time or space!

According to the gospels, Jesus appeared to his apostles and to others after his Resurrection. These appearances were miraculous and, therefore, transcend history. Each of the gospels takes a distinctive approach to the appearances, and each places in time and geographical location what was beyond time or space. None of the gospels tells how long the appearances continued. The Acts of the Apostles says that Jesus appeared to his followers for forty days (Acts 1:3).

In a very real sense, Christ rose from the dead and ascended to his Father at the moment of his death. As a human being he passed through death to the fullness of life in an instant. His Resurrection and Ascension were physical expressions of spiritual realities. His appearances after his Resurrection were miraculous in that he came back from eternity into our time and space and allowed himself to be seen, heard, and touched by his followers.

The gospel narratives show that Jesus' followers were initially reluctant to believe that he had risen. Soon, however, they became convinced of the reality of the Resurrection. Their faith, and the faith of the early Church, was expressed by the apostle Thomas, who first doubted, then fell on his knees before Christ with the words, "My Lord and my God!" (Jn 20:28).

What the enemies of Jesus had thought to be the end turned out in God's providence to be the beginning. The very apostles who had abandoned Jesus at his arrest soon fearlessly proclaimed him as the Messiah foretold by the Old Testament. Though confronted by the same authorities who had intimidated them, they preached that Jesus had risen and was truly the Son of God, sent to bring salvation to the world.

The Development of the Gospels

The story of Jesus just summarized is found in the New Testament documents known as the four gospels. No books have touched the hearts and lives of people so dramatically as have these gospels. Through them, we are put in contact with Jesus himself, with the preaching of the early Church, and with the evangelists and communities who set the gospels into their present form.

The gospels were not written immediately after the Resurrection of Jesus. Catholic Scripture scholars and the teaching office of the Church recognize three stages in the development of the gospels. The first stage was the life and teaching of Jesus himself. The second was the oral preaching of the early followers of Jesus and the creation of written collections of Jesus' sayings and miracles in hymns, testimonies, blessings, prayers, and professions of faith. The third stage was the work of the gospel writers, the evangelists, which consisted of collecting materials about Jesus and adapting them to meet the needs of specific audiences.

It can be hard for us to realize, almost twenty centuries after Christ, how such a process took place. The life of Jesus, the first stage in the development of the gospels, was not like a modern presidential campaign, documented from start to finish. None of Jesus' neighbors thought he was anyone special as he was growing up. When he began to preach, he attracted attention. But at first, people thought he was only a charismatic teacher. Soon his words and miracles caused more speculation about his identity. Some supposed he was an Old Testament prophet or John the Baptist raised from the dead. Some believed he was the Messiah, but even these people could not have imagined that he would be identified as the Son of the Most High, God of the Old Testament.

When Jesus was crucified, all who knew him must have written him off as a failure. His disciples were disillusioned and defeated. Then came the news of his Resurrection, and his followers suddenly had to confront the reality of a miracle they could scarcely believe. They had to come to grips with the identity of someone who could suddenly turn death into life, defeat into victory.

Inspired by the Holy Spirit, the disciples of Jesus began to see that his death was the greatest act of love in the history of humankind, that it was divine love capable of taking away the sins of the world. They understood his Resurrection as proof that Christ was the Son of God, the Savior who could bring believers through death to eternal life. They realized that his teaching was God's own guidance to lead them—and us—to lasting happiness and peace. They began the second stage in the creation of the gospels, oral preaching and the collection of various materials about Jesus.

At first Jesus' disciples simply proclaimed the facts of his death and Resurrection as God's design for salvation. But soon they began to recall more of what he had said and done. They shared narratives of his miracles and preaching. Gradually, these narratives, told and retold, began to take on pattern and form.

It seems that many of the early believers thought that Jesus, who had ascended into heaven, would soon return to bring this world to a close. But as years went by, the community of Christ's followers began to realize that the world as we know it might go on for a long while. They saw a need to preserve their recollections of Jesus in writing. Collections of miracle stories and sayings of Jesus began to appear. Prayers, narratives, testimonies, hymns, and professions of faith were written down and collected. Then, thirty years or so after Christ's death and Resurrection, the evangelists began the third stage in the development of the gospels, actually writing them down as we have them today.

In recent years much research has been done by Scripture scholars to determine when, where, and why the four gospels were written and to discover the communities in which they originated. Such facts are significant because, as the Pontifical Biblical Commission of the Catholic Church stated in 1964, the gospels were written to meet the needs of these communities.

From all the materials handed down to them, the evangelists wanted to provide writings suited to the situation and circumstances of their own communities. One evangelist, for example, might be reaching out to a community of Christians who had been Jews. To such believers, allusions and references to the Old Testament would be expected and easily understood. Another evangelist might be writing for believers who knew little about the Old Testament. These readers would have to be approached in a different way than Christians with Jewish backgrounds.

The latest scholarly research shows that the works written by the evangelists should be considered biographies of Jesus, similar in literary form to other biographies of the time. The evangelists were not as concerned about exact dates and details as a modern biographer might be. But they intended to give an accurate description of Jesus Christ, whose life carried significance for all humanity. The gospels, then, are biographies...and more. They are faith proclamations of the reality of Christ's life, death, and Resurrection, of the significance of his teaching, and of the salvation he offers to the world.

Insight into the work of the evangelists may be found in the Prologue of Luke's Gospel. "Since many have undertaken to set down an orderly account of the events that have been fulfilled among us, just as they were handed on to us by those who from the beginning were eyewitnesses and servants of the word, I too decided, after investigating everything carefully from the very first, to write an orderly account for you, most excellent Theophilus, so that you may know the truth concerning the things about which you have been instructed" (1:1-4).

We can recognize in these words the three stages of gospel development. First, they note the life and teaching of Jesus, seen through "eyewitnesses." Second, they mention the transmission of the Good News through "servants of the word." Third, they show the evangelist himself writing the gospel for a particular audience, for "Theophilus" ("friend of God"), perhaps the leader of the Church community to which Luke was addressing his work.

From such an analysis of how the gospels originated, we can see that they are not only the work of solitary writers. The evangelists may have put the gospels into their present form, but they transmitted materials that had been selected, shaped, and treasured by the Church. The gospels take on a special authority, because they are the witness of not just four people but of the Christian community.

Understanding the Gospels

Knowing the process by which the gospels were formed can help us understand the gospels themselves. Anyone who reads Mark, Matthew, and Luke will realize that there are many similarities as well as some differences. Readers will also note that the Gospel of John is unique in its approach to Jesus.

Most Scripture scholars today hold that Matthew and Luke used Mark as a source. This fact accounts for the similarities of the three gospels and why they are called the Synoptic Gospels ("presenting a similar view"). Luke and Matthew also used another source, commonly referred to as "Q" (from the German word for source, *Quelle),* a collection of the sayings of Jesus. From "Q" they present information that is lacking in Mark. Luke may also have used sources that were unique to him, and Matthew apparently used sources peculiar to him.

The Gospel of John is regarded by many Scripture scholars as having been developed independently of the other three. The most common explanation is that John was written after the others and reflects a longer period of meditation upon the meaning of Christ's life and death. The fourth gospel shows Jesus as the glorified Christ living among his people, facing their conflicts with nonbelievers, and speaking as their representative.

However, scholars are by no means unanimous in their approach to John. Some even say that John is different from the Synoptic Gospels because it was written *earlier* than they were. In this, and in many other areas of New Testament scholarship, we are well-advised to keep an open mind. Not long ago it was believed that John reflected a non-Jewish approach to Jesus. But recent archaeological discoveries have shown otherwise. For example, the pool with "five porticoes" mentioned in John 5:2 was thought by some to have been a stage prop invented by John...until such a pool was actually excavated by archaeologists. Now scholars commonly teach that the Gospel of John demonstrates an insider's knowledge of Jerusalem and of Jewish life and practice.

In short, when we read the gospels, we need to be aware of the stages of development behind these documents. They are not works written by a single individual but are faith declarations of the Christian community. We should understand the various ways they are related to one another. These relationships account for many of the similarities and differences we find in them. Above all, we must realize that the gospels were not written just to preserve information about an interesting person. They were written to invite us to put faith in Jesus Christ as Lord and Savior.

The Gospel of Matthew

The Gospel of Matthew was written in Greek, as were the other books of the New Testament. Its title, "The Gospel According to Matthew," does not come from the author but was added later. (The titles of the other gospels are also later additions.) Some early writers asserted that the apostle Matthew authored this gospel, but there are reasons to doubt such a statement. It is difficult to explain, for example, why the apostle Matthew would have used Mark's Gospel as a source, when Matthew was an apostle and Mark was not. It is possible, however, that Matthew was named as author because an earlier work he wrote in Aramaic was a source for this gospel or because Matthew was a part of the tradition that created the gospel.

The Gospel of Matthew presents Jesus as the fulfillment of Old Testament hopes and prophecies. Its structure seems to be patterned on the five books of the Pentateuch. The main body is divided into five parts, each consisting of a narrative and a discourse. These five parts are preceded by a prologue, the narrative of Jesus' birth and infancy. They are followed by an account of Jesus' passion, death, and resurrection.

The Prologue, or Infancy Account, sets the tone for the rest of the Gospel, spotlighting Christ as the one foretold by the prophets, yet not accepted by his own people. It begins with a genealogy that links Jesus to Abraham, David, and the Jews. Jesus' birth, the visit by the wise men, the flight to Egypt, the massacre of the innocents, the return from Egypt, and the move to Nazareth all happen "so that what had been spoken through the prophets might be fulfilled" (Mt 2.23). Jesus is presented as the new Moses (like Moses, he escaped death as an infant). He is the new Israel (like Israel, he was called out of the desert), but whereas he is persecuted by Herod, the King of Judea, he is worshiped by Gentiles, the wise men.

The five books of the main body of the Matthew's Gospel open with the beginning of Jesus' ministry (3–4) and the Sermon on the Mount, a summary of his message (5–7). The second book spotlights Jesus' miracles and names the apostles (8:1–10:4), then gives Jesus' directives for preaching the gospel and enduring persecution (10:5–11:1). The third book deals with the opposition Jesus faces from Pharisees and others who reject him (11:2–12:50), then presents a discourse in the form of parables (13:1-53). The fourth book contains a series of events and miracles that widen the gap between those who reject Jesus and those who believe, especially Peter, who proclaims Jesus as the Messiah and is called the "rock" on which Jesus will build his Church (13:54–17:27). The discourse that follows contains instructions for the Church, especially guidelines for relationships among its members (Mt 18). The fifth book tells of Jesus' journey to Jerusalem. Controversies increase until they peak with Jesus' denunciation of the Pharisees (19–23). The discourse contains Jesus teaching about the destruction of Jerusalem, the end of time, and the Final Judgment (24–25).

Matthew's Gospel climaxes in the passion, death, and resurrection of Jesus (26–28). Matthew declares that the events of Jesus' passion and death happen in order to fulfill Old Testament prophecy. He indicates that the Old Covenant has come to an end when the curtain of the Temple is torn in two at the moment of Jesus' death. Jesus' Resurrection turns death into life, and the Gospel ends as Jesus commissions the apostles to preach to the whole world and promises to be with them until the end of time.

Because of its attention to the Old Testament, the Gospel of Matthew seems to have been written for Christians who had converted from Judaism. These people had probably believed that all Jews would eventually put their faith in Jesus. Instead, Jerusalem had been destroyed, and the majority of the Jews who survived rejected Christ and his followers.

Matthew reflects this situation from the infancy account through the controversies with the Pharisees to the rending of the Temple curtain. Matthew teaches that Jewish Christians are right to put their faith in Jesus, because the Old Testament points to him as the Messiah. He hints that since Jesus was rejected by so many Jewish leaders in his lifetime, Christians should not be surprised that most of their Jewish contemporaries fail to accept Jesus. What matters is that Christ fulfilled the Old Law; therefore, both Jews and Gentiles can find salvation in Christ, not in the practices of Judaism.

Scripture scholars say that a likely community for the development of the Gospel of Matthew would have been Antioch, the capital of Syria (north of Palestine). Here there would have been Jewish Christians and Gentile converts. The time of composition is usually given as around 80-85, after the destruction of Jerusalem. The final author is unknown but must have been someone well versed in the Old Testament and skilled as a teacher.

Read *Matthew 5-7,* the Sermon on the Mount. It begins with the Beatitudes, in which Jesus turns the values of the secular world upside down and offers us true happiness when we put God's kingdom first. Jesus teaches fidelity to God's law, victory over anger and lust, love of enemies, and generosity that is modeled on God's generosity to us. Jesus teaches his prayer, the Our Father. He bids us to put God above all. He assures us that God loves us and that we are of value because we matter to the Creator of the universe. In the Sermon on the Mount, we find a pattern for living that is psychologically and spiritually sound: healthy self-esteem, generous love for others, belief in God as origin and goal of life.

We who read Matthew's Gospel are led to see Jesus as the Messiah long awaited by Israel. We are encouraged to accept Christ and become members of the Church, the New Israel, for in this way, we inherit the kingdom of God.

The Gospel of Mark

The Gospel of Mark was the first gospel to be written. It is the shortest of the gospels and focuses more on the active ministry of Jesus than on his teaching. Mark's Gospel is a whirlwind of miracles and service, of human relationships and confrontation.

Mark introduces his work with the words, "The beginning of the good news of Jesus Christ, the Son of God" (1:1). He invites his readers to put their faith in Jesus as the one who gave his life in loving service of others. Jesus gave of himself by caring for people, healing the sick, driving out demons, feeding the hungry (1:1–8:26). He gave of himself by persevering in spite of the misunderstanding and persecution he encountered throughout his ministry, even when he knew it would lead to the cross (8:27–10:52). He gave of himself by fearlessly entering Jerusalem and speaking the truth, regardless of the cost (11–13). Finally, he gave of himself by suffering, dying, and rising to new life (14–16).

Mark emphasizes that Jesus was not truly recognized as the Son of God by the crowds, by his apostles, or by the Jewish authorities. Jesus even had to tell people to keep quiet about his miracles, apparently because the crowds saw him only as a miracle worker and potential earthly king. It was only at the moment of his death on the cross that Jesus was properly acknowledged. "When the centurion who stood facing him saw how he breathed his last he said, 'Truly this man was God's Son!'" (15:39).

Some scholars say Mark originally ended his gospel by describing the bewilderment of the women who first witnessed his empty tomb. An angel directed them to "tell his disciples," but "they said nothing to anyone, for they were afraid" (16:7,8). In such a conclusion, Mark would be suggesting that reluctant believers should proclaim the risen Lord as the women eventually did. It is possible also that the original ending of Mark's Gospel has been lost.

In the text as we have it, later endings added to the Gospel by unknown writers show how Christ's followers knew that he had risen and had commissioned them to preach the Good News.

Traditionally, the author of this Gospel has been held to be John Mark, whose mother's house was a place where Christians gathered (Acts 12:12). Mark traveled with Paul and eventually ended up in Rome, with connections to Peter. A few scholars, however, argue that the author was unfamiliar with Palestinian customs and was an unknown Christian of Hellenistic background. Most scholars date the Gospel of Mark around 65-70. Mark's original audience is uncertain but may well have been gentile Christians faced with persecution because of their beliefs. Mark wrote to urge them to be steadfast in every circumstance, just as Jesus had been.

Read *Mark 1* for the beginning of Jesus' public ministry and for a taste of Mark's style. Read *Mark 14–15,* the account of Christ's passion and death.

As we read Mark's Gospel, we are challenged to believe in Christ, still misunderstood and rejected by the worldly wise. We may face persecution as Jesus did, but Mark urges us to put faith in the Son of God and to share our faith with others.

The Gospel of Luke

The Gospel of Luke was written as the first half of a two-part work that included the Acts of the Apostles. Traditionally, the author has been identified as Luke, a Syrian from Antioch who is mentioned several times in the New Testament and who may have been a traveling companion of Paul.

The Gospel of Luke and the Acts of the Apostles have the same purpose, to show that Christ came to save the whole world. These works were written in excellent Greek and are literary masterpieces. They seem to have been composed after the destruction of Jerusalem, perhaps between 80 and 90.

By that time the Good News of Christ had been preached throughout the Mediterranean world by Paul and other missionaries. Many of those who accepted Christ were well-to-do Gentiles. They knew that their religion had its origins in Judaism. But by the 80s, it had become obvious that most Jews had rejected Christ and that Judaism had suffered a serious setback in the destruction of the Temple. If Christianity was the fulfillment of Old Testament prophecy, why had it been rejected by so many Jews? Why were Jewish Christians now outnumbered by gentile Christians? Was Christianity really the true religion and had it actually come from God?

To answer these questions of gentile Christians, Luke took a positive approach. In his Gospel and in the Acts of the Apostles, he viewed the Old Testament as prophecy foretelling Christ, and he showed that faithful Jews had indeed accepted Christ. From Simeon and Anna in the infancy narratives, through John the Baptist and many others in Christ's public ministry, to the great crowd of three thousand believers at Pentecost, the Jews who truly understood the Old Testament had put their faith in Jesus. Christianity was *the* true religion, Luke assured his readers, and God had sent Jesus for the salvation of the whole world. This was the reason why so many Gentiles were becoming Christians. All that had happened was in accordance with God's design, and therefore, Luke's readers should "know the truth concerning the things about which" they had been instructed (1:4).

The Jesus we encounter in the Gospel of Luke, then, is the Savior of all people. He brings joy and peace to those who accept him. He shows special concern for the poor and the lowly. He recognizes the dignity of women, who were often treated as second-class citizens in the ancient world. He teaches that God is merciful and forgiving beyond expectation, a Father who takes back the prodigal son. Jesus offers pardon, peace, and salvation to all. He even prays that forgiveness be extended to those who had crucified him, and he promises paradise to a repentant criminal nailed to a cross beside him.

Luke's beautifully written infancy narrative presents many of the themes found in the rest of the Gospel. Luke's audience of gentile Christians had to deal with skepticism from their pagan neighbors. Luke assures them that Jesus Christ came from God, and that his birth was foretold in the Old Testament and prefigured by John the Baptist's birth. It fit into God's plan for all people, since it happened while Mary and Joseph were in Bethlehem for a census of "all the world." Christ's birth was announced by angels to lowly shepherds who paid him homage. Jesus was recognized by faithful Jews, Simeon and Anna, who testified that Jesus came from God. Jesus' special place in God's plan was shown when, at the age of twelve, he spoke in the Temple and recognized it as his "Father's house" (1–2).

The main body of Luke's Gospel begins with Christ's public ministry in Galilee. Luke paints the miracles of Jesus, his teachings, and his relationships with disciples into an artfully designed portrait of Jesus as the Savior who is gentle, compassionate, wise, and powerful (3:1–9:50).

But Luke wants to show that the Gospel was meant for the whole world. So he tells of Jesus leaving Galilee and beginning his journey to Jerusalem. (In Acts, the risen Christ will guide his followers from Jerusalem to Rome, the capital of the world.) In this journey to Jerusalem, Luke teaches how Jesus willingly accepts his mission to save the world. He weaves the miracles and teachings of Jesus into a beautiful narrative that invites believers to follow Jesus to Jerusalem, to put their faith in him without any thought of turning back. Once in Jerusalem, Jesus is drawn into a confrontation with his enemies. Yet he continues to show compassion, even recognizing a poor widow's contribution to the Temple. He teaches the importance of loving service, even as he is being drawn toward his passion and death (9:51–21:38).

Luke's account of Christ's passion emphasizes the mercy and gentleness of Jesus. He heals the high priest's servant, one of those sent to arrest him. His presence even brings about a reconciliation between Pilate and Herod Antipas. On his way to Calvary, he shows compassion to the women of Jerusalem. He forgives his enemies and promises heaven to a criminal crucified with him. When he has risen from the grave, he gently leads his followers to belief. He commissions them to witness to him, and he ascends into heaven. As risen and glorious Lord he will send the Holy Spirit upon his followers, thus causing the spread of the gospel from Jerusalem to all the world (22–24).

Read *Luke 1–2,* the infancy narrative. Read *Luke 15,* which contains three beautiful parables of God's forgiveness. Read *Luke 24* for the account of Christ's Resurrection and appearances.

Luke's Gospel invites us to put faith in Jesus, our gentle, compassionate Savior, to meet him in the Scriptures and in the breaking of the bread. (See Lk 24:30-32.)

The Gospel of John

The author of the Gospel of John has been the subject of much discussion since ancient times. Parts of the Gospel show a familiarity with Palestine and apparently originate from an eyewitness of the events described. However, there is evidence that the Gospel does not come from a single author. For example, there are duplications in some of Jesus' discourses. (See Jn 14:31 and 18:1.) There are two endings (Jn 20:30-31 and 21:24-25), and chapter 21 seems to be a later addition. Scholars, therefore, believe that the present work shows signs of editing and multiple authorship.

Many scholars teach that the apostle John was the eyewitness behind this Gospel. They identify him with the beloved disciple so often mentioned in the Gospel and theorize that the Gospel arose from a community at Ephesus in Asia Minor.

While others question these opinions, it does seem likely that John the apostle was the original source of the material found in this Gospel. That source was certainly someone close to Jesus and acquainted with Jerusalem. Many scholars date the Gospel around 90, to allow for the development of its thought and organization.

The Gospel of John is a work of art, complex in its thought, symbolic meanings, and dramatic structure. It has been divided by some scholars into a Prologue (1:1-18), a Book of Signs (1:19–12:50), a Book of Glory (13–20), and an Epilogue (21).

The Prologue introduces Jesus as the Word-of-God-made-flesh. Its powerful language is a profession of faith in the divinity of Christ.

The Book of Signs is a rich collection of material about Jesus. There are conversations such as those between Jesus and Nicodemus, and Jesus and the Samaritan woman. There are dramatizations of events, such as the healing of the man born blind and the raising of Lazarus. There are instructions, such as the teaching of Jesus as the bread of life. These conversations, events, and instructions lead us to the conclusion that Christ is Son of God and master of life and death. They present Jesus' miracles and teaching in such a way that the sacramental life of the Church is alluded to, with Baptism and Eucharist especially prominent.

The Book of Glory takes a different approach to the passion and death of Jesus than do the Synoptic Gospels. It shows Jesus, powerful and majestic, fully in control of his destiny. He speaks to his apostles at the Last Supper as the eternal Christ as well as the Jesus about to be crucified; through Jesus, they are united to the Father and the Holy Spirit. His enemies arrest him only because he allows it. Jesus, rather than Pilate, demonstrates dignity and authority. He "gave up his spirit" (dies and sends the Holy Spirit) only when prophecy is fulfilled and all is "finished." As risen Lord, he "breathes" the Spirit and the sacrament of forgiveness upon the apostles. He is acknowledged as Lord and God, and he attends to the future of his Church.

The Epilogue is an early addition to the Gospel that has always been regarded as inspired. Rich in symbolism, it shows the risen Christ nourishing his Church and restoring Peter to his position as shepherd. Finally, it demonstrates that the reports that the Beloved Disciple would not die until Jesus came again were not accurate.

John's Gospel is the result of the Church's reflection on the significance of Jesus' words and deeds. In it we hear Christ speaking through the Christian community that has been guided and directed by the Holy Spirit. There are many layers of meaning, and to appreciate the complexity of thought, the artistic development, and the carefully composed dialogue of John's Gospel, readers should study it carefully and perhaps consult a good commentary.

Read *John 6,* which presents the belief of the Church in the reality of Christ's presence in the Eucharist. Read *John 17* for Christ's beautiful prayer for his followers. Read *John 20* for the Resurrection appearances as related by John's community. Note how Thomas' profession of faith in Jesus as Lord and God is really the profession of faith of the Christian community.

We who study John's Gospel today will receive insights into the humanity and divinity of Christ, the doctrine of the Trinity, and the meaning of the sacraments. We can reflect for a lifetime on these and the many other truths taught in John's Gospel.

Reading the Gospels

Every Christian should read all four gospels. They are four inspired portraits of Jesus Christ, painted by the early Church. In them, we meet Jesus, one of us. In them, we encounter the Christ, our Savior, our Lord, and our God.

Questions for Discussion and Reflection

Each gospel was written to bring the life and teaching of Christ to a specific time and place. It has been said that all Christians are called to be "gospels" bringing Jesus into their homes, neighborhoods, and workplaces. Have you ever thought of yourself as a gospel? What kind of gospel are you to your family? to your friends? to your neighbors? to your coworkers? to your enemies?

Someone has said, "You may be the only gospel that some people will ever read." What do you think is meant by this statement?

Activities

Meditation on the gospels is a traditional method of prayer. The following is a sample meditation on the passion of Christ.

Find a quiet place. Take a few moments to relax and focus on God's presence. Then picture yourself at the crucifixion of Jesus. See him hanging on the cross. Look at the crowd standing around, some weeping, some mocking, some indifferent. Listen to Jesus as he speaks from the cross. Hear the sobbing of Jesus' friends, the mockery from his enemies. Touch the wood of Christ's cross. Feel the temperature drop as clouds roll in and the wind begins to blow. Notice the smell of rain, and taste the raindrops on your tongue. Look into Christ's eyes, and thank him for his great love. Express sorrow for your sins and the sins of the world. Tell Christ of your love for him and your desire to bring his love to the world. Then speak to him about anything else that seems important.

CHAPTER TEN

Acts to Second Thessalonians

The apostles hid in a second-floor room. The windows were shut-tered and the door locked. For a long time they sat in silence. Then Peter said to the others, "I've got a great idea; let's tell everybody that Jesus rose from the grave." "Peter," shouted Andrew, "you may be my brother, but that's the most stupid idea I've ever heard!" "Andrew, keep it down," whispered John, "somebody will hear you. Peter, why tell people that Jesus is alive? The authorities had him crucified. They'll do the same to us. What could we possibly get out of claiming that Jesus is risen?" "Think about it," replied Peter enthusiastically, "we'll be ar-rested. We'll be disowned by our friends and family. Our property will be confiscated. Then we'll be tortured and put to death. Isn't that ter-rific?"

The other apostles looked at Peter with amazement. The death of Jesus must have driven him over the edge. A man would have to be crazy to make a suggestion like that. All they wanted to do was lay low until things quieted down, then drift on back to Galilee and resume their lives.

The Reality of the Resurrection

It would, of course, have been crazy for the apostles to proclaim that Jesus had risen if he really hadn't. They would have gained nothing from concocting such a story except persecution and death.

But the apostles did tell the world that Jesus had risen, and the re-sponse from their enemies was swift and violent. The apostles *were* persecuted, arrested, tortured, and put to death. Yet they never wavered from their testimony to the reality of Christ's Resurrection. None of them ever confessed to a plot fabricating the Resurrection of Jesus. All maintained to the death that Christ had risen. And why? Because he *had* risen.

So the fact of the Resurrection, on the testimony of the apostles, is certain. How it actually happened is beyond the reach of history and science. In some way the mortal body of Jesus was transformed into a glorified body. The Jesus of history became the Christ who transcends space and time.

Christ appeared to his followers after the Resurrection. As Lord and God, Christ had the power to come back in a way that allowed him to be seen, heard, and touched. But he did not return in his *mortal* body. It was his body, now immortal. If an enemy had been able to see him after the Resurrection and had tried to thrust a sword into Christ, he could have done Christ no harm.

But the glorified body of the risen Christ is not less real than our physical bodies, which will one day return to dust. Christ's glorified body is real and perfected, for it cannot be destroyed. The life Christ now leads is the most real life imaginable. As a human being, the risen Christ is united to Life itself, the Life of God.

The apostles somehow realized this, even in the first extraordinary days after the Resurrection. They realized also that the risen Christ wanted to share God's life with them and with all people. This was Good News beyond anything they had imagined, and Christ had asked them to bring it to the world.

The Resurrection Appearances and Christ's Ascension

In the days after the Resurrection, Jesus appeared often to his followers. All four gospels mention these appearances, as does Saint Paul. (See 1 Cor 15:3-8.) The Acts of the Apostles reports that the appearances continued for a period of forty days, after which Christ ascended into heaven. The historical reality behind this statement is that only the more frequent appearances ceased. The New Testament says that Christ appeared to Saint Paul on several occasions. He may have appeared to other believers as well, and there are reliable reports that saints have had visions of Christ on various occasions.

In any event, the Acts of the Apostles sees the Ascension as a sign that Christ would be present to the world and would continue his ministry in and through his disciples. Christ, who could have appeared daily in a miraculous way until the end of time, chose instead to make his real, spiritual presence visible through his followers. He gave them the responsibility of being the "body of Christ" (1 Cor 12:27).

The Acts of the Apostles

Most of what we know about the Body of Christ, the Church, in the years following Christ's death and Resurrection, comes from the Acts of the Apostles. Written with the Gospel of Luke as a two-part work, Acts has the same author and was composed at the same time as the Gospel.

The Gospel of Luke and the Acts of the Apostles were intended for Christians who came from gentile backgrounds. They must have wondered why so many Jews had refused to accept Christ as the Messiah. They must have been asked by their pagan neighbors why they believed in a Jewish Savior.

In his Gospel and in Acts, Luke shows that many faithful Jews did accept Christ and that God had always intended for the whole world to find salvation in Christ. The Gospel discloses how Christ was born in Bethlehem to fulfill Old Testament prophecies. It explains how he began his ministry in Galilee and then journeyed to Jerusalem, where his death and Resurrection occurred, again in fulfillment of prophecy.

Acts reveals how Christ, through his disciples, brought the Good News of salvation from Jerusalem to Judea, Galilee, Samaria, and to the ends of the earth, including Rome itself. Acts focuses especially on the ministry of Peter and Paul. Peter, the leader of the twelve apostles, begins his preaching in Jerusalem on Pentecost and is led by divine revelation to be the first to bring the gospel to Gentiles. Paul, a devoted Jew, a Pharisee who persecuted Christians, is commissioned by Christ with the responsibility of bringing the gospel to Gentiles throughout the world.

Acts, like the Gospel of Luke, was written in polished Greek and was artfully constructed according to contemporary literary conventions. From its elegant formal introduction to its conclusion where the author pictures Paul teaching about the Lord Jesus in Rome, Acts is a book full of action, lively personalities, colorful narratives, and well-crafted speeches.

The historical reliability of Acts is generally regarded as very good. But the purpose of the author is to teach religious truth, not just to record names, dates, and places. Luke writes to proclaim Christ as the Savior of the world, and he selects and arranges his material with this in mind.

One of Luke's favorite tools for proclaiming Christ is his use of speeches and sermons throughout Acts. They occupy about one fourth of the book. It was customary at the time for historians to put speeches on the lips of the main characters in their narratives. The historians were expected to write what should have been said and to do it eloquently. Therefore, the many speeches in Acts are not meant to be word-for-word reports. (This would have been impossible, since Luke wrote twenty to fifty years after the events he was describing.) Rather, Acts presents the themes of early Christian preaching, and scholars generally agree that Acts gives a faithful record of such themes. Peter's sermon on Pentecost, for example, is regarded as representative of early Christian proclamations of salvation and of Baptism as the appropriate response to Christ.

In Acts, Luke has an interesting method of highlighting important material: He uses repetition to emphasize special themes and events. The communal nature of the Church and its Eucharist-centered worship, for example, are spotlighted in idealized summaries of early Christian life (2:42-47; 4:32-35; 9:31). The story of Paul's conversion is told three times (9:1-22; 22:1-21; 26:1-23). The account of Peter's evangelization and Baptism of the Roman centurion Cornelius is repeated three times (Acts 10; 11:1-18; 15:7-11). Three times Paul tells the Jews that he preached first to them and goes to the Gentiles only after rejection by the Jews (13:46-47; 18:5-6; 28:23-28). The decision of the Jerusalem council to receive Gentiles is reported three times (15:19-21; 15:28-29; 21:25). These repetitions, and others as well, call the reader's attention to the most significant messages of Acts.

A summary of the Acts of the Apostles is a summary of the early years of the Church. It can help us understand how the first Christians came to see themselves as the Body of Christ on earth. It can lead us to a better comprehension of what it means to be the Church, the Body of Christ today.

Pentecost

According to Acts, after the Ascension of Jesus, the apostles gathered in an upper room at Jerusalem with Mary, the Mother of Jesus, and with other believers. They chose Matthias to replace Judas Iscariot, who had committed suicide after betraying Jesus. They must have discussed the extraordinary things that had happened since they had first met Jesus. They must have wondered how they, such a tiny group of unimportant people, could possibly make disciples of all nations.

Their misgivings vanished in a mysterious outpouring of strength and wisdom, which Acts describes as a strong driving wind and tongues of fire. These signs indicated the coming of the Holy Spirit, whom Jesus had promised to send to his followers as their advocate and helper. Led by Peter, the apostles began to preach to the crowds assembled in Jerusalem for the feast of Pentecost.

Peter announced that Jesus was the fulfillment of Old Testament prophecies and had been raised from the dead as Lord and Messiah. He invited his listeners to repent and be baptized in the name of Jesus Christ for the forgiveness of sins. He promised that they too would receive the Holy Spirit. Three thousand were baptized.

The believers devoted themselves to the teaching of the apostles, to the breaking of the bread (Eucharist), to prayer, to a communal life, and even to the sharing of possessions. Their manner of life attracted others to join them. But they continued to worship in the Temple and saw themselves as Jews who believed that Jesus was the Messiah (Acts 1–2).

Miracles and Evangelization

Soon the miracles which had marked the ministry of Jesus began to occur through his disciples. After Peter and John healed a crippled beggar, the Jewish authorities arrested them and threatened punishment if they continued to preach in Jesus' name. Peter and John responded boldly that they intended to obey God and to speak about what they had seen and heard. Fearful of the crowds who had witnessed the healing, the Jewish leaders had to release Peter and John. The apostles, strengthened by prayer, continued to proclaim Christ as Messiah and Lord.

The believers became known for their generosity in caring for the needy, and many of them went so far as to sell property and houses in order to make contributions for the poor. Not everything was perfect.

Some, like Ananias and Sapphira, tried to deceive the community. Persecution continued. The apostles were arrested, and after a miraculous escape were arrested again. That time they were tried by the Sanhedrin, warned, and flogged. The moment they were released, however, they resumed preaching.

As the number of Christ's disciples grew, Hellenist believers (probably Palestinian Jews who spoke Greek) complained that some of their poor were being overlooked. The apostles, by prayer and laying on of hands, commissioned seven assistants, called deacons, to care for the neglected. Soon the deacons were also preaching the Good News (Acts 3–6).

Saul's Persecution

This evangelization was met with renewed persecution, and a deacon named Stephen was arrested and stoned to death. Saul, a zealous Pharisee and overseer of Stephen's murder, tried to destroy the Church. He searched out believers and had them thrown into prison. It was about the year 35, five or six years after Christ's death and Resurrection.

The persecutions, however, actually helped the Way (an early name for Jesus' followers) to expand. Many believers had to flee from Jerusalem, and they began to preach the Good News throughout Judea, Samaria, and Galilee. With another deacon, Philip, in the vanguard, they made converts in Mediterranean towns like Gaza, about fifty miles southwest of Jerusalem. They moved north along the coast to Azotus and other places until they reached Caesarea Maritima (Acts 7–8).

Saul's Conversion

Then came a dramatic and unexpected development. Saul, on his way from Jerusalem to Damascus to arrest followers of Jesus, had a vision of the risen Christ. He became a believer and began to proclaim Jesus as the Messiah. He must have thought that people would surely trust one who had formerly persecuted Christians. Instead, some Jews tried to kill him, and he had to flee from Damascus. Eventually, he went to Jerusalem, where another attempt was made on his life, forcing him to return to Tarsus.

Persecution slacked off after that, and the Church flourished in Judea, Galilee, and Samaria. There were more miracles, including Peter's healing of a paralytic at Lydda and his raising a dead widow back to life at Joppa (Acts 9).

Peter and Cornelius: Evangelizing the Gentiles

Up to that time, the Good News had been preached only to Jews and Samaritans. But when Peter was inspired by a vision to evangelize and baptize the household of Cornelius, a Roman centurion at Caesarea, the question arose as to whether Gentiles could become followers of Christ. Peter explained his vision to the believers in Jerusalem, but the matter came up again when Gentiles were baptized at Antioch, an important city in the Roman province of Syria (now part of the southeastern tip of Turkey). The Jerusalem Church sent Barnabas, a trusted missionary, to investigate. He was so impressed that he brought Saul from Tarsus to help him preach to Gentiles at Antioch. It was here that followers of Christ were first called Christians (Acts 10–11).

Paul and Barnabas:
The Mission to the Gentiles Expands

Another persecution broke out in 44, this one started by Herod Agrippa, grandson of Herod the Great and ruler of Judea from 41 to 44. He killed James, the son of Zebedee, and arrested other Christians, including Peter, who miraculously escaped from prison. In spite of such troubles, Christians continued to preach, grow in number, and care for one another. Christians at Antioch, for example, sent relief to famine-stricken believers in Judea through Barnabas and Saul. Such instances of concern brought Christians closer to one another and gave them a sense of identity as a Church. The persecutions against them and the refusal of so many Jews to accept Christ gradually began to change the notion that Christianity was merely a branch of Judaism, still connected to Temple worship and under obligation to all the laws of Moses.

Paul's First Missionary Journey

After Herod's death in 44, Saul (now known as Paul) and Barnabas were sent by the Church at Antioch to preach on the island of Cyprus (about one hundred miles west of the Syrian coast). Accompanied by a young Christian from Jerusalem named John Mark, they preached in the synagogues at Salamis, Paphos and elsewhere with some success. From Cyprus they sailed to the town of Perga in Pamphylia (modern-day Turkey). There John Mark left them and returned to Jerusalem.

Paul and Barnabas continued on to the city of Antioch in Pisidia (modern-day central Turkey, not to be confused with Antioch in the Roman province of Syria). While some Jews put their faith in Christ, others responded with ridicule. Then Paul and Barnabas spoke the words that set the pattern for their future missionary efforts: "It was necessary that the word of God should be spoken first to you. Since you reject it and judge yourselves to be unworthy of eternal life, we are now turning to the Gentiles. For so the Lord has commanded us, saying, 'I have set you to be a light for the Gentiles, so that you may bring salvation to the ends of the earth'" (Acts 13:46-47).

From Antioch in Pisidia, Paul and Barnabas went to Iconium, Lystra, and Derbe (all in modern-day Turkey), preaching and establishing communities of Christians. They then retraced their steps through the towns they had evangelized, appointing leaders and encouraging the believers. From Perga, their original point of entry, they went to Attalia, another port city. There they caught a boat to Antioch in Syria, having traveled about one thousand miles over a period of approximately three years. They returned to the Christian community that had commissioned them and reported on the success of their missionary efforts, especially among the Gentiles (Acts 12–14).

The Council of Jerusalem

It was then about the year 49. Some Christians of Jewish background in Antioch objected to what Paul and Barnabas had done. These Jewish Christians argued that all believers must keep the Law of Moses. Church leaders, including Paul, Barnabas, Peter, and James, assembled in Jerusalem to discuss the matter. The crucial argument was given by Peter: "We believe that we will be saved through the grace of the Lord Jesus" (Acts 15:11). The council decreed that Gentiles need not keep the Jewish law but recommended only that they refrain from certain practices particularly offensive to Christians of Jewish background.

This Jerusalem Council illustrated truths at the heart of Christianity: Jesus Christ is the Messiah sent by God, the Word and Revelation of God; any other word or revelation must be judged in the light of Christ's life and teaching, and salvation can be found only in Christ. Christians now recognized these truths as the foundation of their tradition, and henceforth the Old Covenant would be judged in the light of the New. Christianity was no longer seen as a Jewish sect, but as a religion for all people—a *catholic* religion (Acts 15:1-35).

Paul's Second Missionary Journey

Soon after the council, Paul suggested to Barnabas that they visit the churches they had established in Cyprus and Asia. Barnabas wanted to bring John Mark along again, but Paul objected because he had abandoned them on their first journey. So Barnabas took John Mark and went to Cyprus, while Paul chose another missionary, Silas, to accompany him to Asia Minor (modern Turkey).

Paul and Silas went by land through Syria into the area known as Cilicia (where Tarsus was located), visiting and encouraging Christian churches. At Lystra they were joined by a disciple named Timothy, who accompanied them as they made the round of the churches in the regions of Phrygia and Galatia. At Troas, Paul had a vision that prompted the missionaries to sail to Macedonia (modern Greece). At this point the author of Acts begins to use "we" instead of "they," leading many scholars to believe that Luke accompanied Paul on some of his journeys. The missionaries spent some time in Philippi, staying at the home of Lydia, a dealer in purple cloth and a zealous believer.

While in Philippi, Paul cast an evil spirit out of a slave girl whose owners used her for fortunetelling. Enraged, the slave owners dragged Paul and Silas to court and had them beaten and jailed. That night an earthquake damaged the prison. The guard, thinking that the prisoners had escaped, was ready to kill himself until Paul stopped him. After listening to Paul's preaching, the prison guard and his household were baptized. The next day the city magistrates, alarmed at discovering that Paul was a Roman citizen, convinced him to leave Philippi.

Paul then went to Thessalonica and Boerea, preaching in Jewish synagogues and winning converts, but also encountering hostility. Leaving his companions, he went south to Athens. There he spoke with limited success, then moved to Corinth, a port city notorious for immorality. There he stayed with Aquila and Priscilla, Jews from Rome and tentmakers like Paul. Joined by Silas and Timothy, he preached to Jews until their animosity turned his attention to the Gentiles. The missionaries won many converts and established a church in Corinth, staying there for a year and a half. It was from Corinth that Paul sent a letter to the church at Thessalonica, the first of his New Testament writings.

After further harassment from Jewish foes and a court appearance at which he was declared innocent, Paul decided to sail to Ephesus, a major port in Asia Minor. He did missionary work there, then embarked on the long voyage to Caesarea. From there he returned to his starting point, Antioch in Syria. He had spent about three years on this second missionary journey and had covered over two thousand miles. He had founded or strengthened churches in places like Galatia, Thessalonica, Corinth, and Ephesus, whose names form the titles of New Testament letters and so are familiar to millions today (Acts 15:36–18:23).

Paul's Third Missionary Journey

Paul did not remain long in Antioch. In about the year 54 he embarked on a third missionary journey, following approximately the same route as on his second. He spent over two years in Ephesus preaching to Jews and Greeks, healing the sick, driving out demons, and converting people from superstition and paganism. He survived a riot of Ephesian silversmiths, who were upset because Paul's preaching had hurt their business of making idols. After the riot, Paul went to Greece for three months; during that time, he visited Corinth and wrote his Letter to the Romans. He then moved north to Philippi, where he was apparently rejoined by Luke. They and other missionaries then sailed to Troas.

At Troas, Paul restored to life a young man who had gone to sleep during Paul's preaching and had fallen to his death from a third-story window. The incident occurred "on the first day of the week" when the Christians were gathered "to break bread" (Acts 20:7). This is the first New Testament reference to the Christians assembling on Sunday, the day of the Lord's Resurrection, rather than on the Jewish Sabbath.

After returning to Asia Minor where he bade farewell to the elders (presbyters, priests) of Ephesus, Paul and his companions, including Luke, traveled from port to port until they boarded a ship from Patara to Tyre on the Mediterranean coast west of Mount Hermon. They then moved south down the coast through Ptolemais to Caesarea, where they stayed at the house of the deacon, Philip. In spite of prophecies warning him of dire consequences if he went on to Jerusalem, Paul was determined to go there for the Passover (Acts 18:24–21:14).

Paul's Journey From Jerusalem to Rome

Once Paul had arrived in Jerusalem about the year 58 with Luke and other companions, he met with Church leaders. They approved of his mission to the Gentiles but told of rumors that Paul was encouraging Jews to stop observing the Law of Moses. In order to quell such rumors, they suggested he bring some Jews to the Temple to help them fulfill vows they had made. When he did so, Jews from the province of Asia saw him and started an uproar. Paul was in danger of being torn apart by the crowds when Roman soldiers intervened. Paul's efforts to speak to the Jews resulted in a near riot, and the Romans were about to interrogate and torture Paul until they discovered he was a Roman citizen.

The next day the Roman commander allowed Paul to address the Sanhedrin. Paul cleverly blamed his arrest on his belief in resurrection, and this caused the Pharisees and Sadducees to argue among themselves. Again, the commander had to take Paul into the Fortress Antonia, only to discover through Paul's nephew that there was a plot afoot to murder Paul. So he had Paul escorted under heavy guard to Caesarea.

In Caesarea, Paul was brought before the Roman governor, Felix, who held a trial for Paul but left him in prison in the hopes that Paul would offer a bribe. After two years (58-60), Felix was succeeded by Porcius Festus. Festus gave Paul a hearing, but when he asked Paul to go to Jerusalem to stand trial, Paul appealed as a Roman citizen for a trial in Rome.

While waiting to send Paul to Rome, Festus was visited by King Herod Agrippa II, son of the Herod Agrippa who had killed James, Zebedee's son. Agrippa II was ruler of small parts of northern and eastern Palestine and had no authority over Paul's case. In any event, Paul's speech before Festus, Agrippa, and Agrippa's sister Bernice was a compelling witness to the truth of Christianity and an occasion for Paul to be declared innocent.

Nevertheless, Festus decreed that Paul must go to Rome, because he had appealed to the emperor. Paul and some other prisoners were put under the charge of Julius, a Roman centurion. From Caesarea they sailed to Tyre, then to Myra in Asia Minor. They made their way to the island of Crete and tried to find a suitable place to spend the winter. Unfortunately, they were caught in a terrible storm and blown into the open sea. After two weeks they were shipwrecked on the island of Malta, south of Sicily. Incredibly, all aboard survived and were cared for by the residents. Paul worked miracles of healing and won the favor of the people.

In the spring Julius found passage for Paul and his companions to Italy. When they arrived at Puteoli, they were greeted by Christians, who escorted them to Rome. There Paul was kept under guard but allowed to preach. When he failed to win over Jewish leaders to Christ, he turned once again to the Gentiles. For two years (61-63) he received all who came to him, proclaimed the kingdom of God, and taught the Good News (Acts 21:15–28:31).

Reading Acts

Read *Acts 1–2*, which describes Christ's Ascension, the Holy Spirit's coming on Pentecost, and the community life of the first believers. Read *Acts 9* for the story of Paul's conversion and for a description of miracles worked by Peter. Read *Acts 14* for some of Paul's adventures on his first missionary journey. Read *Acts 26* for Paul's trial before Festus and Agrippa. Read *Acts 28:16-31* for the account of Paul's stay in Rome.

We who read Acts today can gain a better understanding of the basic truths of Christianity. Jesus is the Savior of the world, God's Son sent for our redemption (9:20; 10:34-43). God is the creator of the universe, the God of every nation; in God "we live and move and have our being" (17:28). God the Holy Spirit is our helper and guide (1:8; 13:2). All Scripture points to Jesus Christ, who fulfills Old Testament prophecy (18:28). Salvation is found in Christ, not in observance of the Law of Moses or anywhere else (Acts 15). Christ is present in the world through those who believe in him (9:4-5), and he continues his ministry through them (3:12-16). Therefore, the Church must be a community of love and service, of healing and forgiveness (4:32-35; 5:12-16; 10:42-43; 11:27-30). Christ gives his life and grace to believers at Baptism (2:38), Eucharist (breaking of bread, 2:42), and Confirmation (bestowal of the Holy Spirit, 19:6). Through these sacraments, we become members of the Church, Christ's body on earth. The Eucharist, the teaching of the apostles, and prayer are the heart of Christian worship (2:42-47; 20:7); in them we find the essentials of our present-day celebration of the Mass.

New Testament Letters

Twenty-one New Testament books are called *letters,* or *epistles.* Some of them can properly be identified as letters in our modern sense, but others are actually sermons or theological treatises. They include the earliest and latest writings of the New Testament.

The letters are not arranged in chronological order. Letters attributed to Paul, for example, are placed first, and his letters to communities are placed before those to individuals. Letters attributed to the same author, like 1 and 2 Peter and 1, 2, and 3 John, are kept together. Within these groupings, longer letters are placed before shorter ones.

Other classifications are commonly used as well. Four of Paul's letters are known as "Captivity Letters" because in them the author speaks of being in prison. The First and Second Books of Timothy and the Book of Titus are called "Pastoral Letters" because they offer guidance to Church leaders (pastors).

Most of the letters follow a set pattern. First comes a greeting, which names the writer of the letter and the intended recipients. Next comes a prayer, usually praise, thanksgiving, and intercession. Then the main body of the letter is given, which might include explanations of doctrine, answers to questions, and directions for moral Christian behavior. The letter concludes with requests that greetings be extended to certain individuals or churches, followed by a closing prayer, and a farewell.

For the most part, the letters were written to meet specific needs of early Christians, to offer solutions to problems, and to answer questions. They show the gradually increasing comprehension of Christ's life and message gained by the early Church under the guidance of the Holy Spirit. None of the letters is a complete explanation of Christian doctrine, but taken together, and with the gospels, Acts, and Revelation, they form the foundation for subsequent theological development in the Church.

Many of the problems of the early Church, such as surviving in a secular society, struggling with temptation in a world hostile to Christian morality, and coping with human weakness, are the same as those we face today. Therefore, the letters not only offer insight into the life of the early Church; they address God's word to us and teach us how to follow Christ faithfully.

The letters contain some difficult passages and require study. Attention to Bible footnotes and a good commentary can be helpful. Since the letters contain many references to the Old Testament and to the life and teaching of Jesus, the more familiar we are with the rest of the Bible, the more easily we will be able to comprehend the letters.

Thirteen New Testament letters are attributed to Paul. However, Paul dictated some letters to secretaries, and others may have been composed by coworkers who depended on outlines drawn up by Paul. Some letters attributed to Paul and to other New Testament leaders may have been composed after their deaths by writers who used ideas originating with these leaders.

Because of the number of letters ascribed to Paul and because of his great importance in the missionary efforts of the early Church, students of the New Testament should be acquainted with him. We can learn many details about his life and ministry from the Acts of the Apostles, and Paul gives some autobiographical information in his letters. Other qualities can be read between the lines in his many writings. By all accounts, he is a fascinating personality and a significant figure in the process that shaped the beliefs of the New Testament Church.

The Life of Paul

In his early years Paul was known as Saul; the reasons for his change of name and its significance are uncertain. Here he will be referred to as Paul.

The date of Paul's birth is recorded nowhere. Since the Acts of the Apostles states that he was a young man when the deacon Stephen was martyred (sometime about 32-34), scholars generally estimate that he was born about A.D. 5. His birthplace was the city of Tarsus (Acts 21:39), a prosperous port on the Cydnus River in Cilicia (present-day Turkey). It was a center of learning where Jewish and Greek studies flourished, a place likely to stimulate the mind of a man as brilliant as Paul. Paul, like many scholars and rabbis of his time, had a trade, tentmaking (Acts 18:3), which he no doubt learned as a youth in Tarsus.

Paul was both a Roman citizen and a Jew. As a young man he moved to Jerusalem, perhaps with other members of his family, for Acts mentions his nephew, the son of Paul's sister, as being there (Acts 23:16). In Jerusalem, Paul studied under the famous rabbi, Gamaliel (Acts 22:3), and was known for his devotion to the Law of Moses. When he learned of Christianity, he saw it as a threat to orthodox Jewish belief and became an ardent crusader against Christians, arresting them and striving to have them put to death (Acts 26:1-11).

Sometime about 34-35 Paul had a conversion experience on the road to Damascus. He met Christ in a vision that left him physically blind but spiritually aware of the risen Lord's presence in his Church. Taken to Damascus, Paul was cured of his blindness and baptized by a disciple named Ananias. The exact sequence of events after this is uncertain, but it seems that Paul went to Arabia (Nabatea, southeast of the Dead Sea) for three years of prayer and reflection. This retreat would have occurred between his escape from Damascus and his first visit to Jerusalem (Acts 9; Gal 1). Finding that he was still mistrusted by Christians and hated by Jews, he left Jerusalem and went to Tarsus. He remained there, perhaps frustrated by his inability to win the confidence of either Jews or Christians, until Barnabas contacted him and brought him to Antioch about 42-43. Paul's missionary activities from that time on are well chronicled in Acts until his imprisonment in Rome, which ended about the year 63.

What happened to Paul after 63 is uncertain. Some scholars are of the opinion that he was executed at this time. Others think, on the testimony of early Church authorities, that he traveled to Spain, was again arrested and taken to Rome where he was beheaded at the orders of the Emperor Nero in about 67.

Paul gave his whole heart and soul to what he knew to be important. Once he began his missionary journeys, he was constantly at work, often on the move. He probably dictated some of his letters rapidly, pouring out ideas one after the other with the result that they are at times difficult to follow. Nevertheless, his writings are so powerful, personal, and insightful that they have inspired millions of believers for almost two thousand years.

As a preacher and writer, Paul displayed a fiery temperament and keen mind. He had many friends and speaks warmly of them in his letters. He could quarrel, as he did with Barnabas over John Mark, but he could also forgive and be reconciled. Above all, Paul was possessed by his great love of Jesus Christ. Once he experienced the depth of Christ's love for him, he gave his life completely to his Lord. For Christ he endured harsh labors, imprisonments, beatings, stonings, dangerous journeys, sleepless nights, every difficulty and anxiety (2 Cor 11:23-28). For Paul, life was to be summed up in the words: "I want to know Christ and the power of his resurrection and the sharing of his sufferings by becoming like him in his death, if somehow I may attain the resurrection from the dead" (Phil 3:10-11).

The Letter to the Romans

The Letter to the Romans was written by Paul from Corinth about 57, near the end of his third missionary journey. At the time, he was planning to visit Jerusalem with a gift from Greek Christians for the poor of Jerusalem. After that, Paul wanted to go to Spain and on the way stop at Rome. He wrote this letter to introduce himself to Roman Christians. Paul's plans were, of course, blocked by his arrest at Jerusalem. When he finally came to Rome in 61, he was a prisoner. Groups of believers escorted Paul into Rome after he arrived in Italy (Acts 28:15), so his letter must have made an impression on the Christian community there.

When the Roman church was founded is uncertain, but it probably developed among the large Jewish population in Rome. Paul's friends and coworkers, Aquila and Priscilla (Prisca), had lived in Rome and were forced to leave when the Emperor Claudius ordered all Jews out in 49 (Acts 18:2). They and other Jewish Christians returned after Claudius died in 54. By then the Roman church must have been made up largely of Gentiles. So the community faced the familiar questions about whether to observe Jewish laws, about why so many Jews rejected Christ, and about the universality of salvation. In his letter Paul addressed these issues as well as many others.

After the customary introduction (Rom 1:1-15), Paul explains that Jews and Gentiles had been hopelessly lost before Christ (Rom 1:16–3:20). Sinners, Jew or Gentile, find justification only through faith in Christ. We hope that God will save us because of the great love shown in Christ's death for us (Rom 3:21–5:21).

Paul insists that we must not use God's love as an excuse for sinning, for that love is a call to holiness. We are free from the Old Covenant Law, but this is so that we, baptized into Christ's body, led by the Holy Spirit, and aware of our dignity as God's children, may serve God faithfully. Because of God's great love, we can be sure that God will help us overcome any difficulty, even death itself (Rom 6–8).

Next, Paul struggles with why so many Jews refused to accept Christ. He points out that, even though they rejected Christ, God was able to use their error to bring salvation to the Gentiles. God has never rejected

161

Israel, and there is hope that the Jews will ultimately turn to Christ (Rom 9–11).

Paul then offers an explanation of the duties of Christian life. Because we are the Body of Christ, we are to use our gifts to benefit one another. We are to love others, to respect proper authority, and to remember that this world is passing away. We ought to be aware of the needs of others and to avoid giving scandal to those with tender consciences. In everything, we should glorify God and treat others as Christ treats us (Rom 12:1–15:13). Paul concludes with information about himself, a request for prayers, greetings to his friends in Rome, and a word of praise to God (Rom 15:14–16:27).

Read *Romans 5:1-11* for Paul's theology of justification and salvation. Read *Romans 8:28-39,* Paul's great hymn of confidence in God's mercy. Read *Romans 12* for a beautiful expression of the meaning of Christian life and love.

Some people see Romans as saying that we are saved by faith as opposed to works. They approach others with the question, "Are you saved?" However, this question confuses Paul's understanding of justification with that of salvation. Paul indicates that we *have been* justified (Christ has done everything necessary to free us from sin). He shows that we have every reason to hope that we *will be* saved (achieve eternal life). (See Rom 5:1-11.)

When Paul addresses the issue of faith and works, he is pointing out that we are saved by Christ, not by the works of the Old Law. But the New Law of Christ involves works, especially the work of love.

In Romans 10:9, Paul states that "if you confess with your lips that Jesus is Lord and believe in your heart that God raised him from the dead, you will be saved." In Romans 10:13 he writes: "Everyone who calls on the name of the Lord shall be saved." But what does it mean to "confess" and "believe" and to "call on"? Does it mean just to say the words and not express them in our lives? Of course not. How do we love someone? By expressing it in our actions. How do we believe? By expressing faith in our actions through our works. That's why Paul devotes so much of his letter to the Romans to explaining the duties of the Christian life (Rom 12:1–15:13). That's why Paul writes to the Philippians: "Work out your own salvation with fear and trembling" (2:12). In Paul's theology there is no conflict between faith and works. They are both part of following Christ.

We may read Romans today for an explanation of the primacy of

Christ in our lives. We are not faced with the issue of observing the Law of Moses, but we are tempted to put our reliance in other things. Christ alone can save us. In Romans we are told how to put faith in Christ. We are shown the power of hope. We are taught to love as we are loved by Christ.

The First Letter to the Corinthians

The city of Corinth was the capital of the Roman province of Achaia (now southern Greece). It was a thriving port, bustling with travelers going from Rome to the East and back again with ideas, commerce, money, and vices. People from all over the world, including many Jews, lived there.

Paul went to Corinth on his second missionary journey, remaining for a year and a half. He stayed with Aquila and Priscilla and supported himself by making tents. Assisted by Silas, Timothy, and others, he converted many to Christ and established a vibrant Christian community.

But after Paul left Corinth, problems began to occur. There were rivalries and divisions. Some Christians fell back into the immoral practices so common in Corinth. Some had legal conflicts in the civil courts. Their liturgical celebrations became rowdy, and the poor were neglected. Charismatic gifts, such as speaking in tongues, took precedence over charity. Questions arose about eating meat that had been offered to idols, about sex and marriage, about the Resurrection, and about other issues.

These problems and questions came to Paul's attention while he was in Ephesus during his third missionary journey. He wrote a letter to the Corinthian Christians that has not been preserved (1 Cor 5:9), then in 56 or 57 sent the letter we know as the First Letter to the Corinthians.

Paul begins his letter with the usual greetings and prayer of thanks (1 Cor 1:1-9), then moves immediately into the problem of factions among members of the Christian community. Some of them claimed allegiance to Paul, others to Apollos (Acts 18:24), others to Kephas (Peter). But the Christian community, Paul insists, can be founded only on Jesus Christ (1 Cor 3:11), and each member must work for the upbuilding of the Church on the foundation of Christ (1 Cor 1:10–4:21).

Paul then addresses the moral disorders reported in the Corinthian church. He orders excommunication (expulsion from the community) for a man guilty of incest. He denounces those who haul other Christians into the courts. He urges the Corinthians to avoid immoral practices (1 Cor 5–6).

Next, Paul answers questions presented to him in a letter from the church at Corinth. He gives directives about marriage and divorce, virginity and widowhood. He offers practical guidelines about eating meat that had been sacrificed to pagan idols before being sold in the markets (1 Cor 7–8).

Some Church members who disliked Paul had attacked his credentials as an apostle. Paul defends himself and his ministry, then urges the Corinthians to be faithful to Christ and loyal to one another. He appeals to them especially on the grounds that they share in the Eucharist: "The cup of blessing that we bless, is it not a sharing in the blood of Christ? The bread that we break, is it not a sharing in the body of Christ? Because there is one bread, we who are many are one body, for we all partake of the one bread" (1 Cor 10:16-17). As Paul imitates Christ, so the Corinthians ought to imitate Paul (1 Cor 9:1–11:1).

The problems of the community had been reflected in their liturgical assemblies. Paul makes recommendations to correct abuses and gives the earliest description of Christ's institution of the Eucharist (1 Cor 11:2-34).

Charismatic gifts, such as healing and speaking in tongues, flourished in Corinth. But some had turned these gifts into occasions of contention and spiritual elitism. Paul reminds the Corinthians that we are one body in Christ and must work for the benefit of the body. All other gifts are subordinate to love, the greatest of the gifts (1 Cor 12–14).

Some Christians at Corinth, perhaps influenced by the Greek thinking that had caused philosophers at Athens to ridicule Paul when he mentioned the Resurrection (Acts 17:32), had even questioned the reality of Christ's Resurrection. Paul shows that Christ's Resurrection is a certainty, and because Christ rose from the dead, we who believe in him will rise (1 Cor 15).

In conclusion, Paul sends guidelines for a collection to be taken for the poor of Jerusalem. He gives news about his plans and about other missionaries. He offers greetings from the Christians with him and sends a blessing and his love (1 Cor 16).

Read *1 Corinthians 1:10-25* for insight into the factions at Corinth and for the lesson that we must be one in Christ, who was crucified for us. Read *1 Corinthians 11:23-26* for Paul's account of the institution of the Eucharist. Read *1 Corinthians 12:12–13:13* for Paul's explanation of the Church as the Body of Christ and for his beautiful discourse on the meaning of love. Read *1 Corinthians 15:1-28* for Paul's witness to the reality of Christ's Resurrection and of our own.

The First Book of the Corinthians can show readers of today that the Church was never perfect. Human beings, even those who belonged to the earliest Christian communities, had faults and failings. But as Paul was willing to give his life to avert dissension and division, so we are called to work for unity among members of the Body of Christ. This letter can teach us a great deal about Christian living, especially about love, worship, and our destiny to spend eternity with Christ, our risen Lord.

The Second Letter to the Corinthians

The problems of the church at Corinth were not resolved by Paul's letter. It appears that enemies of Paul continued to question his authority and attack his reputation. Word of this reached Paul some months after he had sent the first letter, so he composed what we now know as the Second Letter to the Corinthians.

Actually, this book of the Bible may be a composite of parts of three or four letters written by Paul to the Corinthians. Scholars have noted that some portions of the letter (for example, 2 Cor 6:14–7:1; 9:1-15; 10:1–13:10) seem out of context and may be taken from other letters. Whatever the actuality may be, Paul wrote with great emotion. He was upset that false teachers should sow discord among believers, and even more upset that the Corinthians should so readily follow those teachers.

After the customary greeting and prayer (2 Cor 1:1-7), Paul speaks of his own condition; he is exhausted and afflicted, even to the point of death. He defends his ministry and explains why he has had to change some of his plans. He intersperses his explanations with testimonies to the glory of God, the love of Christ, and the presence of the Holy Spirit (2 Cor 1:8–7:16).

After several appeals for generosity toward the collection to be taken up for the poor of Jerusalem (2 Cor 8–9), Paul returns to his self-defense. He pours out his feelings in an outburst of love, anxiety, anger, and frustration, and in the process gives us remarkable insights into his own heart. He concludes his letter with a prayer for unity and peace and with a blessing (2 Cor 10–13).

Read *2 Corinthians 11:16–12:10,* part of Paul's defense against the charges made by his enemies. In these verses we see the hardships Paul had to endure as a missionary. We learn of his ecstasies (being "caught up to the third heaven") and of his agonies (the "thorn in the flesh"). We see him as a real human being, totally devoted to his Lord.

The letter offers insights into the mind and heart of Paul available nowhere else. When we are tempted to give up because of opposition, unfair criticism, or rejection by those we try to help, Paul encourages us to persevere as he did, "for the sake of Christ" (2 Cor 12:10).

The Letter to the Galatians

Galatia in Paul's time referred to the central portion of modern Turkey, north of the island of Cyprus. Paul and Barnabas visited cities in the southern part of this region on their first missionary journey, and Paul preached in the northern portion on his second and third journeys. Scholars debate whether Paul wrote this letter to Christians living in north or south Galatia. They disagree about the date of the letter. The most common view is that Paul wrote to Christians in northern Galatia around 54.

Paul was moved to write this letter when he learned, after his evangelization of the Galatians, that some other missionaries had upset his converts with demands that they keep the Law of Moses. Paul believed that the Old Testament pointed to Jesus, but he knew that Christians were no longer bound by its precepts. He realized that if the Christians in Galatia tried to find salvation in the Old Law, they would be abandoning Christ.

Consequently, he was outraged at the false teachers who had followed him to Galatia, and he was upset with his converts, for they seemed all too ready to listen to those teachers. He wrote the Letter to the Galatians to proclaim the uniqueness of Christ and to denounce those who tried to find salvation in observance of Old Covenant laws.

Paul's turbulent emotions may be seen at the beginning of his letter. He shortens the introductory greeting and prayer (Gal 1:1-5), immediately expresses his amazement that the Galatians are abandoning Christ, then calls down a curse upon anyone who would teach a gospel contrary to the one proclaimed by Paul (Gal 1:6-10).

Paul next defends his ministry, explaining his conversion and early years as a Christian. He argues that the church leaders at Jerusalem have certified his preaching as orthodox, even though their conduct was not always in keeping with their words. He asserts that salvation comes through Christ, not through the Jewish law (Gal 1:11–2:21).

Using a series of arguments drawn from the Old Testament, Paul shows that Christ has delivered us from the demands of the Old Law and has given us the freedom of the children of God. This freedom must not be taken lightly or thrown away (Gal 3–4).

Paul demonstrates how our freedom ought to be exercised. We must put our faith in Christ. We are to serve others. We are to live by the Spirit as members of the Christian community, correcting and helping one another. Paul concludes with the assertion that circumcision, the mark of the Old Law, counts for nothing. "May I never boast of anything except the cross of our Lord Jesus Christ, by which the world has been crucified to me, and I to the world" (Gal 6:14). Paul is marked with the scars of his ministry as belonging to Christ. As Christ's servant, he asks God's blessing on the Galatians (Gal 5–6).

Read *Galatians 1:11–2:21,* Paul's description of his first years as a Christian and of his struggles to proclaim the primacy of Christ, even to Peter. Read *Galatians 5:13-26,* an explanation of how to use our freedom well. Note the qualities listed in 5:22-23, traditionally called the Fruits of the Spirit.

In reading Galatians we are encouraged to see Christ as the center of life. We find an explanation of the relationship of faith to works. In Galatians 3:1-9, Paul emphasizes that justification comes through faith in Christ rather than through observance of the Jewish law. By saying this, Paul does not deny the importance of good works. Rather, he shows that faith and works are intimately connected: "The only thing that counts is faith working through love" (Gal 5:6). Faith is essential, but so are good works. We put our faith in Christ. We imitate Christ in the works of everyday life.

The Letter to the Ephesians

Ephesus was a large port city in what is now western Turkey. Paul first preached the gospel there on his second missionary journey, and he spent two years there on his third journey. But it is uncertain if the Letter to the Ephesians was composed in its final form by Paul or if it was originally addressed to the Christians at Ephesus.

The language and development of thought in Ephesians is different from Paul's own letters. The personal references we might expect if

Paul had actually sent this letter to the Ephesians are missing. The letter itself is more of a theological treatise and seems to rely on the Letter to the Colossians. Many early manuscripts do not list the Ephesians as recipients of the letter. Therefore, some scholars contend that the Letter to the Ephesians was actually composed by a writer versed in Paul's teachings, possibly about the year 90, and sent as a circular letter to a number of different churches. Paul's name and references to Paul were used to add authority to the letter, appropriately so because Ephesians is a legitimate development of Paul's theology and writings. Other scholars argue that the letter was, in fact, authored by Paul, perhaps through a secretary.

The letter begins with a statement of God's plan to save us through Jesus Christ. Those who believe in Christ are sealed with the Holy Spirit and form the Church, the Body of Christ. God has generously called the Gentiles into the Church, making them one with the Jews into a "holy temple in the Lord," "a dwelling place for God" (Eph 1–2).

Paul's ministry is recalled as part of God's plan to invite Gentiles into the Church. Since believers are one with Christ, they are to live in holiness, unity, and peace so that the Church may be built up under Christ, the head of his body. Christians must avoid sin and dwell in the light of Christ. Husbands and wives must love each other as Christ loves the Church, and family members must treat one another with respect. We are all to put on the "armor of God" and fight the good fight until the end (Eph 3–6).

Read *Ephesians 3:14-21,* a prayer for the Church. Read *Ephesians 5:1–6:4,* advice for holy living and Christlike family relationships.

Ephesians has long been spotlighted as the letter describing the Church as one, holy, catholic, and apostolic. The Church is one, the Body of Christ (4:4-6). It is holy with the holiness of Christ (5:25-27). It is catholic in that God calls all to be saved through Christ (2). It is apostolic because it is built on "the foundation of the apostles" (2:20). Therefore, we who read this letter are presented with a beautiful vision of the Church. We see our high destiny as members of Christ's Body. We are taught to live in holiness and love, especially with the members of our family.

It should be noted that this letter does not promote dominance of husband over wife. Husband and wife are to be "subject to one another out of reverence for Christ" (5:21). Wives are to be subject to their husbands, but husbands are to love their wives as Christ loves the Church

(5:22-25). Since Christ washed the feet of his apostles and laid down his life for the Church, the Letter to the Ephesians actually recommends that husbands and wives imitate the love, humility, and generosity of Christ in their dealings with each other.

The Letter to the Philippians

Philippi was a prominent city in the northeast portion of the Roman province of Macedonia (part of modern Greece). On his second missionary journey Paul spent some time there, establishing a church that he visited on his third journey. Paul felt close to the Philippians, and they offered him support in his ministry.

The document we know as the Letter to the Philippians seems to contain parts of three letters that were later edited into one work, probably by someone in the church at Philippi who wanted to adapt them for community reading.

In the first part of the letter, Paul begins with the traditional greetings and thanksgiving. He expresses his affection for the Philippians and mentions his imprisonment, possibly at Ephesus around the year 55. Paul urges his readers to remain faithful, to imitate Christ in humble service and holiness of life. He speaks of fellow missionaries Timothy and Epaphroditus and closes with a recommendation to "rejoice in the Lord" (Phil 1:1–3:1).

Another letter begins with Paul warning the Philippians against a familiar foe, those who taught that Christians were bound by the laws of the Old Covenant. Paul encourages his readers to focus their attention on Christ (Phil 3:2-21).

The next verses possibly belong with the first part of the letter; they urge the Philippians to strive for unity and peace (Phil 4:1-9). These verses are followed by a third letter, a short note of appreciation to the Philippians for their generous support of Paul's work. The letter closes with greetings and a farewell (Phil 4:10-23).

Read *Philippians 2:1-18,* a call to live in love and humility in imitation of Christ. This section contains an early Christian hymn to Christ (2:6-11). Read *Philippians 4:4-9,* a beautiful instruction showing the way to joy and peace of heart.

We find in such passages patterns for Christian living. We see in the community life of the church at Philippi a model for our lives as members of the Church today.

The Letter to the Colossians

This letter is addressed to the Christian community at Colossae (a small town in what is now southwestern Turkey). It is attributed to Paul, and there are references to Paul's life and companions in the letter. Traditionally, Paul was held to be the actual author of this letter, and some scholars still hold this position. They believe that Paul dictated it to a secretary during one of his imprisonments.

Others favor the opinion that Colossians was written by one of Paul's disciples. They feel that the style and language do not match Paul's and that the theology is a later development of his thought. They see the work as a sermon written after Paul's death, using Paul as a heavenly spokesman. Colossians shows an acquaintance with Paul's earlier letters and has many parts that are similar to Ephesians.

The Letter to the Colossians was occasioned by doctrinal confusion among Christians. False teachers were suggesting that demigods and heavenly powers had to be placated. They may also have been recommending magic, astrology, and secret cult practices. Some of these ideas may have been part of the development of the Gnostic heresy, which later held that salvation came through mystical knowledge and denied both the divinity and the humanity of Christ.

The Letter to the Colossians shows that such ideas are contrary to Christianity. It expresses orthodox Christian belief in the preeminence of Christ as Savior and Lord, as head of the Church.

The letter begins with greetings, thanksgiving, and a prayer professing belief in the salvation brought by Christ. An early hymn proclaims Christ's unique role as the image of God, the one through whom all things were created, the head of his Body, the Church, and the redeemer of humanity. Christ lives in us to such an extent that we may join even our sufferings to his "for the sake of his body, that is, the church" (Col 1:24).

Next, the author warns against false teachings and occult practices that threaten the orthodoxy of the community (Col 2). He then gives a wonderful outline of life in and with Christ. Christians are to put away vice and put on the virtues characteristic of Christ, such as compassion, forgiveness, love, and peace. Family and human relationships are highlighted. The letter closes with the traditional greetings and a blessing (Col 3–4).

Read *Colossians 1* for the standard opening of a New Testament letter, its magnificent expression of the preeminence of Christ, and its explanation of Christ's life in us. Read *Colossians 3:1-17* for its description of life "hidden with Christ in God."

Colossians invites us to see Christ as our Savior and Lord. It reminds us of our union with Christ and our privilege as those called to be Christ in the world today. It points out our destiny as human beings, directing us to "seek the things that are above, where Christ is, seated at the right hand of God" (3:1).

The First Letter to the Thessalonians

Paul, assisted by Silas and Timothy, evangelized the Macedonian city of Thessalonica on his second missionary journey. When Paul had to move on because of persecution, he left Silas and Timothy behind to minister to the Thessalonians. They later joined him at Corinth. Then Paul sent Timothy back to the Thessalonians to see how they were doing. Probably in the early summer of 51, Timothy brought a report to Paul, and this report motivated Paul to write the First Letter to the Thessalonians. This letter is of special importance because it is almost certainly the first work of the New Testament to be written.

At this time, about twenty years after Christ's Resurrection, Christians seemingly expected that Christ's Coming and the end of the world might occur at any moment. They wondered how those who had died could share in eternal life. Paul explained that those who had died in Christ would share fully in eternal life, no less than those living on earth when Christ returns.

Paul begins his letter with greetings from himself, Silvanus (possibly another name for Silas), and Timothy. He offers a thanksgiving prayer for the courage of the Thessalonians in turning from idols to Christ. Paul recalls his ministry among them, emphasizing his sincerity and affection for them ("like a nurse tenderly caring for her own children"). He acknowledges the persecution they are undergoing, possibly harassment from pagan neighbors, and dissension caused by Jewish Christians who insisted on observance of the Law of Moses. He explains why he sent Timothy and expresses joy at the good news Timothy brought of their faith and love (1 Thess 1–2).

Paul offers guidelines for Christian conduct, especially purity and love. He assures his readers of the reality of the Resurrection and of their share in eternal life through Christ. He speaks of the need to be always ready for Christ's Coming. He recommends obedience to Church authorities and charity toward all. He closes with a prayer, a greeting, and a blessing (1 Thess 3–5).

Read *1 Thessalonians 4:13–5:28* for a sense of how the early Church understood Christ's Second Coming and for Paul's guidelines on Christian vigilance and virtue.

Later New Testament books indicate that Christians gradually began to realize that the end of the world and the Second Coming of Christ might be much later than originally thought. The Catholic Church teaches that we cannot know the time of Christ's Second Coming. For all practical purposes, this world ends for us when we die. We do not know the time of our death, and so reading this letter can remind us of the importance of always being ready to meet the Lord.

The Second Letter to the Thessalonians

In its introduction, this letter is said to be sent from Paul to the Thessalonians. If so, Paul may actually have written it or given the main ideas to a secretary. Some scholars, however, are of the opinion that it was written by an unknown author to Christians in Asia Minor around the year 90. This opinion is based on considerations of style and content. It holds that the author used 1 Thessalonians as a pattern, wanting to give authoritative teaching in a situation where believers were confused about the Second Coming of Christ.

The community to whom the letter is addressed had been shaken by rumors that the "day of the Lord," Christ's Second Coming, was at hand (2:2). Apparently, the rumors had started from a letter falsely attributed to Paul. Some Christians were frightened, and others stopped working to wait for the Lord's coming.

The introduction is modeled on that found in 1 Thessalonians. After the thanksgiving the theme of Christ's coming is presented. The author urges the readers not to be upset by the false report that the day of the Lord is imminent. He lists a number of events that must occur first. These events are vaguely described and certainly do not offer a timetable for the end of the world (2 Thess 1–2).

The author prays that the Lord will direct the hearts of the readers "to the love of God and to the steadfastness of Christ." He then offers a practical application: Christians are not to excuse themselves from work. Those who are unwilling to work should not eat. The letter closes with a short prayer, a greeting, and a blessing (2 Thess 3).

Read 2 *Thessalonians* 2 for advice on staying calm about the end of the world. We need not understand the allusions to the "rebellion" and "the lawless one" made in this chapter to grasp its main message: Do not be "shaken in mind or alarmed" (2:2).

In every age there have been false prophets predicting the imminent coming of Christ. In our own time there are preachers who try to forecast the exact date of the end of the world. Reading 2 Thessalonians should teach us not to take such alarmists seriously. For two thousand years they have all been wrong! What really matters is living each moment in union with Christ.

Questions for Discussion and Reflection

How many of the important personalities and events mentioned in the Acts of the Apostles can you recall? Can you give a summary of the most important points of Paul's theology you have found in his letters?

Activities

Many Bibles have maps illustrating the journeys of Paul. Using such a map, find the places named in the explanation of the Acts of the Apostles.

Study the following outline to become familiar with the main dates of Paul's life. Fill in the outline with any details you wish to add.

The Life of Paul

5(?)—birth of Saul in Tarsus; 30(?)—move to Jerusalem, study under Gamaliel; 34-35—Saul's conversion; 35-38—Arabia; 38—first visit to Jerusalem; 38-41—Tarsus; 41-44—persecution under Herod Agrippa; 42-43—Barnabas brings Paul to Antioch, relief mission to Jerusalem; 45-48—first missionary journey...Paul and Barnabas; 49—Council of Jerusalem; 50-53—second missionary journey...Paul, Silas, Timothy, Luke(?); 54- 57—third missionary journey...Paul and Luke; 58—Jerusalem: arrest at Temple; 58-60—imprisonment at Caesarea under Felix; 60-61—voyage to Rome, shipwreck; 61—arrival at Rome; 61-63—imprisonment at Rome; 64(?)—visit to Spain(?); 67(?)—final imprisonment and execution under Nero(?)

CHAPTER ELEVEN

1 Timothy to Revelation

T he soldiers threw the old man down against the wood of his cross.
"Another Jew," the centurion spat contemptuously. "This one said
he wasn't worthy to die like his Master. So give him his wish. Crucify
him upside down." Soldiers seized the old man's arms and smashed the
nails through flesh and bone into the wood. Then quickly they nailed
his feet flat against the main beam, heaved the cross up, and dropped it
with a thud into the hole they had prepared. Peter moaned with pain,
then whispered again and again, "Lord, you know that I love you."

Paul, arms chained behind his back, knelt down before the execu-
tioner. He spoke, loud enough for the Christians waiting to claim his
body for burial to hear: "To live is Christ, and to die is gain." He slowly
bent his head forward and waited. The heavy sword flashed in a swift
arc, and Paul made the journey through death to the life he had long
desired.

With the martyrdom of Peter and Paul in Rome, an era ended and a
new epoch began. The great apostles had brought thousands to Christianity, had established churches, and appointed leaders. The mission
of spreading the gospel of Christ had been passed on to a second generation of Christians.

The Second Generation of Christians

We do not know the exact date of the deaths of Peter and Paul, but
the most reliable evidence shows that they both were martyred in Rome
during the persecution of the Emperor Nero, sometime about 64-67.
During these years many Roman Christians were condemned to torture
and death. The persecution ceased in 68 when Nero committed suicide.

By this time Peter, Paul, and other missionaries had established Christian churches throughout Palestine, Asia Minor, northern Africa, Greece, Italy, and Spain. Christians numbered in the tens of thousands, the majority of Gentile origin. Writings about Jesus and the Letters of Paul were being circulated. Believers saw themselves as the Body of Christ, privileged to bring Christ's love and truth to the world.

The Destruction of Jerusalem

While Christianity was spreading through the Roman Empire, a spirit of unrest was sweeping through Palestine. The officials who succeeded Pontius Pilate were not up to the task of governing the unruly Judeans, and the Zealots grew bolder in their call for a revolt against Rome. In 66, when the Roman procurator Gessius Florus confiscated a huge amount of gold from the Temple treasury, a crowd of Jews gathered to protest. Florus set his troops upon them and killed thousands. Enraged, the Zealots rallied the entire city and attacked the Roman soldiers. Florus managed to escape, but the Fortress Antonia fell and its garrison was massacred. The Jews seized weapons from Roman arsenals, and rebellion spread like wildfire throughout Palestine.

The first attempts by Syrian-based Roman troops to quell the revolt were turned back. Although the Jews set up a martial-law government and fortified cities throughout Judea, Samaria, and Galilee, Roman reaction was swift. The great general, Vespasian, invaded Galilee in 67 with a huge Roman army. He quickly conquered all of Galilee and took control of the Mediterranean coast as far south as Azotus. There the Jewish commander, Josephus, was captured. He tried unsuccessfully to convince the Jews that further resistance was useless. Years later he wrote a history of the Jewish people.

In 68 Vespasian moved inland toward Jerusalem. Conquering city after city, he was ready to attack Jerusalem when Nero committed suicide. In 70 Vespasian was named emperor. Leaving for Rome, he put his son Titus in charge of the military operations in Judea. Titus moved against Jerusalem with an army of eighty thousand. He besieged the city in the spring when Jerusalem was packed with perhaps half a million pilgrims who had come for Passover. Casualties were heavy on both sides, and the Romans relentlessly pressed forward, breaching the outer walls and invading the city. But the Jews held out behind the walls of the Temple, the Fortress Antonia, and the inner city.

Titus decided to starve the rebels out by sealing off Jerusalem. Those who tried to escape or smuggle in food were caught and crucified by the thousands. Soon famine and disease were rampant. According to the Jewish historian Josephus, this situation became so desperate that some women were reduced to eating their own children. Still the rebels refused to surrender, and Titus attacked the weakened defenders with a vengeance. The Romans battered down the walls of the Fortress Antonia and the Temple. They slaughtered, burned, and pillaged until the city was a ruin of rotting corpses, smoldering timbers, and blackened stones. Historians estimate that hundreds of thousands of Jewish men, women, and children perished in the misery of famine and disease, in the storm of battle, and in the crucifixions. The few who survived were carried off as slaves.

From Jerusalem the Romans attacked remaining pockets of resistance. The last, the fortress at Masada, overlooking the Dead Sea, fell in 73. When the Roman troops finally broke through the Zealot defenses, they found a thousand corpses of men, women, and children. Rather than be taken captive, the Jews had committed suicide.

For almost sixty years Judea was quiet. The population of Palestine, decimated by war, gradually began to increase. In 131 Emperor Hadrian decided to rebuild Jerusalem as a Roman city with a temple to Jupiter. Jews were outraged, of course, and a new rebellion broke out under the leadership of Simon bar Kokhba. Skilled in guerrilla tactics, he would attack Roman garrisons, then fall back to hideouts in the wilderness of Judea. He forced the Romans to abandon Jerusalem and gained control of much of Judea. But the Romans sent another huge army to put down the rebellion. Simon fought back with ambushes and raids but was finally cornered and killed with the last of his troops in 135. The Romans enslaved or slaughtered all remaining Jews who had not escaped from Palestine. They settled Jerusalem with Gentiles, built a temple to Jupiter, and decreed that Judea no longer existed. Although colonies of Jews survived throughout the Roman Empire, the Jews would remain without a homeland until the twentieth century.

Christianity and the Roman Empire

It might seem incredible that hundreds of thousands of Jews would go to Jerusalem for Passover when an attack from a Roman army seemed imminent. However, Jews might have felt safer in Jerusalem because its walls and fortifications appeared to be impregnable. Furthermore, most Jews believed that God would not allow the Holy City to be destroyed. In fact, the Zealots refused to surrender even after Jerusalem's outer defenses had been breached, because they were certain that God would send a Messiah to save them from the Romans.

Christians, however, knew that the Messiah had already come, and the gospels record that Jesus had predicted the destruction of the Holy City (Mt 24:1-28). They had no illusions about the invulnerability of Jerusalem. Consequently, many of them escaped from Palestine when the Roman invasion began. They settled in cities throughout the Roman Empire and brought their faith to others.

The spread of Christianity was facilitated by the Roman system of roads and Roman policing of sea lanes. Missionaries traveled freely to preach the Good News of Jesus. Its promise of Christ's salvation to all people was well received in an age when paganism was losing its appeal.

Christian communities sprang up everywhere. Christians met for worship in private homes, forming churches ministered to by deacons, priests (elders, presbyters), and bishops (overseers). Most new believers were Gentiles who saw themselves not as a branch of Judaism but as a distinct religion. By the end of the first century, there were 300,000 to 500,000 Christians from India to western Europe.

Such a vast number of believers needed leadership if they were to see themselves as one Church. After the destruction of Jerusalem, such leadership came from cities like Antioch, Ephesus, Alexandria, and Rome. Of these, Rome became the most prominent. It was, after all, the center of the Mediterranean world. It was the city where Peter, first among the apostles, had been bishop. It was the place where Peter and Paul had died. By the end of the first century, Clement, Bishop of Rome, was showing concern for other churches. During the second century, sacred writers were expressing the view that all other churches must be one with the church of Rome in doctrine and policy.

Persecution

The Roman Empire had an official religion and a state cult that worshiped pagan gods and the emperor himself. Christians, unwilling to participate in such pagan worship, found themselves at odds with the state and were often accused of being disloyal. Nero was the first emperor to persecute Christians, seemingly to distract attention from his own shortcomings, but his persecution was localized in Rome. The Emperor Domitian (81-96) launched the first general persecution of Christians late in his reign. After him, there was an official policy under which Christians were liable to arrest, confiscation of property, slavery, torture, and death. Some emperors did not actively pursue Christians, but others did, including Trajan (98-117), Marcus Aurelius (161-180), Decius (249-251), and especially Diocletian (284-305). Historians debate about how many Christians died during the persecutions; the numbers probably ran into the tens of thousands.

In spite of persecution, Christianity continued to spread, and there were several million believers by the year 300. Christianity entered a new era in 313 when the Roman Emperor Constantine issued the Edict of Milan, granting religious tolerance to Christians. They were then free to worship and evangelize. The power of Christ's love had conquered the might of Rome.

Later New Testament Books

Most, if not all, of the New Testament books were written by the year 100. By 200 the twenty-seven New Testament books along with the forty-six Old Testament books of the Alexandrian collection were recognized as inspired by God. In the late fourth century a list of these seventy-three books was acknowledged in Catholic Church councils.

Many New Testament books reflect the historical circumstances current when they were composed. For example, we can see the development of lines of authority in the Letters to Timothy and Titus, and we find evidence of persecution by Roman authorities in the Book of Revelation.

The exact time when many New Testament letters were written is uncertain. Some of those attributed to Paul and Peter may have been composed by followers after the fall of Jerusalem. In this book we can only mention a few of the more notable opinions about authorship of these letters. There are many other opinions, of course, but the most important fact to keep in mind is that these books are inspired by God, regardless of who the human authors were.

The Pastoral Letters

Paul's letters to Timothy and Titus differ from his other letters in that they are directed to leaders of the Church rather than to the congregations of the churches. Because they offer guidance to pastors, they are known as the "Pastoral Letters."

Some scholars feel that the Pastoral Letters were actually written by one of Paul's disciples after his death, probably in the 80s or 90s. They point out that the language and style of these letters differ from Paul's other writings. The Pastorals seem to reflect a later era in the Church; for example, 1 Timothy 3:6 says that a bishop should not be "a recent convert." They deal with different issues, including the need to be faithful to the teaching of the apostles and to avoid the false knowledge that came to be called Gnosticism (1 Tim 6:20). Other scholars, however, state that these reasons are not conclusive and do not rule out the possibility that Paul wrote the letters through a secretary.

In any case, the doctrine of the Pastoral Letters is consistent with and faithful to Paul's theology. The author, if not Paul, certainly intended to teach with Paul's authority and was familiar with Paul's writings. One possible opinion is that the author of the Pastorals gathered excerpts from letters Paul had written to Timothy and Titus and incorporated them into a set of directives to Church leaders that we know as 1 and 2 Timothy and Titus.

The First Letter to Timothy

Timothy was a native of Lystra (modern south-central Turkey). Paul founded a church there on his first missionary journey, and on his second journey he welcomed Timothy as a fellow missionary. Timothy accompanied Paul on his third journey and was sent on several important assignments by Paul. He clearly was one of Paul's most trusted associates.

The First Letter to Timothy presents Paul as writing from Greece to Timothy, whom Paul had set over the church at Ephesus. After a short greeting, Paul warns Timothy to guard against false doctrine. Remembering God's mercy to him, Paul urges Timothy to "fight the good fight, having faith and a good conscience" (1 Tim 1).

Next, Paul asks for prayers, especially for those in authority. He offers directives for dress and decorum at worship assemblies, directives that reflect the customs of that particular time and place. He recounts qualifications for bishops and deacons. He describes the Church as "the pillar and bulwark of the truth." He sings a hymn of praise to Christ, "the mystery of our religion" (1 Tim 2–3).

Paul next attacks the false doctrines of those who taught that only the spiritual side of humanity was good. For Paul, "everything created by God is good," the body as well as the spirit. Timothy is to be faithful to his duties and to his office, conferred "through prophecy with the laying on of hands by the council of elders." Paul commissions Timothy to treat members of the community with respect. He offers regulations for widows, who fulfilled special roles in the early Church. He advises Timothy to guide the elders (presbyters), mentioning the laying on of hands, a reference to what later came to be known as the ordination of priests (1 Tim 4–5).

Paul mentions relationships of slaves and masters, then again warns against false teachings, especially the notion that religion should be used for material gain. He closes with exhortations to keep the commandments and hold to the truth (1 Tim 6).

Read *1 Timothy 1*. Note the references to false teaching and to the vices so common in the pagan world. Note also the reference to Paul's own past and to God's great mercy toward him. Read *1 Timothy 3* for the qualifications of bishops and deacons and for the brief hymn honoring the mystery of Christ's Incarnation. Note that the expression, "married only once" (3:2) does not mean that the bishop had to be married (Paul was not), but only that the bishop could not be married more than once.

The First Letter to Timothy offers insights into the development of Church authority and structure. Even in the first century, Church leaders saw the importance of organization if unity was to be maintained. We see in 1 Timothy that false teachings had to be opposed. It should be no surprise to find similar problems today.

The Second Letter to Timothy

The Second Letter to Timothy shows Paul writing from prison at Rome to his beloved disciple. It is more personal in tone than 1 Timothy, and even if set in its present form after Paul's death, it may contain passages originally written by Paul himself. Paul relates the trials he is undergoing and asks Timothy to visit him, bringing some documents and a cloak Paul left in Troas. Paul describes his work as finished and himself as ready for death.

The letter begins with a greeting and an expression of gratitude that mentions the faith of Timothy's mother, Eunice, and grandmother, Lois. Paul encourages Timothy to be faithful to the gospel, which proclaims Christ as Savior. Paul may be in chains, but "the word of God is not chained" (2 Tim 1:1–2:13).

Paul cautions Timothy to beware of false teachers and to avoid useless disputes. He warns of the wickedness that will come in the "last days," an admonition found often in the New Testament. Timothy is to follow Paul's example and to be faithful to the sacred Scriptures, for "all scripture is inspired by God" (2 Tim 2:14–3:17).

As the letter draws to a close, Paul offers another exhortation to Timothy to carry out his ministry. He speaks of his own approaching death with confidence and hope. He gives news about fellow missionaries, sends greetings, and concludes with a blessing (2 Tim 4).

Read *2 Timothy 1–2* for the opening words and some of Paul's exhortations. Note how Paul advises Timothy to pass on the gospel to other teachers, just as Paul has handed it on to Timothy.

The letter reveals the heart and mind of Paul during his last days on earth. We see the trials endured by the first missionaries and the dangers of false doctrine. In spite of such trials and dangers, Paul faced the future with hope, and he inspires us to do the same.

The Letter to Titus

Titus was a gentile Christian, a disciple and companion of Paul. He is mentioned in 2 Corinthians as a trusted associate sent by Paul to Corinth on several missions. In 2 Timothy 4:10, Titus is said to be in Dalmatia (modern Croatia). In this letter he is on the island of Crete. The letter is shorter than 1 Timothy but deals with many of the same concerns.

The Letter begins with the customary greeting and states that Titus was sent to Crete to appoint elders (presbyters) and bishops. Qualifications for such leaders are listed, with special attention paid to the ability to refute false teachers. Apparently, these were plentiful on Crete, and among them were Jewish Christians who preached that believers were obliged by the Law of Moses and Jewish dietary laws (Titus 1).

Next, guidelines for moral behavior are given to Christians of every age and class. God's grace has been given to all, and all await Christ's Coming. Christians are to be good citizens, peaceful and gracious, in response to the kindness and generous love of Christ. The letter closes with advice to Titus about dealing with false teachers, with personal remarks, greetings, and a blessing.

Read *Titus 2:11–3:7* for guidelines on Christian life as a response to God's goodness. Note the reference to Baptism in 3:5.

Like the other Pastoral Letters, Titus helps us understand the problems faced by the Church as leadership passed from the apostles to the second generation of Christians. We also find instructions on how to live Christlike lives in an imperfect world.

The Letter to Philemon

This letter is the shortest of those ascribed to Paul and is therefore placed last. It was written by Paul while he was in prison, perhaps at Ephesus around 56 or at Rome around 62, and sent to Philemon, a wealthy Christian who lived at Colossae (southwestern Turkey; see Col 4:9).

Onesimus (a name meaning "useful") was a slave who escaped from his owner, Philemon, and ended up with Paul. Paul converted him and wrote this letter to urge Philemon to welcome Onesimus back as a brother. There is a subtle hint that Paul would like Philemon to free Onesimus and allow him to return to Paul as an assistant.

Paul does not address the institution of slavery. The first Christians realized that they could not change Roman laws, and they expected that Christ would soon return. But the attitudes that Paul encourages in this Letter and elsewhere (see Gal 3:28) would eventually lead Christians to repudiate slavery altogether.

Read *Philemon.* Note how Paul addresses the letter not only to Philemon but to Apphia, Archippus, and other members of the church meeting at Philemon's house. This, of course, would provide additional incentive to Philemon to accede to Paul's wishes. Note how Paul praises Philemon, then begs him to listen to his pleas for Onesimus. Paul closes with the hope that he will soon visit Philemon, with greetings, and a blessing.

We who read Philemon today cannot fail to be touched by the appeal of Paul, "as an old man, and now also as a prisoner of Christ Jesus." We are encouraged to imitate Paul's affection for others and to open our hearts to people of every social class.

Hebrews

This writing has traditionally been called the Letter to the Hebrews. The title is a later addition, however, and the work is actually a sermon. "Hebrews" became part of the title because of the many Old Testament references in this book, but the actual audience of this sermon is unknown. Its author is also unknown. In the past some scholars thought it might have been composed by Paul because of a reference to Timothy in the last chapter. But the style and language differ so much from Paul's that few scholars today feel that Paul could be its author.

We can learn a great deal about the work by studying its contents. Its Greek is excellent, and it was written by someone skilled in language, composition, and literary style. The author quoted frequently from the Alexandrian (Greek) version of the Old Testament. He, therefore, had to be knowledgeable in Greek and in the Old Testament. This has caused many scholars to suggest that Hebrews might have originated in Alexandria, Egypt.

Whether it was intended for the Christian community at Alexandria or elsewhere, or for the entire Church, is uncertain. To judge from statements in the letter, those who were meant to hear the sermon had been Christians for some time and were tempted by persecution or routine to fall from their early fervor. Some may have stopped coming to regular worship services and abandoned their Christian faith.

Because of the many references to Temple worship, some scholars feel that Hebrews was composed before the fall of Jerusalem in 70, but this is uncertain. It may have been written as early as 60 or as late as 90.

Whatever questions may exist about the author, audience, and date of composition of Hebrews, there is no doubt about the value of the work itself. It is a masterful presentation of Christ as the Word of God, the priest who saved us by his death, and the leader who opens heaven to us. Theological explanations are mingled with moral exhortations throughout the work. It accomplishes its purpose of encouraging Christians to follow Christ with courage and zeal.

The author begins by stating that God, who has spoken to our ancestors in many ways, has in these "last days" spoken to us through his Son. Christ is above all creation, higher than the angels, therefore, we ought to be faithful in following him through suffering and death to eternal life (Heb 1–2).

Christ is our "high priest," greater than Moses. He leads us to the

Promised Land and "sabbath rest" of heaven. He understands our weakness, and we should trust in him (Heb 3:1–5:10).

Hebrews encourages us to go beyond the basic teachings of our faith to realize that Christ is a high priest who ministers to us forever. He surpasses the priesthood of Aaron, and like the Old Testament priest Melchizedek, he receives his priesthood directly from God. The heavenly ministry of Jesus exceeds the worship of the temple, and Christ's sacrificial death alone saves us. His sacrifice on the cross has replaced the sacrifices of the Old Covenant. Therefore, we must hold to our faith, perform good works, and participate in the liturgical assemblies of the Church (Heb 5:11–10:39).

We strengthen our faith by considering the great believers of the Old Covenant. God has granted us what they hoped for. They watch over us as we "run with perseverance the race that is set before us, looking to Jesus, the pioneer and perfecter of our faith." We must endure our trials courageously, for sufferings strengthen us in our journey to "the city of the living God." We ought to live in holiness. With God as our helper, we can imitate the great leaders who have gone before us, for "Jesus Christ is the same yesterday and today and forever" (Heb 11–13).

Read *Hebrews 1:1-4,* the introduction to this great sermon. Read *Hebrews 2:14-18,* an expression of our oneness with Christ. Read *Hebrews 4:1–5:10* for an example of the author's use of Old Testament references and a beautiful explanation of Christ as the priest who shares even our sufferings. Read *Hebrews 10:19-39* to see how the author uses both promises and warnings to encourage us to be faithful to the end. Read *Hebrews 12:18-24,* which states the only real goal of human existence.

These are only samples of the doctrine of Hebrews. This book, if read in its entirety, will give a clearer understanding of the constant presence of Jesus as our teacher, leader, and priest. It will offer new insight into faith (11:1), hope (6:18-19), and love (10:24) as virtues that bind us closely to Christ.

The Letter of James

"James, a servant of God and of the Lord Jesus Christ, To the twelve tribes in the Dispersion, Greetings." This salutation begins the Letter of James, but it does not reveal the identity of James or of the tribes. James may be the relative of Jesus and leader of the Jerusalem church, or someone else. The term, "twelve tribes," designates Israel, and "the dispersion" refers to Jews living outside Palestine. In this New Testament context, these expressions may refer to Christians of Jewish background or to all Christians, who saw themselves as the new Israel.

Because this letter and those that follow it are addressed to believers in general, they are sometimes called the "Catholic (Universal) Letters." This designation is found in some Bibles, but is not a part of the title of these letters.

The Letter of James is actually a written sermon encouraging its readers to lead moral lives and emphasizing that faith must express itself in good works. Its style is Jewish, with similarities to Old Testament Wisdom literature in its sayings and exhortations. It employs dialogue (2:18-26) and diatribe (aggressive debate, 4:3-4 and 5:1-6). While Jewish in style, it is written in excellent Greek.

If the Letter of James comes from the leader of the Jerusalem church, it antedates 62, the year of his death. If it comes from another James, it could have been written any time in the second half of the first century.

After the introductory greeting, James explains the value of trials and temptations. He encourages his readers to be "doers of the word," to let religion find expression in actions, and to avoid favoritism toward the rich and powerful. For James, faith must lead to action, for faith without works is dead. James preaches control over the tongue and teaches the meaning of true wisdom. He cautions readers against divisions and presumption, warns of the transitory nature of riches, and teaches the value of prayer, especially for the sick. He closes with a promise that those who bring about the conversion of sinners will be saved from death (Jas 1–5).

Read *James 2:14–3:12*, a clear statement of the importance of good works and a fine sermon on controlling the tongue. Read *James 5:13-16* on the power of prayer. Note how prayer is mentioned in each verse. The reference to the anointing of the sick is understood by the Catholic Church as referring to the Sacrament of Anointing of the Sick.

We who read James today will find solid, common-sense advice about living our faith in the real world. Indeed, this whole work might be seen as a commentary on the words of Jesus: "Not everyone who says to me, 'Lord, Lord,' will enter the kingdom of heaven, but only the one who does the will of my Father in heaven" (Mt 7:21).

The First Letter of Peter

This letter is addressed from Peter the apostle to churches in Pontus, Galatia, Cappadocia, Asia, and Bithynia, regions in Asia Minor (now modern Turkey). Until recently, most scholars believed that the letter was sent by Peter from Rome (called "Babylon" in 5:13) and written through Silvanus (see 5:12) about the year 64.

Some modern scholars, however, are of the opinion that the language and circumstances found in the letter imply a later date, perhaps 80-95, and an author writing in Peter's name. Still others think that the letter was composed by someone who used sermons and letters of Peter as sources.

In any event, the letter is inspired by God and is a beautiful sermon encouraging faithfulness to the Christian life. There are many references to Baptism, and the letter may contain portions of early baptismal instructions and liturgies. It quotes Christian hymns, prayers, and sayings as well.

The letter refers to sufferings and a "fiery ordeal" (4:12). These may point to Nero's persecution, to the trials of living in a pagan world, to hostility from Jewish neighbors, or to the persecution of Domitian late in the first century.

This letter and the one that follows indicate the special place of Peter in the early Church. The Gospel of Matthew reports that Jesus said to Peter, "You are Peter, and on this rock I will build my church....I will give you the keys of the kingdom of heaven, and whatever you bind on earth will be bound in heaven, and whatever you loose on earth will be loosed in heaven" (Mt 16:18-19). This passage mandates a special place of leadership and authority for Peter. Many other New Testament passages reinforce this view. Peter is named first in the lists of the apostles (Mk 3:16-19). He is the central figure in gospel events such as the Transfiguration (Mt 17:1-8). After denying Jesus, he is singled out by the Lord to shepherd the flock (Jn 21:15-19). He is the first to proclaim the gospel publicly and is the chief spokesman for the apostles (Acts 2:14-40). Eventually, Peter went to Rome, where he was martyred; according to tradition (referred to in the introductory part of this chapter), he was crucified upside down. Those who succeeded Peter as bishops of Rome were recognized as having a special authority and as leaders among bishops, just as Peter had been leader among the apostles.

The First Letter of Peter begins with the greeting, a reference to

Father, Son, and Spirit, and a blessing. There follows an explanation of the new birth of Baptism and of the virtues of obedience, reverence, and love that ought to be part of Christian life. Christians are privileged to be living stones in the spiritual house of God's Church. They are a chosen race, a royal priesthood, a holy nation...God's people (1 Pet 1:1-2:10).

Peter advises Christians to give good example to nonbelievers and to be loyal citizens. Slaves may imitate the long-suffering and generous love of Jesus. Husbands and wives should honor and reverence one another. All should live in love and goodness. When Christians must undergo trials, they should respond like Christ, who suffered for us. They should live morally, even in an immoral world, doing everything in the love and grace of God (1 Pet 2:11–4:11).

Peter assures Christians who must endure a "fiery ordeal" that they are sharing in the sufferings of Christ. Church leaders should care for their people. Believers should be obedient to their leaders, humble toward one another, vigilant in resisting the devil, and reliant upon God's mercy. After these admonitions, Peter closes with personal greetings and a blessing.

Read *1 Peter 1:1–2:10* for an explanation of Baptism and the Christian life. Read *1 Peter 5:6-11* for a short exhortation reminding us to put our trust in God and in God's promise of eternal life.

The First Letter of Peter will help us understand the great privilege of being baptized Christians. It encourages us to look to Christ for strength when we experience difficulties. It gives sound advice to us in our efforts to imitate Jesus.

The Second Letter of Peter

This letter is said to be from "Simeon Peter, a servant and apostle of Jesus Christ." But from the beginning, the notion that the letter actually came from Peter the apostle has been questioned. Its language and style differ from 1 Peter. It speaks of the apostles as already dead (2 Pet 3:2-4) and refers to a collection of the letters of Paul as part of the Scriptures (2 Pet 3:15-17). Its chief concern is that heretics are scoffing because Christ's Second Coming has not yet occurred; this would hardly have been a problem in Peter's lifetime. Finally, there is a passage about false teachers (2 Pet 2:1-18) that seems to depend on the Letter of Jude, and it is not likely that Peter would have quoted from a lesser authority.

For these reasons, some Catholic scholars believe that 2 Peter was actually written by a later preacher who wanted to appeal to Peter's prestige and who may have used some of Peter's sermons as a source. Speaking as Peter, he recalls the Transfiguration (1:16-18), refers to an earlier letter (3:1), and talks of being near death (1:13). It is as if the author were saying: "If Peter were here now, this is what he would tell you." This, of course, testifies to the special reverence for Peter held by the early Church.

After a greeting and a prayer, the author encourages his audience to put faith in God. Christ, who was transfigured before Peter, can be depended on, and God's prophetic message is entirely reliable (2 Pet 1). False teachers, on the other hand, must be shunned. They mislead people with empty promises (2 Pet 2). Those who scoff at Christ's Second Coming are foolish, for "with the Lord one day is like a thousand years." God is patient in giving us time to repent, but this world will one day pass away. We must, therefore, be ready for judgment (2 Pet 3).

Read *2 Peter 3* for the main point of this letter, that God's judgment will certainly come, even though the exact time is unknown.

This message is true today. The world will end for us at the moment of our death, and we ought always to be ready. The author of 2 Peter speaks of the earth being dissolved with fire. He is using apocalyptic language, not teaching science. But, as a matter of fact, scientists say that eventually our own sun will grow into a red giant and incinerate the earth. (This is not an immediate cause for concern, since scientists estimate that it will occur roughly five billion years from now!)

The First Letter of John

This letter is actually a theological instruction, for it lacks the salutation and close of New Testament letters. Many scholars believe that it was written by a disciple of the author of John's Gospel, perhaps by the same person who added Chapter 21 to the Gospel. The date of composition is probably about 95-100. This letter appears to have been addressed to a church or churches in Asia Minor, possibly Ephesus and nearby communities.

The First Letter of John emphasizes belief in the humanity of Jesus Christ and in the reality of Christ's divine Sonship. It gives special attention to the themes of faith and love. We must believe in Jesus Christ and in the truth that flows from him. We must love one another as God has loved us. Our faith and love must find expression in good deeds, particularly in keeping the commandments.

This letter also addresses the problem of false teachers who reject Jesus as Messiah and Son of God (2:22) and deny the Incarnation (4:2). These false teachers came from the community, but left and are now considered "antichrists" (2:18-19).

The First Letter of John is full of beautiful teachings about Christ, God's love for us, and ourselves as children of God. But it is not organized in a way that can be followed easily by modern readers. It places loosely connected sayings one after another and follows a circular pattern, restating ideas in slightly different words. Even so, if we do not expect carefully prepared, logical arguments, and instead accept the author's approach, we can draw much profit from his sayings, explanations, and exhortations.

The First Letter of John begins with a prologue that has some resemblances to the prologue of John's Gospel. The author then proclaims God as light and admonishes his audience to walk in this light. They are to keep the commandments, above all the commandment of love. The author speaks to groups within the community, then addresses the issue of the antichrists, those who have denied Christ. The faithful must reject these teachers and cling to the truth of Christ. The faithful are God's children and should live in God's love and truth (1:1–3:11).

Because God has loved us so, we ought to love one another. Because Christ laid down his life for us, we ought to lay down our lives for one another. We put our trust in God when we believe in Jesus Christ. Our faith is true when we believe that Jesus came in the flesh, a fact denied by the antichrists. The God we believe in is a God of love. We are to accept God's love; loving God, we must love one another. Faith in God and in Jesus brings victory and eternal life (1 Jn 3:12–5:13).

Apparently, the letter originally ended at 5:13. The remaining verses were added later. They counsel believers to pray for sinners, and they reiterate the necessity of putting faith in God and in Christ (1 Jn 5:14-18).

Read *1 John 1,* the prologue, followed by a reflection on God as light. Read *1 John 4:7-21,* which teaches that we must believe in God's love for us and love one another.

We who read 1 John will find that it deepens our belief in God's love and in the reality that Christ is one of us *and* God's own Son. We will find the simple and profound explanation of who God is...."God is love" (4:16).

The Second Letter of John

This short letter and the one that follows are addressed by the "elder" (presbyter, priest) to specific recipients. The identity of the elder is unknown to us, but the fact that he did not have to give his name means that he must have been a prominent leader in the early Church. He is generally believed to have come from the community that produced John's Gospel and 1 John. He may be the same individual who wrote 1 John. The First and Second Letters of John are generally dated around 95-100.

The Second Letter of John is sent to the "elect Lady and her children," a designation for a Christian church. Unlike 1 John, it has the classic form of ancient letters: salutation, thanksgiving, body, and closing, with greetings from an "elect sister" church. It is brief, possibly designed to fit on a single sheet of papyrus. It may have been sent to a church community that inquired about the same problems addressed in 1 John. The elder mentions these issues briefly—truth, love, false teachers, the antichrist—then promises to visit the church, no doubt to explain matters in detail.

Read *2 John.* This letter may be seen as a brief summary of the themes of 1 John. Its admonition to reject false teachers comes not from a lack of charity but from the need to keep the truth of Christ undefiled by error.

In this letter we are encouraged to seek the truth, live in love, keep the commandments, shun error, and build our lives on the teaching of Christ.

The Third Letter of John

The letter is another message sent from the elder, this time to Gaius, apparently the leader of a Christian community in Asia Minor. The letter is concerned with missionary activity in the early Church and with problems of authority.

After an introductory greeting and words of praise, the elder asks Gaius to welcome and support missionaries he has sent. He complains that another leader, Diotrephes, has refused to acknowledge his authority. The elder mentions that if he comes he hopes to rectify the situation. He recommends a certain Demetrius, perhaps the one who delivers the letter. He closes with the hope of visiting Gaius soon and with a brief prayer and greeting.

Read *3 John*. This letter shows that problems of authority existed in the early Church. In spite of them, Christianity flourished in the truth of Christ and in the love of God. We should not be surprised, therefore, that we face problems in the Church today. We can be confident that with God's help the Church will continue to live in truth and love.

The Letter of Jude

The author of this letter is given as "Jude, a servant of Jesus Christ and brother of James." The person referred to is probably the individual called the brother (relative) of the Lord (Mk 6:3). If this Jude is the author, the letter could have been written any time around 60-80. However, the letter seems to refer to the apostles as being in the past (Jude 17), and many scholars hold that it was actually composed late in the first century by someone who used Jude's name to give the work a special authority. The intended recipients of the letter are unknown; they might have been members of any Christian community or the Church taken as a whole.

The occasion for this letter was the false teaching of some who denied Christ and turned Christian freedom into license to indulge in immorality. Jude attacks the false teachers and encourages true believers to be loyal to the faith.

Jude begins with a greeting and a prayer, then mentions the false teachers as intruders and godless persons. He condemns their immoral actions and threatens them with God's judgment. Jude refers to several apocryphal (not belonging to the Bible) books from Old Testament times (6,9,14–15); he uses them to illustrate certain points, without affirming them as historical. Then he turns to the recipients of his letter. He urges them to build themselves up in their "most holy faith," to remain in the love of God, and to look forward to eternal life. He closes with a prayer of praise.

Read *Jude*. We live in a world where false teachers deny sin and misinterpret freedom as license to do anything, however wicked. Jude can help us avoid immorality that surely leads to destruction.

The Book of Revelation

The Book of Revelation belongs to a category of literature called apocalypse, popular two hundred years before and after Christ. This literary form is found in the Old Testament Book of Daniel, in parts of other biblical books, and in many nonbiblical works.

Apocalyptic literature originated during times of persecution and was intended to encourage readers in their trials. It used language the writer and his audience could understand but the persecutor would find meaningless.

This apocalyptic language included symbols like strange animals and bizarre creatures. It assigned special meanings to numbers. In the Book of Revelation, four stands for the whole world (north, south, east, and west). Seven symbolizes perfection (seven days of creation). Twelve recalls the tribes of Israel and the apostles; it represents God's people. A thousand means a multitude.

Apocalypse employed dramatic visions often interpreted by an angel. It described contemporary events in veiled language. It referred to past events to show that God's grace could be counted on in the present and future. It offered picturesque descriptions of the struggle of good against evil, with assurances that good would ultimately triumph.

Apocalyptic literature dealt with contemporary events. The Book of Daniel was composed to give hope to Jews during the persecution by Antiochus IV. The Book of Revelation was created during Domitian's persecution to encourage Christians threatened with execution because they refused to worship the emperor as a god. Neither book intended to give a timetable for future events, such as the end of the world.

Unfortunately, many people have attempted to read the Book of Revelation as if it were a crystal ball foretelling events in their century. Again and again they have misused Revelation to predict the end of the world. They have always been wrong. Such predictions supposedly based on the Book of Revelation approach blasphemy because they contradict the words of Jesus: "But about that day or hour no one knows..." (Mk 13:32).

The Book of Revelation was not devised by a fortune teller gazing into a distant future. The author was writing for the people of his time, and he would have done them no good by foretelling events to take place centuries later. What he predicted was to happen "soon." God gave "the revelation of Jesus Christ" to show "what must soon take place" (Rev 1:1; 22:6). The revelation was Christ's victory over evil (see 1 Cor 1:7; 2 Thess 1:7; 1 Pet 1:13). God had always won in the past (as shown by numerous references to the Old Testament), was winning even as Revelation was being written, and would win in the future.

Revelation repeats this message in letters, symbols, dramatic settings, and colorful actions: God wins!

Revelation demonstrates that Christ has already defeated Satan by his death and Resurrection (Rev 1:5; see Col 2:13-15). This victory, however, must be expressed in the lives of individual believers and in historical events (Rev 3:21; Rev 18; see Eph 6:12). It will be completed at the end of time (Rev 21:1-8; see 1 Cor 15:24-26).

To understand Revelation, we must be familiar with its literary form, terminology, symbolism, and frequent use of the Old Testament. It is not a traditional story with beginning, middle, and end. Rather, it repeats in cycles of seven the epic battle of good against evil. Reading Revelation might be compared to going to a theme park where we take half a dozen exhilarating rides. The rides bring us through frightening visions of evil monsters and impending dangers, but all perils are overcome and we exit each ride with a sense of victory.

Throughout history the Church has been challenged by evil. There have been shadowy passageways, demonic forces, and terrifying battles. But against all odds the Church has emerged from each confrontation because Christ has conquered Satan. If we see the Book of Revelation as a pattern for confidence in Christ through every age, we can enjoy its twists and turns. We will grow in faith and hope, in our assurance that God wins.

In addition to the main theme that God triumphs over evil, many other important lessons are taught in Revelation. God the Father is adored as Creator of all. Jesus is proclaimed as Savior of the world and is worshiped as divine. The Holy Spirit is shown to touch the lives of believers. The absolute perfection of the Trinity is displayed through symbols of wisdom, power, holiness, and majesty. The universe is God's handiwork, subject to divine Providence. Mary stands radiant in heaven as the Mother of Christ. The saints in heaven join us in prayer and worship. People have free will and can sin, but God will vindicate the just and punish the guilty. God does not view earth's events as a disinterested bystander, but invites us to accept grace and salvation. Christ is represented in glory as being close to his Church. He is one with believers and acts on their behalf. He rejects lukewarmness, and urges us to follow him with all our hearts. Christ expects us to be courageous in challenging false values in society or government. Revelation invites us to trust God, who will bring us through every trial, even death itself, to eternal life.

The Book of Revelation begins with a prologue announcing the author as John. We do not know the identity of this person; some have suggested John the Apostle or the author of John's Gospel, but there is little evidence to back these claims. However, the author must have been a leader of some prominence in the early Church (1:1-3).

Revelation next moves to a collection of letters addressed to seven Church communities in Asia Minor (modern Turkey). Seven signifies completion, and so the letters are probably addressed to the whole Church. John is said to be writing from Patmos, an island fifty miles south of Ephesus used by the Romans for prisoners in exile. Christ appears and tells him to write. The letters that follow are full of symbols, often related to the city addressed. They encourage believers to persevere in the faith and to turn away from laxity and sin (1:4–3:22).

Next comes a series of visions of heaven. These visions are not photographic images. Christ is portrayed as a lamb with seven horns and seven eyes. We ought not suppose that the author actually saw such a strange creature; instead, the horns symbolize power and the eyes all-seeing wisdom. The visions show that heaven and earth are interrelated. The saints in heaven, for example, offer up the prayers of those on earth (4:1–5:14).

The next section introduces sets of visions: seven seals, seven trumpets, seven plagues, and seven bowls. Within these patterns of seven are placed other visions involving angels, prophets, a woman (representing Mary and the Church), a dragon (Satan), beasts (probably the Roman Empire and its rulers). These visions depict the clash between good and evil, the persecution of the innocent, and God's punishments upon the wicked (6–16).

Rome is then shown as "Babylon the great," the wicked persecutor of Christians. Rome's downfall is announced and a thousand-year period proclaimed...probably a symbolic representation of the time between Christ's Resurrection and the end of the world. The end of the world will see the ultimate victory of God over the forces of evil (17–20).

With the end of this world will come "a new heaven and a new earth." The beauty of heaven is shown in dramatic portrayals of the new creation and the new Jerusalem. The Book of Revelation closes with assurances of its truth and of the certainty of Christ's Coming (21–22).

Read *Revelation 1:1–2:7* for the introduction, the first vision of Christ and the first of the seven letters. Read *Revelation 12* for the vision of the woman and the dragon, representing the ongoing struggle between God's people and Satan. Read *Revelation 21:1-8,* an image of heaven and of the union with God promised to the just, as well as a warning of the punishment to be endured by the wicked.

We who read Revelation will find it a fitting conclusion to the whole Bible. Genesis assures us of the existence of God. It proclaims that God created the world and gave life to human beings because God wanted them to share God's love (Paradise). The remainder of the Bible is a commentary on the tragedies that have come upon our world because people refused God's friendship and on how God constantly reached out to call us back. Above all, the Bible assures us that God sent Jesus Christ to offer salvation and eternal life. The Book of Revelation acknowledges the struggles we have undergone because of sin, but it also lets us know that God's love and Christ's salvation are the greatest powers in the universe. No matter how badly human beings have failed, no matter how terrible the wounds sin may inflict on the world, no matter how desperate our situation may seem to be, God will surely prevail.

So the victory is not yet complete, but it is already certain! Revelation and the entire Bible invite us to trust God and accept God's kingdom offered us through Jesus Christ:

"See, the home of God is among mortals. He will dwell with them as their God; they will be his peoples, and God himself will be with them; he will wipe every tear from their eyes. Death will be no more; mourning and crying and pain will be no more, for the first things have passed away."

The one who was seated on the throne said, "See, I am making all things new....I am the Alpha and the Omega, the beginning and the end" (Rev 21:3-6).

"Amen. Come, Lord Jesus!" (Rev 22:20).

Questions for Discussion and Reflection

Imagine yourself living in the first century. You belong to a Christian community in Greece and are gathering with other members at a home for the Sunday Eucharist. The priest enters the room and announces that Peter and Paul have been martyred in Rome. These great leaders, and most of those who had seen Jesus face to face, are now gone. Christianity now depends on you, the second generation of believers. How do you feel about this? What do you talk about with your friends? Paul's letters warning of false teachers had been read to your community in years past. Who will now speak authoritatively about truth and falsehood? Will Roman officials now persecute Christians all over the Empire? Does your little group have any chance of surviving such a persecution? Then the priest asks for quiet. He addresses the community: "We have all heard the news of the deaths of Peter and Paul. We have been sharing our thoughts and feelings. Now I would like to ask you to think about the life, death, and Resurrection of Jesus, and about his teaching." Then the priest turns to you and addresses you: "You have been a Christian longer than the rest of us. Please tell us what you think Jesus himself would say to us about these events and about our future...." What is your response?

Activities

Read Revelation 21:1-4. Take a few minutes to relax in silence and peace. Then try to imagine what it will be like to enter heaven. The beauty is breathtaking. You are surrounded by the loving presence of God. You see members of your family and your closest friends walking toward you. The last time you saw them alive, they were worn with age and illness; now they are so alive and so beautiful that you are overwhelmed. You embrace and talk and laugh. Suddenly, the realization fills your whole being: "We'll never again be parted. There is nothing to fear, nothing to be anxious about. No more sadness, no more hatred, no more sickness, no more tears, no more death. This is what I've always wanted; this is what I was made for."

Pray for as long as you like, reflecting on the beauty of heaven, on the love of God, and on the joy of being with family, friends, saints, and all the great people who have ever lived on earth and died in the love of God. Reflect that, as the Book of Revelation and the whole Bible point out, heaven is our true home. Ask Jesus to help you keep this always in mind. Talk to your favorite saints and to friends and family who have died. Ask them to stay close to you, watch over you, and help you to live in such a way that one day you *will* join them in heaven.

CHAPTER TWELVE
The Bible:
A Book for Life

How did I like your book? I knew that question would come up," said the Believer, smiling at Jesus. "I enjoyed reading it, but there are quite a few things I still don't understand." "Ask me," replied the Lord; "we do have forever, you know."

"First of all, why were you silent for so long before you finally talked to Abraham? People were on earth for hundreds of thousands of years before him. And why did you speak only to the Jews?" "As a matter of fact," Jesus said (the Believer was relieved to see that Jesus was smiling too), "I wasn't silent until Abraham and I didn't speak only to the Jews. It was just that they listened. Things could have been so much better if more people had done the same."

The Believer pondered Jesus' words for a moment, then spoke again: "Another thing I don't understand is how the Bible can be so beautiful in some places—I loved what you said in John 17, for example—but so ugly in others...wars, treachery, confusion, heartaches. From Cain's murder of Abel in the first book to persecutions in the last, there's so much that's evil." "That's true," admitted Jesus, "because that's the human condition. People were entrusted with the gift of freedom at the beginning. I never took that gift back. So I could only invite and love and teach in ways that allowed them the freedom to say yes or no to the goodness of God. The Bible reports my love and my invitation. It shows the goodness and love that touch human lives when people say yes. It also reports the terrible consequences when people say no."

"But," the Believer insisted, "there is so much evil. The Bible shows it on almost every page. Why?" "Freedom, freedom, freedom," countered Jesus, gently. "Without freedom, people are not human. It is true that without freedom no one could choose evil. But it is also true that without freedom no one could choose good or love or enjoy the unity of heart with others and with God that is the greatest human endeavor. Yes, there is evil, but the Bible shows that God's goodness cannot be defeated by evil. God makes nothing evil, but God is willing to risk giving human beings the freedom to do evil so that they might have the freedom to do good. One pure act of love outweighs all the evil in the universe. Remember Paul's words to the effect that nothing, not even death, can separate you from the love of God. And I remind you that my Resurrection proved this long before Paul wrote Romans 8!"

The Believer would have blushed had this been possible in a spiritual body. There was a long pause, then… "One more question, Jesus, and I'll be still. Why has the Bible led to so many arguments and caused so much confusion? Why have you allowed even your own words in the New Testament to be understood in so many different ways?" "Let me ask a question of my own," said Jesus. "Now that you've had a chance to see the universe in your new spiritual body, what do you think of it?" "It's magnificent," the Believer responded, "billions of stars, billions of galaxies. I'll need an eternity to take it all in." "That's right," declared Jesus, "and even the most powerful of human beings couldn't make even the smallest star! God's knowledge and love are like the universe, immense beyond human imagining. Even the wisest of human beings can grasp only the smallest portion of God's wisdom, can hold only a tiny droplet from the vast ocean of divine knowledge. If only people could admire that tiny droplet with reverence and humility. If only they could refrain from trying to make truth to their own image and likeness. If only they could resist the temptation to judge, criticize, and attack others. If only they would remember that I sent the Holy Spirit to teach and guide them through the Church. Then the Bible would be for all a source of wisdom and of unity. As you will soon discover, those who live here have learned these lessons. That's one of the reasons this place is called heaven!"

The Bible: God's Word to the World

There will come a day when all our questions will be answered. But for now we must do our best to learn what we can with courage, enthusiasm, and humility. The Bible is God's way of addressing us as dearly beloved children. It has all the grandeur, wisdom, and love we can take in because it comes from God. But because it comes through human beings, it also has limitations. These, however, should not blind us to the grandeur, wisdom, and love.

For God wants the whole world to come, through the Bible, to the "knowledge of the truth" (1 Tim 2:4). We have seen that the Bible answers the most basic questions that face us as human beings. Questions like:

1. "Is there a God?" Without a doubt! The Bible helps us to realize that everything, except sin, must come from an all-powerful Creator, or from nothing. It shows God as the Source of all that exists. The Bible opens us up to the knowledge that God is a loving community of three Persons—Father, Son, and Holy Spirit—who long to draw us into their family of love.

2. "Is there meaning and purpose in life?" Certainly! The Bible teaches us that God gave life to human beings so that we might come to know God, to walk with God in the garden that is earth (Gen 3:8), to experience God's goodness, knowledge, and love, and to use our freedom well to mold this planet into all it is meant to be. Life here is a journey beginning with birth and leading through death to an even closer union with God, as death strips away our limitations and opens us to the fullest possibilities for knowledge and love. This union with God is our purpose and goal.

3. "Why then is life sometimes so painful? Why is there so much evil, sin, and sorrow?" Because God has made us free to love and therefore free to say yes or no. Evil is surely the most difficult of the problems we face in human existence, and there are no easy answers. The story of Adam and Eve shows how human beings have misused freedom by sinning, by saying no to God instead of accepting God's word about what is good and what is evil. The rest of the Bible relates the sad consequences of sin.

4. "Has sin made life unbearable and defeat inevitable?" By no means! While human beings have far too often said no to God, God has never said anything but yes to us. God's love has reached out to us, as we see in every page of the Bible, in the beauty of nature, in every blessing that has ever touched a human being, in moments of prayer and worship, in the teaching of spiritual leaders, and in the good lives of those who have followed God's way. Above all, God has said yes through Jesus Christ, God-became-one-of-us. Jesus truly entered into our hu-

man condition and endured what we must endure, even suffering and death, so that we might never be alone. We admit the reality of evil; but with Jesus at our side, we know that we can triumph over every evil, even death itself.

5. "How can we find real happiness and peace?" By accepting Jesus Christ, by living according to the guidelines he has given, by recognizing his continuing presence in the Church, and by becoming a part of that presence. Just how we do this, of course, becomes clearer the more we know about the Bible and the more we live as members of Christ's Church. For it is through the Bible and the Church that Christ teaches us and shares with us his life and love. To live the Bible and to live as members of the Church should be the work of a lifetime, the greatest challenge we face as human beings and the most noble human enterprise.

6. "What happens to us when we die?" We are born to new life! If we believe in Jesus Christ and live according to his word, we are united to his life, death, and Resurrection in such a way that death becomes birth to everlasting life. There is in our hearts a longing for something this world cannot provide. That is because we are made for God, and our hearts will be restless until they rest in God. This rest in God will bring us to the Source of knowledge and love, and therefore eternal life will bring everything we long for. We will have the happiness, security, and peace we can only hope for here. We will have that loving union with God and one another that seems so elusive now. From the first page of the Bible to the last, God assures us that what we need and desire will be ours.

"In the beginning when God created the heavens and the earth" (Gen 1:1), God planned that human beings should enjoy God's knowledge and love. In the end, for those who say yes to God, thanks to the goodness of God, the grace of Jesus Christ, and the love of the Holy Spirit, there is "a new heaven and a new earth...the home of God among mortals. He will dwell with them as their God; they will be his peoples, and God himself will be with them" (Rev 21:1,3).

The Bible, Tradition, and the Church

Catholics believe in the Bible as the word of God. We believe that the Bible is a gift granted by God to the Church to be treasured and used. The answers to the most basic questions in life may be found in the Bible.

But many other questions are not answered in the Bible. Catholics believe that answers to these questions may be found in the sacred Tradition of the Church, for we know that God reveals truth through sacred Tradition as well as through Scripture.

Here we may be challenged by those who contend that Christians must believe only what is in the Bible. However, this contention contradicts the Bible itself, for Scripture offers a great deal of evidence for the existence of sacred Tradition.

John's Gospel closes with the statement: "But there are also many other things that Jesus did; if every one of them were written down, I suppose that the world itself could not contain the books that would be written" (Jn 21:25). Clearly, the Bible does not contain all of God's revealed truth.

Scripture acknowledges the existence of traditions handed down by oral teaching as well as by the Bible. Saint Paul wrote to the Thessalonians: "...stand firm and hold fast to the traditions that you were taught by us, either by word of mouth or by our letter" (2 Thess 2:15).

Jesus promised to continue speaking through his disciples, "Whoever listens to you listens to me" (Lk 10:16). After the Resurrection, the apostles preached God's word and appointed others to teach after them. The New Testament reports this mandate of Paul to Timothy: "And what you heard from me through many witnesses entrust to faithful people who will be able to teach others as well" (2 Tim 2:2). Sacred Tradition *is* Christ teaching the world through the Church's leaders he guides and directs.

Jesus promised to send the Holy Spirit to lead the Church to the truth: "When the Spirit of truth comes, he will guide you into all the truth" (Jn 16:13). Such guidance is necessary if we are to apply biblical principles to modern problems.

If asked, "What is the pillar and bulwark of the truth?" people who deny sacred Tradition will reply, "The Bible, of course." But that is not what the Bible says! The Bible declares that the Church is the "pillar and bulwark of the truth" (1 Tim 3:15).

The Church, of course, came before the Bible, and this proves that there is divine revelation not found in the Bible. The first Christians had no New Testament. If all teaching had to be drawn from Scripture, the early Church would have had little to teach. Further, Church councils made the decisions about which books should be accepted into the

Bible. Without sacred Tradition there would have been no way to determine which books belonged in the Bible and which did not. Without sacred Tradition, there could be no Bible.

History has provided another proof of the need for sacred Tradition. One of the principles taught by those who broke away from the Church in the sixteenth century was "Scripture alone." This is the notion that God reveals the truth to each individual without the need for sacred Tradition or a Church to interpret and clarify what the Bible says. But history has shown that this cannot be the way God acts, for it has resulted in the formation of thousands of denominations, each with its own version of the truth. If God guided each individual to the truth, everyone would believe the same thing. Jesus did not promise that each person could find truth without recourse to the Church. Instead, Jesus established a Church and promised that the gates of Hades would not prevail against it (Mt 16). Catholics today believe what the first Christians believed about the Eucharist and other essential doctrines. This is because they are guided by God's revelation in sacred Tradition, by Christ's Church, rather than by the whims of some individual or by the changing currents of a passing world.

Finally, there is no passage in the Bible which says that the Bible is the only source of divine revelation. Therefore, anyone who claims we must believe only what we find in the Bible is asking us to believe something that is not in the Bible!

Sacred Tradition and the Bible are not in opposition. Most dogmas of our faith can be found explicitly in the Bible. All our Catholic beliefs are in harmony with the Bible. (See *"We Believe..." A Survey of the Catholic Faith* by Oscar Lukefahr, C.M., Liguori Publications, 1990, 1995.) Some, like the doctrine of the Assumption of Mary, are taught implicitly in the Bible and are revealed more clearly by God to the Church under the guidance of the Holy Spirit.

We Catholics, then, depend both on the Bible and on sacred Tradition. We do this on the authority of the Bible itself!

Interpreting the Bible Through the Church's Tradition

The sacred Tradition of the Church helps Catholics understand and interpret the Bible. The Catholic approach to the relationship of Bible and Tradition may be seen in the question of the "brothers and sisters" of Jesus and the related issue of Mary's perpetual virginity.

The New Testament speaks of "brothers and sisters" of Jesus (Mt 13:56-57). But the Catholic Church teaches that Jesus had no blood brothers or sisters and that his mother Mary always remained a virgin. These truths have been arrived at from the Bible and from sacred Tradition.

In biblical times, as now, "brothers and sisters" could be used in many ways. When we hear speakers address audiences as "brothers and sisters," we assume that the words refer not to blood relatives but to friends or to members of a particular nation, group, or race. In the Old Testament, "brothers and sisters" might refer to members of the same tribe (Deut 15:12) or race (Deut 23:7), or to nephews (Gen 13:8) or cousins (Lev 10:4), or to relatives in general (2 Kings 10:13).

The New Testament never speaks of other children of Mary, so it is impossible to prove from the Bible that Jesus had blood brothers or sisters. But there are many passages which indicated that he did not.

Two of those who are called brothers of Jesus, namely James and Joseph (Mt 13:56-57), are later identified as sons of another woman, possibly Mary's sister (Mt 27:56). If Mary had other children, they would have been mentioned in the description of the pilgrimage to the Temple when Jesus was twelve years old. If Mary had other children, it is difficult to explain why Jesus, as he hung on the cross, would have given Mary into the care of the beloved disciple. "When Jesus saw his mother and the disciple whom he loved standing beside her, he said to his mother, 'Woman, here is your son.' Then he said to the disciple, 'Here is your mother.' And from that hour, the disciple took her into his own home" (Jn 19:26-27). Entrusting Mary to the beloved disciple would have made no sense if Mary had other children.

The word *brothers* is used in the New Testament for the followers of Jesus more than one hundred times. For example, the risen Jesus asked Mary Magdalene to "go to my brothers." Mary "went and announced to the disciples, 'I have seen the Lord'" (Jn 20:17-18). Jesus said that those who do the will of his Father are his brothers (Lk 8:21).

Some people argue that Luke 2:7, referring to Jesus as Mary's "firstborn son," suggests that Mary must have had children after Jesus. But "firstborn" was a legal term for Jewish people: The "firstborn" was to be presented in the Temple, as Jesus was (Luke 2:22; see Exodus 13:2). "Firstborn" does not imply other children. An inscription dating to 5 B.C. on the grave of a Jewish woman in Egypt says that she died "giving birth to her firstborn son."

The expression in some English translations stating that Joseph "had no marital relations with her [Mary] until she had borne a son" (Matthew 1:25) also seems to point to other children. But our English word *until* implies "only up to and not beyond." The Greek and Semitic words translated by *until* usually meant "up to" without ruling out beyond. *Until* in English suggests that Joseph did have relations with Mary after the birth of Jesus. But *until* in the Greek or Semitic does not suggest that he did. It focuses only on the time up to the birth of Jesus and says nothing about what happened thereafter. A similar expression in 2 Samuel 6:23 states that Michal "had no child to the day of her death." The English translation uses *to* instead of *until,* but the Semitic expression behind both phrases is the same, and obviously Michal did not have children after her death. In Matthew 28:20, Jesus says, "I am with you always, to the end of the age." (The word translated here as *to* is the same as the *until* of Matthew 1:25.) Here Jesus means that he will be with us until the end of the world and beyond the end of the world, that is, forever. In the same way, Matthew 1:25 carries the meaning that Joseph had no marital relations with Mary until and beyond the time she gave birth to Jesus.

Early Christian writers agreed that Jesus had no blood brothers and sisters and that Mary remained a virgin. Jerome (345-420) wrote that "Ignatius, Polycarp, Irenaeus, Justin Martyr and all the other learned men going back to apostolic times" testified to the perpetual virginity of Mary. These writers had no reason for stating that Jesus was an only child except that he was an only child!

History supports Catholic belief in Mary's perpetual virginity. There is no record of anyone claiming to be a descendant of Mary and Joseph. If there were cause for such a claim, it certainly would have been made known. And we can be sure that people today would be tracing their genealogy back to a blood brother or sister of Jesus!

Our Catholic teaching, therefore, goes back to the earliest days of the Church and has been a constant belief for almost two thousand years. Since the Holy Spirit guides the Church, we can be certain that the Holy Spirit led believers to the fact of Mary's perpetual virginity.

This fact points to the uniqueness of Jesus as the only Son of God. The Bible states that Mary was a virgin when she conceived Christ by the power of the Holy Spirit (Lk 1:31-35). The tradition of the Church teaches that Mary remained a virgin. Why? Because she and Joseph witnessed the miracle of Jesus' conception and birth. They realized that

God had entrusted them with the greatest treasure in the history of the world, God's only Son. They understood that their task in life was to nurture and protect the Savior of the human race. Many years later, Jesus would speak of those who renounced marriage "for the sake of the kingdom of heaven" (Mt 19:12). It cannot be surprising that Mary and Joseph would have wanted to renounce their right to have other children in order to dedicate their lives to the care of God's Son.

The Church's belief in the perpetual virginity of Mary is significant because of what it says about Jesus and about us. The fact that Jesus was Mary's only child underlines his uniqueness as the only Son of God. The fact that Jesus was Mary's only child results in a special relationship between Mary and us. Since we are the Body of Christ (1 Cor 12:27), Mary is our mother, and she has the same mother's love for us that she has for Jesus. Jesus says to us as beloved disciples, "Here is your mother."

These facts, rooted in the Bible and clarified by the Church's sacred Tradition, help us to see Christ in the clearest possible light. They help us to know Mary as the Virgin Mother of Jesus and as our Virgin Mother. These beliefs, old as the New Testament, have enriched the lives of countless generations of Catholics.

Applying Bible Teaching to Modern Problems

The sacred Tradition of the Church and the official teaching office of the Church also help Catholics apply Bible teachings to modern problems. An example of this is the issue of abortion.

Some Christians argue that abortion is morally acceptable and state that abortion is not forbidden in the Bible. Catholics, and many other Christians, believe that abortion is forbidden by the commandment "You shall not kill" (Ex 20:13).

The official teachers of the Church, the pope and bishops, begin with the Bible pronouncement "You shall not murder." They see the Church's tradition as forbidding the killing of unborn children. They look also to the findings of modern medical science, which show clearly that the unborn child is not merely a blob of tissue but a human being. They clarify for Catholics what the Bible teaches in a matter that is crucial to the moral standards of every individual and of society.

"Where Do We Go From Here?"

This *Catholic Guide to the Bible,* then, must conclude with an invitation to continue reading the Bible *and* to study the sacred Tradition of the Church. Both are the word of God, and together they guide us to eternal life.

You who have followed this Bible introduction from the beginning have already read passages from every book of the Bible. You have studied the Bible in the light of the Church's teaching and Tradition. I encourage you to read, study, and pray the Bible, and to look further into the many resources that are available to help you. (See the Bibliography.)

Perhaps the best way to continue is to read some books of the New Testament from beginning to end. I recommend that you read first the Gospel of Luke, then the Acts of the Apostles, then Paul's Letter to the Romans. After these books, you may want to turn to the Gospel of John, to Paul's Letter to the Philippians, and to the rest of the New Testament. Then you might begin reading the Old Testament. Pray for guidance and ask God to open your heart and mind to the word. You have begun, and the Bible is a collection of treasures waiting to be discovered.

Parents who have small children should purchase a children's Bible and frequently read Bible stories to them. Many families keep a New Testament at the dinner table and read a few verses at the evening meal. Husbands and wives should consider reading the Bible together.

You may wish to purchase a set of audiotapes of the New Testament. You can listen to such tapes while driving, while working around the house, or during times of prayer.

Those familiar with computers can use them to study the Bible. Search programs allow Bible students to go to any passage of Scripture, or to view all the passages containing a certain word.

If your parish has a Bible study group, consider joining, for there is a special value in studying the Bible with others. If no such group is available, you may wish to start one, using this book or some other guide to the Bible. You can seek advice and guidance from your pastor or parish religious-education director.

Pray the Bible, especially in the liturgical prayer of the Church. Passages from the Bible are proclaimed and prayed at every Mass, and those who attend daily Mass have the best possible opportunity to be touched by God's word. Some parishes have morning and evening prayer based on the Church's Liturgy of the Hours. Many Catholics use the Liturgy of the Hours, the Church's official daily prayer, as a way to pray the Bible in union with the Church throughout the world. You may get more information about the Liturgy of the Hours from your pastor or at any Catholic bookstore. Catholic bookstores also have prayer books based on the Bible with selections for every circumstance and situation.

You may wish to memorize favorite Bible passages to guide your thinking and emotions. When you are disturbed, for example, you can quiet turbulent feelings or overcome temptation by reflecting on the words, "The LORD is my shepherd, I shall not want" (Ps 23:1), or on the promise of Jesus, "I am with you always" (Mt 28:20). Such passages help believers to live each day in God's presence and to rest peacefully at night. Many Catholics memorize one short Bible passage from the Sunday liturgy, then pray it often during the week. Some post quotations from the Bible on the refrigerator door or have a calendar with a Bible verse for each day. Some keep a Bible handy so they can open the Scriptures and hear God speaking to them at various times during the day.

The possibilities are endless. And in all the ways we turn to the Bible, we must remember that it is the word of God, who knows us better than we know ourselves, who loves us more than we can imagine, who wants to walk through each day with us until we arrive at perfect union with God in heaven.

When we pick up the Bible, we dial God's number. And God is always eager to answer.

Questions for Discussion and Reflection

The section, "The Bible: God's Word to the World" (pages 198-200), lists six basic questions whose answers are found in the Bible. Can you think of passages that answer these questions?

You have spent a great deal of time studying the Bible. In what ways has your study helped you to understand the Bible? to understand your Catholic faith? to grow as a believer? to pray?

Activities

Place yourself in God's presence. Pick up the Bible reverently. Think of all the believers who have held the Bible. Think of the believers whose stories are told in the Bible. Consider your attitudes toward the Bible and your knowledge of the Bible before you began this study. Compare them with what they are today. Consider what you'd like them to be at the moment of your death. Thank God for the Bible and for opportunities to know and love the Bible as God's word. Kiss the Bible reverently, and open it to a favorite passage. Allow God to speak to you.

Bibliography

Atlas of the Bible: An Illustrated Guide to the Holy Land.
Pleasantville, NY: Reader's Digest, 1982.
Catechism of the Catholic Church. Washington, D.C.: United States
Catholic Conference, 1994.
Collegeville Bible Commentary. Collegeville, MN: The Liturgical
Press, 1989.
Jesus and His Times. Pleasantville, NY: Reader's Digest, 1987.
Jesus Christ, Word of the Father. Theological-Historical Commission
for the Great Jubilee of the Year 2000. New York: Crossroad
Publishing Company, 1997.
Keller, Werner. *The Bible As History.* Second Revised Edition. New
York: Bantam Books, 1983.
Lukefahr, Oscar, C.M. *"We Believe..." A Survey of the Catholic
Faith. Second Edition.* Liguori, MO: Liguori Publications, 1995.
McKenzie, John, S.J. *Dictionary of the Bible.* Bruce, 1965.
New Revised Standard Version of the Bible: Catholic Edition.
Nashville, TN: Catholic Bible Press. 1993.
New Revised Standard Version of the Bible: Catholic Edition.
Computer version. Liguori, MO: Liguori Publications, 1994.
New American Bible—New Testament. Twelve cassette tape set.
Hosanna, 2421 Aztec Road NE, Albuquerque, NM 87107. Phone
1-800-545-6552, www.faithcomesbyhearing.org.

Index

Index

Index

Index